Languages at War

Palgrave Studies in Languages at War

Series Editors: **Hilary Footitt**, University of Reading, UK and **Michael Kelly**, University of Southampton, UK.

Languages play a crucial role in war, conflict and peacemaking: in intelligence gathering and evaluation, pre-deployment preparations, operations on the ground, regime-change, and supporting refugees and displaced persons. In the politics of war, languages have a dual impact: a public policy dimension, setting frameworks and expectations; and the lived experience of those 'on the ground', working with and meeting speakers of other languages.

This series intends to bring together books which deal with the role of languages in situations of conflict, including war, civil war, occupation, peacekeeping, peace-enforcement and humanitarian action in war zones. It will offer an interdisciplinary approach, drawing on applied linguistics, sociolinguistics, translation studies, intercultural communication, history, politics, international relations and cultural studies. Books in the series will explore specific conflict situations across a range of times and places, and specific language-related roles and activities, examining three contexts: languages and the military, meeting the other in war and peace-making, and interpreting/translating in war.

Titles include:

Hilary Footitt and Michael Kelly (*editors*)
LANGUAGES AT WAR
Policies and Practices of Language Contacts in Conflict

Hilary Footitt and Michael Kelly (*editors*)
LANGUAGES AND THE MILITARY
Alliances, Occupation and Peace Building

Forthcoming:

Hilary Footitt and Simona Tobia
'WAR TALK'
Foreign Languages and the British War Effort in Europe 1940–46

Michael Kelly and Catherine Baker
INTERPRETING THE PEACE
Peace Operation, Conflict and Language in Bosnia-Herzegovina

Palgrave Studies in Languages at War
Series Standing Order ISBN 978–0–230–35516–3 Hardback
9780–230–35517–0 Paperback
(*outside North America only*)

You can receive future titles in this series as they are published by placing a standing order. Please contact your bookseller or, in case of difficulty, write to us at the address below with your name and address, the title of the series and the ISBN quoted above.

Customer Services Department, Macmillan Distribution Ltd, Houndmills, Basingstoke, Hampshire RG21 6XS, England

---

Languages at War

Policies and Practices of Language Contacts in Conflict

Edited by

Hilary Footitt
University of Reading, UK

and

Michael Kelly
University of Southampton, UK

First published 2012 by
PALGRAVE MACMILLAN

Palgrave Macmillan in the UK is an imprint of Macmillan Publishers Limited,
registered in England, company number 785998, of Houndmills, Basingstoke,
Hampshire RG21 6XS.

Palgrave Macmillan in the US is a division of St Martin's Press LLC,
175 Fifth Avenue, New York, NY 10010.

Palgrave Macmillan is the global academic imprint of the above companies
and has companies and representatives throughout the world.

Palgrave® and Macmillan® are registered trademarks in the United States,
the United Kingdom, Europe and other countries.

ISBN 978–0–230–36877–4

This book is printed on paper suitable for recycling and made from fully
managed and sustained forest sources. Logging, pulping and manufacturing
processes are expected to conform to the environmental regulations of the
country of origin.

A catalogue record for this book is available from the British Library.

A catalog record for this book is available from the Library of Congress.

10 9 8 7 6 5 4 3 2 1
21 20 19 18 17 16 15 14 13 12

Printed and bound in the United States of America
by Edwards Brothers Malloy, Inc.

Contents

Tables

Preface

We started examining languages at war with some trepidation, conscious that little had been written on the subject. We were, however, relieved and greatly encouraged to discover that our work found support in many quarters and has resonated with colleagues from different disciplines. The whole *Languages at War* project was funded by the Arts and Humanities Research Council and we gratefully acknowledge their support and that of the partner institutions in the project: the University of Reading, the University of Southampton and the Imperial War Museum, London.

Our colleagues in the Imperial War Museum have been a pleasure to work with, and we express our particular thanks to Samantha Heywood and James Taylor for their generous and vital contributions and to the Director of the Churchill War Rooms, Phil Reed. Our lively Advisory Group of academics and practitioners patiently provided guidance and support throughout, and we are grateful to Christine Adamson, Dr Robin Aizlewood, Professor Mark Cornwall, Professor Anne Curry, Professor Christopher Duggan, Professor Debra Kelly, Dr Charles Kirke, Professor Andrew Knapp, Lt Col Justin Lewis, Lt Col Andrew Parrott and Dr Frank Tallett. Those who read papers, chaired sessions and contributed to the discussions in the workshops we held in the Imperial War Museum in 2009 and 2010, and in the *Languages at War* conference in 2011, played a key role in developing the themes in this book.

Above all, we are grateful to the many men and women who shared with us their own experiences of languages at war, who offered their insights and whose voices and words echo throughout this volume. Without their contribution it would have been impossible to begin to appreciate the language experiences 'on the ground' of those involved in war.

Languages at War has been a collaborative enterprise in which themes and chapters have been discussed and developed by all participants, with individual members of the group leading on particular chapters. Hilary Footitt wrote Chapter 1, Chapter 4 and Chapter 7 and co-wrote the Introduction and Chapter 8. Michael Kelly wrote Chapter 5 and the Conclusion and co-wrote the Introduction. Simona Tobia wrote Chapter 3 and Chapter 9 and co-wrote Chapter 11. Catherine

Baker wrote Chapter 2 and Chapter 10 and co-wrote Chapter 8 and Chapter 11. Louise Askew wrote Chapter 6. Catherine Baker copy-edited the text.

We hope that this first book in the *Languages at War* series will contribute to a re-mapping of conflict in which foreign languages are seen to be central to our future understanding of war.

HILARY FOOTITT
MICHAEL KELLY

Acknowledgements

The authors are grateful to the following publications for permission to republish parts of the material:

Catherine Baker

'The Care and Feeding of Linguists: the Working Environment of Interpreters, Translators and Linguists during Peacekeeping in Bosnia-Herzegovina', *War and Society*, 29 (2), 2010, 154–75. Maney Publishing (http://www.maney.co.uk/journals/war, and www.ingentaconnect.com/content/maney/war).

Hilary Footitt

'Another Missing Dimension? Foreign Languages in World War II', *Intelligence and National Security*, 25 (3), 2010, 271–89, Taylor & Francis Ltd., http://www.tandfonline.com

'Languages at War: Cultural Preparations for the Liberation of Western Europe', *Journal of War and Culture Studies*, 3 (1), 2010, 109–21, Intellect Journals.

'Incorporating Languages into Histories of War: a Research Journey', *Translation Studies*, 5 (2), 2012, 217–31, Taylor & Francis Ltd., http://www.tandfonline.com

Michael Kelly

Some elements of Chapter 5 were originally published in 'Issues in Institutional Language Policy: Lessons Learned from Peace-Keeping in Bosnia-Herzegovina', *European Journal of Language Policy/Revue européenne de politique linguistique*, 3 (1), 2011, 61–80.

Abbreviations

AD	Archives Départementales
BAOR	British Army of the Rhine
CCG	Control Commission Germany
CCG (BE)	Control Commission Germany (British Element)
CEF	Common European Framework for Language Learning
CIMIC	Civilian/Military Cooperation
CSDIC	Combined Services Detailed Interrogation Centres
DOLSU	Defence Operational Language Support Unit
DSL	Defence School of Languages
EUFOR	European Union Force
GCCS	Government Code and Cypher School
IFOR	Implementation Force
IPTF	International Police Task Force
IWM	Imperial War Museum
JACIG	Joint Arms Control Implementation Group
JAG	Judge Advocate General
JSSL	Joint Services School for Languages
LSB	Linguistic Services Branch
MECAS	Middle East Centre for Arab Studies
MND (SW)	Multi-National Division (South-West)
MODLEB	Ministry of Defence Languages Examination Board
NA	National Archives, London
NATO	North Atlantic Treaty Organization
NCO	Non-Commissioned Officer
NGO	Non-Governmental Organization
OSCE	Organization for Security and Co-Operation in Europe
POW	Prisoner of War
RAEC	Royal Army Educational Corps
RAF	Royal Air Force
RS	Republika Srpska
SHAEF	Supreme Headquarters Allied Expeditionary Force
SFOR	Stabilization Force
SOE	Special Operations Executive
SSEES	School of Slavonic and East European Studies
STANAG	Standardization Agreement

UN	United Nations
UNMO	United Nations Military Observer
UNPROFOR	United Nations Protection Force
WAAF	Women's Auxiliary Air Force
WCIU	War Crimes Investigation Unit
WRNS	Women's Royal Naval Service

Notes on Contributors

Louise Askew has been a professional translator, interpreter and reviser working between English and Bosnian/Croatian/Serbian for, amongst others, the International War Crimes Tribunal in The Hague and the NATO Stabilization Force HQ in Sarajevo, where she set up and headed the translation and interpretation service from 2000 to 2004. She has a PhD in international language policy in post-Dayton Bosnia-Herzegovina.

Catherine Baker is a Research and Teaching Fellow at the University of Southampton and Teaching Fellow in Nationalism and Ethnic Conflict at University College London. Her research interests are in the socio-cultural impact of international intervention and in the politics of popular culture and entertainment, drawing on research in former Yugoslavia. She is the author of *Sounds of the Borderland: Popular Music, War and Nationalism in Croatia since 1991* (2010). Her articles have appeared in journals such as *War and Society, Europe–Asia Studies, Nationalities Papers* and *Ethnopolitics*.

Hilary Footitt is Senior Research Fellow in the Department of Modern Languages and European Studies in the University of Reading and was Principal Investigator for the AHRC project *Languages at War*. She has three areas of research activity. Firstly, she has written on the role and discourse of women in politics (*Women, Europe and the New Languages of Politics*, 2002), and was a participant in the nine-country 'Media Representation of Women in European Elections' project. Secondly, she has worked extensively on Allied–French relations in the Second World War (*War and Liberation in France: Living with the Liberators*, 2004) and is a member of the EURO-HISMEDIA European network, 'Médias, guerre et imaginaires en Europe'. Her articles have appeared in *Intelligence and National Security, Journal of War and Culture Studies* and *Cold War History*. She is on the editorial board of *Journal of War and Culture Studies* and is currently an investigator in the Leverhulme 'Liberal Way of War' programme. Over the past ten years she has been active within fora that promote foreign language study in the UK and was chair of the University Council of Modern Languages and a trustee of the Association for Language Learning. She wrote the government report *HE and the National Languages Strategy* (2005) and is currently co-convenor of the Language Alliance.

Michael Kelly is Professor of French at the University of Southampton. He is a specialist in French cultural history, particularly intellectual history, and in language policy. He has written extensively on the experience of war in France and his most recent monograph is on the intellectual and cultural reconstruction of France after the Second World War. He is editor of the Francophone journal *Synergies Royaume-Uni & Irlande* and the *European Journal of Language Policy/Revue européenne de politique linguistique*. Over the last ten years he has worked on contemporary issues of language policy in Europe and published books on language teacher education and intercultural communication. He is actively involved in bringing about change in language teaching practice and theory and promoting linguistic and cultural diversity in the UK and across Europe. He leads a national support centre for language teachers in the UK (LLAS Centre for Languages, Linguistics and Area Studies), which runs a programme of professional development for teachers in schools and universities. He is Secretary of Speak to the Future, the UK campaign for languages, and Secretary of the Conseil européen pour les langues/European Language Council.

Simona Tobia currently teaches Modern European History at the University of Reading, where she has also contributed to the major project *Languages at War*. Her main interests are focused on war and culture in the twentieth century. She is the author of *Advertising America: The United States Information Service in Italy, 1945–1956* (2008), and of several academic articles.

Introduction

Languages at war

Traditional historical scholarship on war has been markedly ethnocentric. Military historians, in what is still predominantly an Anglophone discipline, tend to adopt a nation-state ontology of conflict, eschewing what Tarak Barkawi calls the 'cultural mixing and hybridity of war' (2006: x), in favour of a state-against-state, them-against-us framework in which 'foreignness' is positioned as an unproblematic given whose qualities are largely irrelevant to the themes that are being considered. In general, when languages appear in these narratives, they do so at the end of the story, represented as elements which are essentially benign, ancillary parts of those diplomatic relations which bring a conclusion to war (Roland 1999), or as sources of useful pedagogic lessons for the post-war period, like those which could be drawn from the US Forces' communicative language teaching techniques in the 1940s (Goodman 1947; Parry 1967). To date, the only detailed historical examination of a language policy within war itself is Elliott and Shukman's work on the secret classrooms of the Cold War (2003), and this is a study which concerns itself not with languages themselves but rather with the social and cultural impacts that a programme of national language training might have on the servicemen concerned. More recently, however, historians engaged with pre-twentieth-century conflicts have begun to question the traditionally accepted linguistic nationalism of the armies that were fighting in Europe in the medieval and early modern periods. Thus Kleinman (2009) traces the presence of Irish participants in the French armies of the late eighteenth century and Butterfield (2009) challenges the monolithic 'Anglophoneness' of British identity taken for granted by the majority of historians of the Hundred Years War. Such instances of the historical inclusion of languages are, however, rare. On the whole, the historiography of war continues to be a largely foreign language-free enterprise. In the Western historical academy, the business of military action conducted with or against national and ethnic groups is typically understood as a monolingual operation, achieved through the language of the dominant force, or at least that of the observing historian or war studies commentator.

If war historians are largely uninterested in languages, however, linguists and translation scholars have shown themselves to be increasingly curious about war and conflict, and in particular about the role that language intermediaries, interpreters and translators, might play in military situations (Apter 2006; M. Baker 2006; Dragovic-Drouet 2007; Inghilleri 2008, 2009; Rafael 2007; Salama-Carr 2007; Simon (ed.) 2005; Stahuljak 2000, 2010). Often informed by a legacy of thought from cultural studies and literary theory (Bermann and Wood 2005), such researchers have sought to enlarge contemporary concepts of translation in ways which might be appropriate to 'translating culture in an age of political violence' (Tymoczko 2009: 179). Stahuljak (2000), for example, has called on frameworks of testimony and witness in order to understand the voices of interpreters in conflict, whilst Mona Baker has drawn on narrative theory to position translators as participants in the construction of war narratives (M. Baker 2006, 2010a), and Inghilleri's Bourdieusian approach positions interpreters within the social and professional contexts of war (2005, 2009). The result of this not inconsiderable body of research has been to emphasize the complex and multifaceted role of translators in conflict situations, thereby making important contributions to broader debates in translation studies concerning, for example, translator agency and the ethics of translation itself. For these translation specialists, languages, far from being absent from military activity, are in effect part of the very institution of war, 'essential for circulating and resisting the narratives that create the intellectual and moral environment for violent conflict' (M. Baker 2006: 2).

It would be true to say, however, that there is still a wide gap between these two distinct parts of the academy – between the perception of translation studies scholars that language intermediaries are vital to war, and the total absence of languages, their occlusion, in the narratives which most historians construct of conflict and peace support. To some extent, this failure to connect the two approaches has a great deal to do with the very different methodological traditions of the two disciplines – translation studies and history. In translation studies, much of the most innovative work on languages and war has been stimulated by recent Western deployments in Iraq and Afghanistan: ' "You don't make war without knowing why": the decision to interpret in Iraq' (Inghilleri 2010); 'The ethical task of the translator in the geo-political arena from Iraq to Guantánamo Bay' (Inghilleri 2008); 'Relationships of learning between military personnel and interpreters in situations of violent conflict' (Tipton 2011); 'Translation, American English, and the national insecurities of empire' (Rafael 2009). In this research, conclusions about the place of languages in war are generally made on the basis of data relating to these contemporary deployments, with an implicit assumption that the position of the interpreter in such conflicts is likely to be somewhat similar to that in other wars; that war, and therefore the interpreter's role within it, will not necessarily change a great deal from one conflict to another. Historians, on the other hand, whilst accepting that there are clearly constants in war – killing, the victimization of the innocent, the inequality of army/civilian relationships – generally view the activities associated with conflict as being radically context-dependent, as being framed by the particular historical and geopolitical circumstances which have produced the war in the first place. This book aims in some measure to bring the two sides of the debate into dialogue: to show how integral foreign languages should be to our accounts of war, and to illuminate the place of languages, and therefore that of language intermediaries, within the contexts of different sorts of conflict situations.

The Arts and Humanities Research Council project on which the book is based, *Languages at War: Policies and Practices of Language Contacts in Conflict* (http://www.reading.ac.uk/languages-at-war/), takes as its starting point the need to contextualize the role of languages in war, to see languages as integral to the constitution and development of each particular conflict. Any war, the authors assumed at the outset of the project, has its own peculiar context, bringing together a range of variables: the purpose and focus of the mission, the constitution of the military forces, the modes of encounter with civilians and the composition and attitudes of local people. These variables frame the conflict itself and the potential role of languages within it. What tasks, for example, have the military been given in any particular conflict? Are they to occupy a country, liberate an area, pacify a region, make peace between warring groups or build a long-term and stable peace? Is their deployment expected to be short-term or extensive? Are the armies drawn from one nationality or several? Have they been deployed as a national group or are they organized with others, either in a loose coalition of foreign partners, or in a tighter treaty organization? On the ground, do they seek to have direct relations with foreign civilians through their own personnel, or do they delegate most of these encounters to third party nationals, recruited on the ground or brought in by a civilian agency? How do local attitudes towards the military differ according to the particular groups involved, and how do such attitudes change over time, perhaps mirroring the behaviour of the armies concerned and/or the evolution of the conflict itself?

To examine languages in this context-specific way, the *Languages at War* project selected two case studies which seemed likely to provide different settings for the role of languages in war: the liberation and occupation of Western Europe (1944–7) and peace operations in Bosnia-Herzegovina (1995–2000). In the Second World War, the mission given to Allied armies was to liberate enemy-occupied territories and then to set up an occupation administration in Germany. In Bosnia-Herzegovina, the military were positioned first as peacekeepers between hostile ethnic groups and finally as peace-builders, seeking to contribute to new relationships for the future. In the 1940s struggle, Allied troops, although brought together in a coalition from a range of nations, largely fought on the ground as separate entities in different theatres of war. In Bosnia-Herzegovina, Western armies were deployed as part of a wider peace operations force under the auspices of the United Nations (UN) or the North Atlantic Treaty Organization (NATO), operating under national orders but within a loose supra-national framework. In the Second World War, the huge armies of the Allied military were largely conscript soldiers and overwhelmingly male. In Bosnia-Herzegovina, the forces came from smaller professional armies into which women had been at least partially integrated. In the Second World War, local attitudes towards incoming troops varied from initial welcome to irritation and growing hostility in liberated territories. In occupied Germany, civilians found themselves living in a country dominated by foreign armies and burgeoning foreign bureaucracies, with little personal freedom of manoeuvre. In Bosnia-Herzegovina, different ethnic groups, both before and after the Dayton Peace Agreement, developed a range of relationships with these foreign contingents who were peacekeepers and then peace-builders.

The role of interpreters/translators in both case studies was of key importance, but the *Languages at War* project sought to contextualize their position within the specifics of each conflict – linguists working for a section of the British administration in Germany, for example, were likely to operate in a very different situation from those engaged by NATO in Bosnia-Herzegovina. Rather than concentrating solely on the work of interpreters/translators, the project aimed to investigate those military perspectives on languages which had created the operational environments in which language intermediaries worked. Understanding the attitude which the military took towards languages – their policies – seemed to be as important as understanding the language experiences of those on the ground of war – the practices of military, civilians and translators/interpreters.

Policy and practice

The project therefore began with the aim of testing the frameworks set by language policies for war against the experiences of those at the sharp end of conflict and examining how the results of experience have in turn inflected policy. Testing policies through their practical outcomes appeared likely to provide a deeper understanding of the realities of language practice by exploring how they diverged from the premises on which policy was based. It appeared likely to lead to a clearer understanding of the ways in which policies were modified in the light of practical experience. And it seemed likely to yield insights that could inform the future development of language policy in conflict situations, and perhaps more broadly in other contexts. The early stages of the research brought these assumptions into question and suggested a more productive approach, which took practice rather than policy as its starting point, and focused on the lessons that could be learned.

An approach based on language policy was a promising point of departure, since it is a well-established field of study, which continues to develop. However, the issues of languages in conflict have rarely been studied, and it became clear that the available frameworks of analysis needed to be significantly extended in order to address them. Language policy emerged from the work of Joshua Fishman, Joan Rubin and others on the sociology of language (Fishman 1972, 1974; Rubin *et al.* (ed.) 1977). It developed principally as an academic basis for understanding and developing language planning at the level of states, an emphasis which still predominates (Kaplan and Baldauf 1997). As a result, language policy has often been regarded as synonymous with language planning, and has referred to the efforts of states or political movements to manage language use within a country in response to, or in pursuit of, social change (Cooper 1989; Schiffman 1996). This is a particular focus for journals such as *Language Policy* and *Current Issues in*

Language Planning, which have developed an extensive research community (Kaplan *et al.* 2000). Work in this area has provided detailed descriptions of a wide range of contexts and has been taken in a number of different directions, exploring, for example, the policy implications of European integration (Coulmas (ed.) 1991), issues of linguistic rights (Skutnabb-Kangas and Phillipson (eds) 1994), and the emergence of globalization (Wright 2004). At the same time, the field has been marked by growing diversity in approaches (Ricento (ed.) 2006). As a result, as Bernard Spolsky noted, 'no consensus has emerged about the scope and nature of the field, its theories or its terminology' (Spolsky 2004: ix).

The field of language policy has remained firmly focused at the level of states and international bodies. In this context, Spolsky's work has been influential in defining the scope of language policy, using a three-part division into 'language practices, language beliefs and ideology, and the explicit policies and plans resulting from language management or planning activities' (Spolsky 2005: 2154). In principle, it was the relationship between the first and third of these elements, practice and policy, which formed the initial framework for the *Languages at War* project. It was a framework well adapted to the analysis of language planning at the level of the state. However, neither the Allied forces in occupied Europe nor the UN/NATO forces in Bosnia-Herzegovina were explicitly concerned with language planning, and as a result the framework did not prove helpful for analysing their experience.

More recently, some attention has been devoted to the 'micropolitics' of language policy within particular institutions. Anthony Liddicoat has directed attention towards language planning at local level (Liddicoat and Baldauf (eds) 2008), Charles Alderson and others have looked at the micropolitics of language education (Alderson (ed.) 2009) and Spolsky's most recent work has addressed the areas of the family, religion, the workplace, the media, schools, legal and health institutions and the military (Spolsky 2009). Their work has been concerned to identify the complexity of issues involved in the management of language at an institutional level and opens up the area of language policy in social activities below the level of the state. In a similar spirit, Georges Lüdi has explored institutional issues of language policy at the level of individual business enterprises (Lüdi and Heiniger 2007; Lüdi *et al.* 2009).

From the experience of addressing issues at the level of military institutions, it has become clear that there is a need for other concepts than those designed to help understand the actions of states. This point has been usefully developed by Michael Hill, in relation to the different levels at which public policy is formed and carried out (Hill 2009). He suggests that a broad concept of 'discretion' may be required to account for the importance of delegated decision-making (Hill 2009: 225). He also endorses Michael Lipsky's notion of 'street-level bureaucracy', a concept used to explore the delivery of state services by teachers, social workers, police officers and others who embody authority at a local level (Lipsky 1983). Lipsky's analysis of the critical role of these agents is particularly helpful in understanding processes within stable bureaucratic structures, but may well be applicable to more dynamic contexts, such as those encountered in military operations. It intersects with the military concept of the 'strategic corporal', under which greater responsibilities are devolved to more junior leaders in contexts of more complex military tasks and greater media attention (Krulak 1999; Szepesy 2005; Liddy 2005).

The specific purposes which policy serves at institutional level may be better expressed in terms of functional needs rather than in terms of political or ideological aims. Claude Truchot and Dominique Huck's work on enterprises adopts this approach to analyse the real or supposed needs of business (Truchot and Huck 2009). A needs-based approach brings with it a focus on problem-solving and strategies for action. Sharon Millar and Astrid Jensen emphasize the role in this of common sense expression, which is essential for effective knowledge production and transfer, and gives the key agents in an enterprise the means to make sense of their own needs and strategies (Millar and Jensen 2009).

These approaches that seek to understand language policy below the level of the state share the common feature of beginning with practice and working towards policy implications, rather than beginning with policy. Their concern is with operational needs and with the people who carry out the operations. Their approach converges with the preliminary findings that emerged from research into languages in the two fields of conflict that the project addresses. The concepts of delegated decision-making, the critical role of agents, needs analysis and problem-solving provide valuable tools for understanding policy development at the level of institutions in general and military institutions in particular.

At the same time, the armed services have an integral relationship with the state. They are coercive state agencies, and military operations are conducted on behalf of a state, embodying the state's political and legal authority. In that sense, even though the armed forces may behave as institutions, they are also subject to the broader language policies prevailing within their state. Similarly, by their actions and example they also represent their state and function as an 'ideological state apparatus', which aims to embed the aims and aspirations of the state in the hearts and minds of those with whom they engage, in war or peace (Althusser 1984). Consequently, an analysis of the language practices of the military must take account of both state and institutional dimensions. On the one hand, the military have operational requirements, to which they respond, and a specific ethos that has developed historically. On the other hand, the armed forces are instrumental in implementing the broader social, cultural and policy framework of the state they serve. There is often a tension between these two dimensions, and militaries may be the vanguard or the rear-guard of changes in civil society as well as embodying or representing them.

Examining the situation of the Allied forces in 1945 and the NATO forces in 1995, it rapidly became clear that there were both too few and too many different policies to provide a coherent framework within which to evaluate the interaction between policy and practice. There were too few policies in the sense that the overall language policy of the Allies and NATO was at an extremely general level. Their first concern was to ensure that the forces could communicate effectively with one another. To a large extent, this was taken for granted in the case of the Allies, who were largely drawn from English-speaking countries, with only small contingents from non-Anglophone Allies. The issue of linguistic 'interoperability' was a more serious issue for the NATO forces (Crossey 2005). NATO policy is officially that English and French are the two working languages. However, since France placed itself outside NATO military command between 1966 and 2009, the use of French has largely been abandoned in practice for communication between contingents. The policy directions in this area are therefore primarily concerned to enhance the ability of different NATO forces to achieve an adequate level of competence in English. NATO also maintains a framework for language testing, based on a Standardization Agreement (STANAG), which defines language proficiency levels in a scale entitled STANAG 6001. The policy directions in this area are primarily concerned with the dissemination and implementation of good practice. This relative dearth of policy has been reinforced in most recent times by the view held by military personnel that 'policy' is a civilian activity and therefore mainly the responsibility of the appropriate government bodies.

In other respects, conversely, there are too many language policies. In particular, each participating country has its own policies relating to language use and language education. This is as true for 1995 as it was for 1945, though the number of contributing countries differs significantly. Each country had its own distinctive approach, which was often in itself quite complex, particularly where countries had more than one official language. Most of the larger contingents in both conflicts used their own national language or languages for internal communications, and English or (more rarely) French for their communications with other contingents. Each country had its own approach to issues of interaction with other units, such as when internal documents would be translated, when officers would use an interpreter to converse with each other, which ranks of military personnel would be required to have language proficiency, at what level, and with access to what training. Each country also had a different approach to communications with the local populations, and frequently different approaches for different linguistic, national or ethnic communities. Different policies also applied to different operational functions. This was a significant problem in the situation after 1945, where the Allied military were tasked with a wide range of activities, including many which were later transferred to civilian agencies or contractors, such as government and administration, judicial systems, humanitarian aid, reconstruction and conference interpreting.

Both of the interventions were transnational operations, and contingents from different countries were frequently required to cooperate on the same operation. In some cases, a single contingent might be formed of brigades from several countries. On the other hand, looking in detail at some of the individual countries, it rapidly becomes clear that the relationship of a contingent to national policy frameworks is extremely variable. In this context, the concept of delegation is particularly helpful, since national frameworks range from highly centralized procedures in which authority is focused at the most senior levels to highly devolved procedures in which a wide discretion is allocated to forces on the ground at lower levels.

The diversity of what might potentially be included in the policy domain is so great as to render it impossible to draw up a coherent statement of policy relevant to language, against which to measure the experience of practice. Yet this diversity is in fact an indication of how deeply language is embedded in the experience of conflict in its multiple dimensions. Language practice exceeds language policy to such an extent that an analysis beginning with policy cannot hope to grasp the complexity of practice. Much better, then, to begin with practice in all of its diversity and work towards a sense of what lessons may be learned to inform future practice and even future policy.

Recovering languages in war

There are, however, methodological problems in investigating the practices of languages in war and uncovering their presence in conflict.

Even in the case of wars for which archival material abounds, the 'architecture' of many of the archives involved – the ways in which the material was originally collected and is now organized – initially presented challenges. How do you, for example, locate the 'foreign' within archives of war which have been created and catalogued in order to represent a particular national story? In the first case study, the Second World War, the catalogue of the British National Archives in Kew detailed thousands of files relating to the period. The search terms 'translator' and 'interpreter', however, revealed fewer than 170 references. Of these, 26 related to operational requirements for translators/interpreters and systems of recruitment for particular sectors – interpreters for hospitals, interpreters for war crimes trials, and so on. By far and away the largest group of interpreter/translator files were captured enemy documents which concentrated not on language intermediaries who had been working for the Allies but rather on those employed by the enemy – indeed, 60 per cent of this collection consisted of memoranda of debriefings with Hitler's chief interpreter, Paul-Otto Schmidt. This weighty archival positioning of translating/interpreting as being connected with an axiomatically suspect 'foreignness', that of the enemy, was replicated in one of the next largest sections in the catalogue for interpreters/translators, the Security Service holdings, which had personal files on captured enemy interpreters. The picture that emerged from this group of catalogue entries was one of interpreters as marginal figures, unreliable and prone to changing allegiances:

> Jakob Gamper, alias Georges Vernier: Swiss. A petty criminal, Gamper was recruited in Dijon in 1944 as a translator/interpreter for SD. His contribution was not great and, as might be expected, he was unreliable, is said to have double-crossed his masters, stolen their money, and finally deserted (catalogue entry KV2/555).

> Arthur Gordon William Perry, alias William Gordon-Perry, British. Before 1939 he held Fascist sympathies and had connections with the German Intelligence Service. He later claimed to have worked for British Intelligence in 1939 in Bucharest. He was interned by the Germans in 1940 and released in 1942 when he worked as a translator for the German Foreign Office and was connected with the publication of the German propaganda newspaper, 'The Camp', which was circulated amongst British prisoners of war (catalogue entry KV 2/619).

Those formally designated as 'translators/interpreters' in the National Archives were thus framed as outsiders, as marginal figures who provoked intense suspicion. This archival eccentricity was reinforced incidentally when the larger number of catalogue entries (359) for 'languages' were examined. In this case, 'languages' generally connoted material actually written in a foreign language: decrypts of German cypher messages; the foreign language press in the USA; foreign language journals of exile groups in London; pamphlets written in French to be dropped by the RAF. In the architecture of the archives, the ways in which material was organized and catalogued, language intermediaries were positioned as marginal, their foreignness a cause for suspicion, and foreign language material was insulated away in a separate category of the foreign, 'languages'.

Despite this, however, foreign languages are indeed present in the archives of war, in those inevitable connections with the 'foreign' which conflict forces upon us when we seek to conceptualize war not as nation-state against others but rather as a process of potential interconnection, what Barkawi calls 'making together' in world politics (Barkawi 2006: 17). In the archives of war, instead of looking for a specific category associated with languages, 'translator/interpreter'/'languages', a more productive approach was found to be following the development of the conflict, the stages of war, and investigating those points at which such connections existed, where languages were actually embedded within military strategy and operational concerns. Military operations, whether invasion or peace support, tend to be organized in broad phases: pre-deployment, deployment (itself understood in discrete operational stages), and post deployment. Foreign Office committees, War Office reports, situation analyses, all followed this trajectory. Connections with the 'foreign' were made either explicitly or implicitly within these stages, through information provided, through intermediaries chosen and through the physical presence of the armies deployed. Thus, for example, the archives showed that preparing 3.5 million troops to land in continental Europe in 12 different countries in 1944 was an exercise in which foreign languages were firmly embedded. A special Foreign Office sub-committee had been tasked with producing a suite of guides to be issued to all soldiers. These guides, information on the countries concerned, were to have a vocabulary list, drawn up by the Foreign Office Vocabulary Sub-Committee, with linguistic suggestions on how to deal courteously and thoughtfully with the liberated civilians whom the soldiers would be meeting. Language intermediaries were present in the archives at almost every stage of the conflict. Far from being marginal, as in the case of the catalogued 'interpreters', these figures were often so tightly integrated into the processes of war that their functions as linguists appeared to 'bleed into' what were considered to be the primary objectives of war. One classic case of this phenomenon, of the processes of war archivally subsuming language intermediaries, was the previously unremarked presence of translators at the heart of the British Intelligence operation at Bletchley Park (the Government Code and Cypher School, GCCS): 18,000 translations per month being processed in the spring of 1944 alone. In this instance, the distinction between intelligence analysis and translation had become essentially notional. Doing one necessarily implied doing the other, so that the job, and the personnel engaged to do it, became indistinguishable. On the ground of war, too, the archives revealed a clear linguistic dimension to the physical presence of the military. Thus, for example, setting up a British zone of occupation in Germany involved the establishment of a huge British bureaucracy with an English-only policy, creating what became in effect a hermetically-sealed space for an English-speaking community, deliberately distanced from the locals. Despite their catalogued marginality, then, foreign languages could indeed be found in the national archives of war. Whether recognized explicitly or implicitly, languages were embedded within the preparations and operations of conflict, providing connections which could be read in the documents of war: connections of information, connections of communication and connections of physical presence.

But, of course, not all wars and conflicts can be approached through a large corpus of archived resources. Documents relating to the second case study in Bosnia-Herzegovina, for example, are still classified and hence currently closed to researchers. In this situation, recovering languages in war had to involve developing a largely interview-based study, one which resulted in more than 50 oral history interviews with participants: locally-recruited interpreters, military linguists, other military personnel and people working with NGOs and peace support organizations. As suggested by the experience of our partner in the project, the Imperial War Museum (IWM) in London, these extended interviews – the shortest one lasted 50 minutes and most were an hour and a half to two hours – followed a broadly biographical trajectory. By stimulating such biographical testimony the project sought to embed languages within the trajectory of the individuals concerned, with the interviewer asking participants in a non-intrusive way about their earlier language learning experiences and bringing to light the diverse biographies of mobility that had served to constitute notions of the local and the foreign within the Bosnia-Herzegovina experience. The NATO-led peace enforcement force, for example, was continually visiting the three main Bosnian armed groups which had taken part in the war, carrying out weapons inspections and holding military liaison meetings. The interviews showed that, whilst some officers in charge of these units refused to use interpreters of a different ethnicity from the armed force they were going to see, others were prepared to do so. For some of the locally-recruited interviewees, at least, military policy dictated that they would be visiting territory under the control of a different ethno-national army from the one which currently held power over the place in which they lived.

Rather than observing the role of languages in documents which had been selected for archiving, this case study listened to the personal testimony of those who had a story to tell about languages in peace operations in Bosnia-Herzegovina and who were still endeavouring to understand their experiences over time. Interviews of this sort did not produce precise data of the type that might be available in contemporary archives (the exact nature of language preparation given to soldiers, the precise number of language intermediaries engaged at any point in the conflict, and so on), but the voice of the language experience itself was a key part of what this project sought to recover, believing that what participants had to say about foreign languages was an integral and valid part of the whole narrative of war. In the Second World War case study, we were able to listen to participants' oral testimonies which had been recorded by the IWM before 2000 and then re-interview them ourselves, listening more specifically for the languages element in the personal stories they told. Interviewees who had barely mentioned languages in the original recordings became voluble about their language experiences and the role which languages had played in their war activity when someone was actually asking them how languages were involved in the jobs they had been given to do. The voices of those actually talking about their experiences of languages in war – whether at the time through archival quotations, in material recorded after, or in interviews specifically undertaken for the *Languages at War* project – are key elements in the recovery of languages for our historical and contemporary understanding of war.

The *Languages at War* project

This volume, *Languages at War: Policies and Practices of Language Contacts in Conflict*, brings together the results of the AHRC-funded project also known as *Languages at War*. The project was a joint one, involving a core group of six researchers, drawn from two UK universities and from the IWM, with additional expertise offered by an Advisory Group of academics and practitioners, including representatives of the Ministry of Defence. Whilst separate chapters are written by different members of the core team (see Preface for details of authorship), the book is very much a product of those lively discussions and reflections which have taken place amongst us as the project has developed.

The book is structured around four themes which broadly mirror the chronological stages of military activity. Part I (Intelligence) investigates the place of languages in what is usually a pre-deployment period. What role do foreign languages play in an intelligence community? How do we approach understanding the other? What place does the 'human' have in human intelligence? Part II (Preparation and Support) examines the role that languages play in military preparations for warfighting and peace operations. How do armies prepare their forces linguistically to liberate territories and to deploy in peace support operations? How does the language infrastructure of the countries concerned affect and modify the preparations they make? Parts III and IV tackle issues relating to the on-the-ground language experiences of war and conflict. Part III (Soldier/Civilian Meetings) looks at the role which an armed force's perception of its own language may have in conditioning the terms of exchange between incoming military and local inhabitants. What is the linguistic context in which 'fraternization' operates, and are such relationships determined by the type of mission in which forces are engaged? Part IV (Communication through Intermediaries) examines the lived experiences of language intermediaries, both military and civilian, allowing the voices of those who play the role of translators/interpreters to tell us about the jobs they do and the lives they lead in conflict. The Conclusions bring together some of the key themes which have emerged from the case studies and set them in the context of lessons which might usefully be learned by government, the military and linguists themselves when they consider future armed conflicts.

Depending on the particular characteristics of the case studies concerned, the four themes are developed through chapters which deal specifically with one or other of the conflict situations. For example, with Intelligence, there is more documentation on the earlier Second World War conflict (Chapters 1 and 3) than on the later case study, whilst the case study on Bosnia-Herzegovina is arguably a more challenging example of the difficulties Western forces face when seeking to 'understand the other' (Chapter 2). In looking at pre-deployment language preparation, the Second World War case study showed what happened when a centralized organization, with a relatively long lead-in time, was preparing for a large continental deployment (Chapter 4), whilst the Bosnia-Herzegovina case study illustrated preparations for an unexpected small-scale deployment which had particularly complex ethno-national realities (Chapters 5 and 6). Chapters 7 and 9 examine occupation and military interpreters in war from the 1940s perspective and Chapter 10 explores the role of civilian interpreters in Bosnia-Herzegovina. Two of the chapters (Chapter 8, Fraternization; Chapter 11, Being an Interpreter) adopt a comparative framework between the two situations in order to see the extent to which the actual practice of languages on the ground in soldier/civilian relations may have changed in the intervening years. Are there clear differences between 1945 and 1995, or is there some consistency of experience for the military, the civilians and the language intermediaries?

As we discovered in this project, war and conflict engage the interest of many different disciplines: history, International Relations, translation studies, peace studies, cultural studies. Above all, they are of major importance to governments and military which prepare for action, and they are of life-threatening danger to those soldiers, civilians and interpreters who become physically involved in what happens on the ground. For all these groups, directly affected by war and conflict, or studying the history and consequences of armed struggle, this volume seeks to present a new map of war, one which is framed by the 'foreignness' of armed conflict and which for the first time places foreign languages at the core and centre of war.

Part I
Intelligence

Gathering and analysing intelligence is vital to national security. Failures of intelligence – when states are taken by surprise by events or misinterpret what is happening to them – are sometimes systemic, caused by lacunae in the intelligence-gathering processes, or failures to share relevant information between the diverse agencies involved. However, other causes of intelligence failures relate not to these organizational issues but rather to the frameworks of analysis, interpretation and reception which have been applied to information once it has been gathered.

This Part addresses one aspect of these frameworks of understanding: the 'foreignness' of the intelligence material and the processes by which this 'foreignness' becomes domesticated enough for the users of intelligence to be able to make strategic intelligence assessments. Typically, intelligence is drawn from an eclectic range of sources: directly available open material, covert operations and signals and human intelligence. In the majority of cases, this information arrives from foreign sources, and appears in its raw form, written or spoken, in a language which is normally not our own. The process of mediation, of rendering the foreign intelligible and therefore assessable, is an integral part of the way in which our understanding of 'the other', and hence our intelligence, is formed and constructed.

The following chapters in this Part explore the 'foreignness' of intelligence in war and peace support operations. Chapter 1, 'Languages in the Intelligence Community', investigates the ways in which institutional language policies are developed for intelligence work and explores the working practices of linguists in intelligence. Chapter 2, 'Frameworks for Understanding', examines how perceptions of a foreign country are closely related to the existing corpus of knowledge about it, with popular constructions of the 'usefulness' or 'relevance' of the foreign language combining with historical myths and recent political experience to create particular representations of the country which are crucial starting points for intelligence analysis. Chapter 3, 'The Human in Human Intelligence', shifts attention towards the experiences of those who act as language intermediaries in particularly tense intelligence situations: interrogations and investigations. The physical placing of the foreign language speaker between the interrogator, who wants to obtain information, and the person interrogated, reluctant to provide this information, is potentially one of the most personally fraught situations for any linguist in war.

Languages, these chapters argue, are key to effective intelligence work. Their presence in intelligence necessarily raises questions about the process of translation itself. Explaining the foreign 'other' places a particular burden upon the language intermediary, a responsibility which can shape responses and events or serve to subvert and challenge those national orthodoxies which intelligence communities develop.

1
Languages in the Intelligence Community

> 'a translation linguistically sound, but without background knowledge is worse than no translation at all...it may be dangerous'.
>
> (NA, HW 50/15, discussion 5 April 1943)

Finding out about the operation of intelligence in war is notoriously problematic, and the closer the conflict to our own times, the greater the difficulties: files are not open, those most involved are bound by the Official Secrets Act not to discuss what they might have been doing. In the case of the Second World War, however, a great deal of information about the working of signals intelligence is now in the public domain. This chapter exploits the opportunity offered by the existence of such documentation in order to examine the role of languages in the processes of understanding signals intercepted, translating what adversaries were actually saying. At the government Second World War Code and Cypher School (GCCS) at Bletchley Park, the Naval Intelligence operation alone processed an average of 18,000 translations per month in the spring of 1944, with 433 messages translated in just one eight-hour watch.[1] In addition to coded sources, there was information to be obtained from captured documents and from prisoner of war interrogations. All these were in the foreign language. The volume of German documents at Bletchley Park rose from 1000 in January 1943 to a staggering 10,000 in July 1944, and those in Italian from 500 in January 1943 to well over 4000 in the summer of 1944.[2] After the Liberation of France, 10 tons of German material appeared, needing to be processed and translated. Obtaining raw intelligence is of no strategic or operational use if its recipients cannot understand what is being said. Without the input of translators and interpreters, most intelligence systems are simply unworkable. Despite this, however, the critical role of languages in intelligence has never been examined, even in those historic cases like Bletchley Park where the structures and successes of intelligence work have been subjected to extensive and detailed historical analysis (Hinsley, Simkins and Howard 1979: 90; Hinsley and Stripp 1994; Lewin 1978; Patterson 2008; Welchman 1982).

This chapter explores how national authorities, in this case the British, have dealt with some of the issues surrounding the foreign language element of intelligence: for example, how do you recruit intelligence operatives with language skills who can be regarded as trustworthy? What is the effect of working in intelligence on the linguists recruited, people who not only have an informed understanding of the enemy culture but who may also retain strong emotional links to it? How does the presence of foreign languages explicitly affect established orthodoxies around intelligence-gathering? How do foreign languages become institutionalized in intelligence in war situations?

Recruiting language specialists

For the authorities who need to employ linguists in intelligence, effectiveness on the job clearly has to be balanced against overriding security requirements. Paradoxically, understanding information about a foreign enemy generally relies on people who have a history of close and sustained contact with that enemy's language and culture. In the most extreme manifestation of this paradox, agents sent into an enemy occupied country during the Second World War were expected to take on the whole persona of the foreign national whilst remaining loyal to the institution which had sent them. Special Operations Executive (SOE) personnel described this phenomenon as 'passing', using their foreign language expertise and cultural knowledge as a mask: 'I was to pass for an average Frenchman, whilst secretly organising the sabotage of selected targets' (Pattinson 2011 [2007]: 15).

Developing language policies for intelligence work thus meant that issues of trust and security had to be set against the need for developed language skills. In practice, it was the technical environments in which language specialists were to be placed that appeared to have the greatest influence on the ways in which government agencies represented their language requirements and on the type of personnel they recruited, both at Bletchley Park/GCCS and in the related listening posts (Y stations), connected by teleprinter landline to Bletchley Park, which had been established all around the British coast, from Peterhead in Scotland down the east and south coasts of England to Wales.

In the case of wireless listening in the Y stations, the need for the authorities to recruit linguists had initially caught everyone by surprise. Wireless interception of enemy transmissions had first been exploited by the military during the First World War. By 1939, each of the services had listening capabilities, bolstered by voluntary amateur radio operators, often using equipment set up in their own homes. The British had expected the Germans to impose radio silence once war began, but instead, as Axis forces invaded more of Europe, listening stations picked up an increasing amount of enemy wireless communications. At one Folkestone listening post in early 1940, the Royal Air Force (RAF) was forced to make a hasty search over the whole station before locating someone who could actually understand the messages they were now receiving in German (Clayton 1980: 29). At the outset, a variety of ad hoc measures were used to fill the gap in competent linguists. Freddie Marshall, one of the few available naval officers able to understand German, spent the early months of the war trying to cope with the radio traffic on his own, occasionally helped out by recruits drafted in at the last minute – three Cambridge undergraduates and one naturalized Swiss with broken English.[3] By March 1940, the Army was arguing that foreign language expertise was urgently needed, although at this stage the definition of what sort of language skills were exactly required was vague – officers with 'a very considerable knowledge and a high degree of imagination particularly if the Germans talk in jargon, intended to be unintelligible to a secret listener' (Skillen 1990: 5). Soon, however, the context in which German linguists would be called upon to work – wireless stations – began to frame a more precise conception of desirable language competences. Knowledge and imagination gave way to a sharper emphasis on receptive language skills and on operational wireless listening ability.

A two-week training course for naval personnel about to work in listening posts was established with the aim of giving German speakers practice in handling wireless receivers, as well as in understanding German and English nautical terms. A mock Y station helped trainees to get an idea of the future job by listening through headphones to transmissions from the control room: 'It seemed a long way from Goethe ... to the deep baritone voice of Lieutenant Freddie Marshall shouting "Achtung! Achtung! Feindliche Zerstörer an Steuerborg!" This, he taught us, was the sort of thing we might hear from a German E-boat near the English coast, and which we would have to intercept and send to our nearest Intelligence Centre.'[4] Excellent hearing and listening skills were as important for recruiters as German language competence. Indeed on occasions a candidate without any German at all could slip through the selection procedure and complete most of the course, until they were asked to actually translate the texts they had taken down: 'I had a well-trained W/T [wireless transcription] ear and...because German was always spelt as it was pronounced, I had no problem taking it down.'[5] Linguists were positioned by their new employers as wireless operators, expected to hear and transcribe a variety of messages transmitted. Foreign language competence was in effect a subset of the general wireless interceptor skills of listening and then reproducing exactly what had been communicated.

Given the volume of traffic, it now became a matter of extreme urgency to find candidates who had these language skills and whom the authorities would be able to regard as trustworthy. The quickest way to recruit personnel who were security-cleared was to draw upon those German-speakers who had already been called up, existing members of the British armed services. By the summer of 1940, however, potential male candidates in uniform were being conscripted for fighting at the front line. The next best alternative was to search for linguists among service personnel who were not destined for active combat, namely women. The authorities therefore trawled through their personnel records to locate female German-speakers currently allocated to other posts who might be speedily transferred. The RAF records office at Ruislip in Middlesex provided a selection of possible WAAF (Women's Auxiliary Air Force) German-speakers who were duly interviewed by a language expert on 13 June 1940 (Clayton 1980: 29), and the first batch of linguists found in the WRNS (Women's Royal Naval Service) arrived in Y stations in the early summer of 1940. Inevitably, some German-speakers were missed on the first trawl and were only recruited later, often by chance. Daphne Baker, for example, then working as a WRNS cypher officer, was recovering in the sanatorium from an ear infection when a chief officer came into the room, looking worried, and asked 'Does anybody here speak German?'[6]

The demand for linguists to work in listening stations grew at such a pace, however, that the pool of existing servicewomen could not satisfy it. Accordingly, in a second wave of recruitment, advertisements in newspapers and on the radio urged women with the desired language skills to join up as quickly as possible. A third wave of female recruits arrived with the 1941 national call-up of women aged 21 to 30. Women could thus find themselves 'hijacked' into linguist posts when it was discovered that they had Higher Certificate German: 'If I could speak German well enough, I was wanted in the WRNS.'[7]

Finally, when the supply of linguist servicewomen looked as if it was drying up altogether, the authorities considered employing civilian German refugees or German-speaking foreigners. This move, however, was cautious – the security vetting procedure was long, and stations with non-British-born employees might find their security classification downgraded, so that they would not get access to highly secret information (Bonsall 2008: 828). Nevertheless, some non-British personnel – Poles, Austrians, Germans, Greeks, Czechs, French and Belgians – were given permission to work at RAF listening stations (Clayton 1980: 56).

As well as the vital security clearance, linguists selected were expected to have fluency in contemporary colloquial German, a fluency which was most likely to have been acquired through an extensive period of residence in the country before the war. The first wave of recruits accordingly tended to have been educated outside the UK, and came from wealthy, often cosmopolitan backgrounds, people who had for example gone to German boarding schools in Switzerland or who had lived abroad for most of their lives.[8] As war progressed, however, and the second wave of recruits came on stream, it was much less likely that these younger women would have had the opportunity to spend time in Germany. Instead, candidates tended to possess formal academic qualifications in the language and arrived at the Y stations often straight from university.[9]

Overall, the problem of identifying people who were closely acquainted with the enemy's language and culture but who were still deemed to be sufficiently trustworthy to operate in intelligence was solved by looking for female service recruits. In order to have the requisite language skills, these women, almost by definition, came from backgrounds not dissimilar to those of the male officers who were recruiting them. In class and attitude, they were close to the norm of the contemporary British officer. The unusual fact that in 1940 women were being employed in this role was to some extent masked by their prior assimilation into the armed services and by the way in which the particular intelligence tasks they had been given were positioned as passive, non-fighting duties, integrated into the essentially mechanical processes of wireless operation.

In contrast with the initial ill-preparedness of Y stations at the outbreak of war, GCCS, in view of what it regarded as the inevitability of war, had begun looking for personnel as early as 1937. The Chief of the Secret Service, Admiral Sir Hugh Sinclair, had issued instructions calling 'for the earmarking of the right type of recruit' (Andrew 2002: 5). Leonard Forster, a Cambridge German lecturer, was one of those lined up for future employment, going on preparatory courses in the Easter vacation.[10] The Head of GCCS looked for what he described as 'men of the Professor type,'[11] using his contacts with two fellows of King's College, Cambridge, who had previously served in the First World War Signals Intelligence Agency – Frank Adcock, Professor of Ancient History, and Frank Birch, a historian. Inevitably, these two sought out recruits in the places they knew best: no fewer than twelve dons from one Cambridge college, King's, were brought in to work at Bletchley Park. The range of disciplines covered by these early recruits was wide – physics, maths, history, classics and languages. What was important was less the particular subject studied, rather the level of intelligence displayed by the candidate, the capacity to think: 'What is required is good general intelligence coupled with an ability to sort out and weigh evidence, and present conclusions in an intelligible form.'[12] The mentality they looked for was that of the inspired and dogged problem-solver. Foreign languages were thus represented as being on a par with any other discipline which might foster these qualities. Instead of the colloquial German and listening skills necessary for Y station workers, Bletchley Park recruiters considered foreign languages in much the same way as classical Greek or Latin – evidence of general intelligence and puzzle-solving ability – a positioning incidentally not uncommon in university foreign language departments at that period. The language skill specified was that of reading competence – 'enough German simply to read it (not to speak nor write it)' – and this only if the other attributes – intellect, energy and common sense – were demonstrably present as well.[13]

In order to recruit language-qualified people whom they would consider trustworthy in this security context, the authorities relied on the tried and tested networks from which the ruling class had long been drawn. Membership of these networks – public schools, universities, London clubs – was seen as a proxy for institutional loyalty, and the initial search for suitable intelligence candidates among linguists was thus conducted within these networks, by word of mouth and personal recommendation. Those who had been students of university Germanists already recruited to Bletchley Park – Leonard Forster (from Cambridge), Trevor Jones (from Cambridge), Frederick Norman (from King's College London) – might find themselves discreetly taken aside and invited to join. On the second day of the war, Edward Thomas, a London university student, was told 'you are a pupil of Professor Norman. I think we can use you' (Thomas 1994: 41). A smaller number of linguists came to intelligence work through family connections. Often, the process of personal recommendation could be quite circuitous. Suitably qualified Newnham College graduates, for example, were contacted via the sister of a senior cryptographer at Bletchley Park who had formerly been a member of the College (Calvocoressi 1980: 12). All staff, including linguists, had to be British-born, although in rare cases exceptions were made if a potentially useful recruit could be seen as fully integrated into key national networks. The Jewish refugee Walter Ettinghausen/Eytan, for example, claimed that, whereas he and his brother would have been debarred from intelligence activity in the USA because of their German birth, they had been approached at Oxford in the summer of 1940 and asked to work for British intelligence (Eytan 1994). Soon, however, the volume of specifically language-related work grew to such an extent that this civilian well of personnel was in danger of drying up. A second wave of recruitment targeted candidates who had already been called up but whose service records suggested they had the right sort of qualifications or experience (Millward 1994).

When it became apparent that Japanese linguists would also be required for intelligence, it was evident that a similar pool of suitable civilian or service candidates simply did not exist in the UK and that the authorities would need to get on and train their own cadre as quickly as possible, in specially-designed courses. The selection procedure for potential students, however, followed much the same process as that for German linguists: discreet word of mouth recommendation, within the established networks of influence. Thus the Master of Balliol College, Oxford, and the President of St John's College, Cambridge, were invited to suggest the names of undergraduates, or young people now in the forces, who had the capacity to learn Japanese in an accelerated programme (Loewe 1994).

As the war progressed, the organization of the translation operation at Bletchley Park became increasingly sophisticated. In January 1940, translation in the Army/RAF intelligence centre, Hut 3, had been handled by a small team: one civilian, three or four typists and a service officer who might or might not be able to understand German.[14] By 1941, the Hut had a whole series of specialist sections, each of which needed well-qualified staff, typically a Head of Department, two senior civilians, a service officer and half a dozen assistants. To support this operation, a second sort of linguist personnel was drafted in: staff who would have to index glossaries, type up records of German messages received and translate and classify the growing stock of captured documents. In this case, language needs were contextualized within an ancillary/support framework. Instead of critical intelligence, what was seen as necessary was a secretarial-type profile, with language competence an adjunct of other practical skills and often interchangeable with them: 'It was realised that we should never be able to employ German-speaking typists and ... it was easier to teach linguists to type rather than to teach typists German.'[15] This representation of a linguist's task as back-room support, coupled with the dearth of possible male recruits, again encouraged the authorities to look for suitable female candidates already in the services. A few could be found by redeploying language-proficient WRNS from Y stations.[16] As the war went on, and this source of recruits dried up, more and more female university graduates were recruited to staff the language support areas: 'nearly all the indexers were university graduates with at least a fair knowledge of German'.[17] To observers, the Bletchley Park translation operation came to resemble a series of specialist sections, each one run by a professor, 'supported by a sprinkling of high grade minions ... (the professors were male, the minions mostly female)' (Jackson 2002: ii). This mixture of male civilian section heads and female support staff mirrored the overall organization of GCCS by this time: out of the approximately 10,000 staff employed, roughly one third were civilians and three quarters female (Hill 2007).

Linguists in intelligence

On an institutional level, linguists who worked in listening stations were largely invisible. Y Service workers in the WRNS initially had to struggle for the right to attend officer training courses, and WAAF linguists found it difficult to get a rank and pay-grade which was equivalent to their non-linguist code and cypher colleagues. In their working environments, too, these language specialists were positioned as somewhat apart, not entirely fitting into the intelligence systems in which they had been placed. It was almost as if the language abilities which had got them the jobs in the first place also gave them a quasi-foreign identity which the prevailing intelligence and service cultures could find occasionally unsettling. When Freddie Marshall, for example, first started translating intercepted German messages, he observed that his superiors regarded him 'with complete disbelief and I was even charged with being a spy'.[18] A senior British-born linguist who regularly participated in selection boards for Y station workers found that the Director of the WAAFs was ill at ease in her company, wondering whether or not she was totally English: 'You are English, aren't you ...? You have quite an accent yourself', and concluded: 'I do not think that the Director approved of having "foreigners" in the WAAF' (Clayton 1980: 55). In practice, Y service linguists appeared to develop an allegiance to an internal group identity based at least partly on their shared involvement in the enemy's language and culture. As one linguist suggested of her fellow workers: 'The great bonus... of Special Duties was that needing to be a German linguist meant that we mostly had this background in common.'[19] Within the already closed world of intelligence, they operated rather as a type of inner secret group – Freddie Marshall, who trained Y service operatives, described them as a sort of 'private army' within Naval Intelligence.[20]

Whereas staff at Bletchley Park encountered the foreign culture almost solely via its written form, and then usually from anonymous sources, in decodes or captured documents, linguists in the Y stations were often listening in to the actual voices of individual enemy servicemen who were communicating with each other or with their headquarters: 'Sometimes during the night when there seemed to be fewer German pilots about, they would have a chat about their girlfriends and what they were going to do when they had finished their shift and which town they would visit' (Flanders 2004). This direct if clandestine contact with a native of a country which they would have known well before the war could be disorientating for those who were listening: 'A year before when I was a student in Germany, I would never have believed that by the following summer I would be in such a secret way the opposite number of the young German Air Force officers with whom I had danced' (Clayton 1980: 32). Dalma Flanders (2004) remembered her feelings of ambivalence as she warned Spitfire and Hurricane crews to prepare for incoming Messerschmitts: 'It seemed so stupid to me as I also had German friends on the enemy side and to be fighting one's friends was hard to come to terms with.'

In comparison with linguists in Y stations, those who worked at Bletchley Park were far more removed from direct contact with the enemy's voice. Translators in the Army/RAF and Naval Intelligence Centres received the German messages on which they had to work at second hand, after they had been decrypted from their original code. Rather than an individual one-to-one contact with foreign material, the translators operated in a highly organized system, 'an assembly line in a factory for mass-production',[21] as one described it. Raw decrypted messages arrived at one end, and were turned, by a variety of processes, into the end-product, namely finished intelligence material for Anglophone clients. Those involved identified 15 discrete stages in this process, each taking an average of 24 minutes.[22] William Millward, who came to work in Intelligence in April 1942, described the key points as emendation, translation, evaluation, commenting and signal drafting (Millward 1994: 20). Decrypts arrived in the Hut with the decode still in five-letter word-groups, on a gummed strip. The first stage, emendation, was thus dividing the groups of letters into German words and numbers and trying to replace missing or corrupted words, in order to arrive at a German text which could be translated. From the beginning, then, the German material with which the linguists were dealing was a highly manufactured text, which would already have passed through a number of hands – the drafter of the original message, the original signaller, followed by the decoder and the typist at Bletchley Park who were receiving the message and passing it on. Wireless reception conditions meant that there were often a number of corrupt words, or sometimes whole sentences, which needed correction or had gaps to be filled in (Freedman 2000: 53). Rather than the direct experience of an enemy voice which listening operatives sometimes had, linguists at Bletchley Park received the enemy culture in a form not unlike a manufactured jigsaw puzzle, with apparently unrelated bits and pieces, appearing at different times. Inevitably, this context produced a distancing effect from the enemy culture: 'here lay a pile of dull, disjointed, and enigmatic scraps, all about the weather, or the petty affairs of a Luftgau no one had ever heard of . . . the whole sprinkled with terms no dictionary knew'.[23]

Translation thus became a process of dealing with the multiple problematics of a partially realized text, and trying to replace each text within its wider, largely unknown context; examining each piece of the jigsaw, as it were, and then seeking to fit it into the overall puzzle. Rather than searching after meaning, translators at Bletchley Park tended to talk about their work as grappling with a range of obscurities in order to establish the basic foreign text before it could be translated. Quite apart from the text's problematic origin, messages had usually been deliberately constructed in German in order to mask their meaning from prying eyes: 'The first task . . . was to produce out of these gaps, abbreviations and technical terms, a reliable and intelligible text, and to put that text into English.'[24]

Given the fact that individual texts were having to be reconstituted before translation and that the volume of translation work was growing in intensity by the hour, translators argued that their priority was to develop a system which would provide some linguistic order amidst the chaos. A corporate linguistic memory had to be established, logging German words coming in, English equivalents proposed and translation difficulties as yet unresolved: 'a prime requirement was stability in translation; right if possible, but stable at all costs'.[25] The first step towards this was the constitution of a continuous record of equivalents and abbreviations in a properly referenced card index. Translators who found particularly difficult words and expressions in the course of a day's work were asked to indicate this on the text with green pencil, and the Navy developed a 'waiting index' for each language, which held worksheets of unsolved translation problems, with progress so far, and a copy of the original text in which the unsolved problem had first appeared. At one stage, at the end of October 1943, a weekly update digest, *Widsith*, was produced, reminding translators of current linguistic snags and giving early warning of apparent changes in nomenclature.[26] In effect, the translators had constructed a large and well-organized linguistic infrastructure to provide stability and coherence in a situation of chronic fluctuation and vagueness. By the end of the war, Army/RAF language indexes had grown to 16,000 equivalents and 10,000 abbreviations in German and Naval language indexes to 13,000 equivalents and 6,000 abbreviations in German, with 2,500 equivalents and 100 abbreviations in Italian.[27]

Relating the disparate texts that came in for translation to the whole surrounding context from which they had come was a particular challenge for translators: 'They had to learn what was in effect a new dialect as they worked; to build up something of a background from fragments that came to hand.'[28] Quite soon it became clear that the best way to construct this as yet unknown background was to develop specialized sub-sections to deal with the various areas that were likely to be relevant: radar/scientific developments, enemy topography, railways, air intelligence, military intelligence, naval intelligence, cover names and so on: 'Hut 3 (Army/RAF Intelligence)...had become an organisation of specialists in more or less restricted fields.'[29] Each sub-section kept detailed indexes on their subject, assembled from the messages translated, as well as from any other useful additional material. As one indexer described it: 'We had a big table with thousands of brown cardboard shoe-boxes full of index-cards...I had to keep a card index of the name of every Italian officer and other rank mentioned in any signal...We were also supplied with cuttings from Italian newspapers, and given interminable lists of men in the Italian Air Force who had been decorated' (Hill 2004: 42–3). Peter Calvocoressi argued that it was precisely these indexes of words which were the backbone of intelligence: 'The cards – about 5x9 inches – were stacked in specially designed stands which stood in rows down the length of a long room. As the war went on their ranks grew until they represented a vast corpus of knowledge beyond even the most retentive human memory' (Calvocoressi 1980: 62).[30]

The working practice of linguists, as it developed, closely resembled that of an academic: 'all the technique of the academic editor, with the great disadvantage, as compared with an academic editor, that the work generally had to be done in a hurry'.[31] The professional methods of university language researchers were transposed into an intelligence context with apparent ease: 'It was very noticeable that those of us who took most easily to the work were people already acquainted with the technique of research in some other field.'[32] Rather than an identity which was uneasily split between an enemy culture they knew well and loyalty to their own native culture, these linguists progressively attached their allegiance to broader professional objectives and qualities – the disinterested pursuit of knowledge, 'the scholar's approach to problems'[33] – which they had espoused in their pre-war activities. A certain collegiality grew up around this shared concept of what they were trying to do: 'The encouragement we derived from knowing that similar work to our own was being competently done, by a person with a similar approach'.[34] The goal of the translation system they established was ambitious: to access the enemy's lexicon in its entirety – 'the whole of this ever-expanding vocabulary was being used somewhere, by someone, all the time, and it was our task to cover as much of it as humanly possible'.[35] The scholar's never-ending struggle to understand was displaced from pre-war university activities to that of wartime intelligence: 'Research-work has a snowball tendency. The more one knows, the more one finds one does not know.'[36] As Trevor Jones summed it up, they were, in their way, 'scrabbling after infinity'.[37]

Languages and the intelligence orthodoxies

Translating in this professional context implied attitudes towards background information and to the inter-relatedness of texts which seemed initially to disrupt traditional intelligence orthodoxies. The received intelligence wisdom was that translators at Bletchley Park should treat each of their texts as a separate entity, and not 'contaminate' it by referring to other texts or to external background material: 'We were merely to break, decode and translate'.[38] Intelligence practitioners in early 1940 maintained that a distance should be kept between raw intelligence and the analysis and interpretation of this intelligence, and that the analysis should be carried

out separately by intelligence professionals. Given the highly problematic nature of the texts with which translators were dealing and
their ambition to relate each text to the overall context which had
produced it, this official approach was rapidly seen by them as
unacceptable.

There ensued a long struggle between the linguists at Bletchley Park
and the official authorities – a battle of attrition, nicknamed by those
involved 'the Battle of the Books'. Linguists demanded that the information blackout to which they were subjected should be lifted. If they
were to be able to translate, it was vital to obtain relevant supporting
material. The official response was negative. Requests for German books
to be bought via the naval attaché in Stockholm, for example, resulted in
just one technical dictionary being sent, together with a note explaining
that since the rest of the books were already held in an Admiralty department in London they would not be sending another one to Bletchley
Park.[39] Basic tools for the translator (the *Oxford English Dictionary*) were
not provided: 'we fought for a year... for an Italian encyclopedia, but
although there are copies of such publications in various libraries in
the country, somehow the Foreign Office was unwilling to obtain one'.
When the translators themselves finally tracked down a copy in a
London public library, 'It was... alleged that considerations of security
(!) precluded the Foreign Office from taking steps to obtain it on loan'.[40]
The depths of the misunderstanding between the official intelligence
culture and translation practice were evident when linguists, needing
to deal urgently with material coming from the Spanish Navy, asked if
the Admiralty could get them a basic Spanish Navy manual. The reply
was: 'Are you suggesting that the Spanish Navy has anything to teach
us in seamanship and gunnery?'[41] In the event, translators sought to
fill the vacuum in background books by a variety of personal shopping
expeditions to the Charing Cross Road, or by haphazard borrowing from
friends' homes when suitable material, like *Meyers Konversations-Lexikon*
(*Meyer's German Encyclopedia*), for example, happened to be spotted on
the bookshelves.[42] As one linguist concluded, 'The truth is of course that
we use books, English and foreign, for purposes for which they were
never meant to be used.'[43]

The practice of linguists as it developed at Bletchley Park made any
distinction between raw intelligence and the evaluation of this intelligence essentially redundant. Reconstituting the German original from
the decode, and seeking to extract its full meaning by referring to the
massive subject indexes which had been established, meant that the

process of translation and analysis had become one: 'By the time a man has emended and translated a decode, he has all the points at his finger ends.'[44] In 1941, an argument erupted at Bletchley Park about who was actually going to control the complex translation/intelligence system which was developing – whether 'mere translators' could be allowed to operate without being under the close supervision of qualified intelligence officers. To translators, the conflict was by then irrelevant: 'The controversy ought...never to have arisen.... With the increasing complications and ramifications of our work, we were...in fact doing intelligence.' Translation and intelligence analysis had become inseparable: 'It may seem strange that the foundation of exacting full and accurate information from a German mine or torpedo, a fleet order or a shore's telephone list, should be a matter of philology – of the accurate use and definition of terms.'[45]

A contributory factor to the success of Hut 3 as an intelligence organization was undoubtedly this notion that translation as an activity was inseparable from evaluation and analysis; that translating was an integral part of a holistic intelligence system: 'The actual situation, no doubt very distasteful to these officers and their superiors, was that Hut 3...had turned itself into a far more efficient intelligence organisation than its Whitehall counterparts.... With their ever-growing indexes, research facilities, technical experts, specialised "back room" groups...Hut 3 had become an intelligence organisation the like of which had never been seen...in the...stuffy military establishment' (Freedman 2000: 55). For later historians, it was indeed this close integration of intelligence processes, established for the first time, which had spearheaded Bletchley Park's success: 'The interaction between cryptanalysts, translators and intelligence analysts enhanced the effectiveness of all three and was one of the great strengths of British communications intelligence in World War II' (Headrick 1991: 227).

At the root of this successful challenge to prevailing intelligence orthodoxies was the practice of the linguists who held the gateway between the raw intelligence and its clients and who insisted that their translation process necessarily included evaluation and analysis. The success with which linguists subverted official conceptions of raw intelligence and analysis crucially depended on their monopoly of the means to understanding, namely the foreign language itself: 'Hut 3 always and rightly, remained the final arbiter on...German language'; 'we had an enormous pull in being able to work in constant contact with the German originals'.[46]

Conclusions

The role of linguists in intelligence in the Second World War raises issues which continue to be relevant to later intelligence situations and systems. How governments and the military interpret their foreign language needs and the status which they accord to languages tend to be closely related to the ways in which the authorities describe the technical environments in which languages are expected to operate. In 1940–5, the contexts in which intelligence work was going to be carried out – wireless intercepts, decoded texts and written documents – conditioned, at least to some extent, the institutional status accorded to the linguists concerned. Officials represented the language skills they required as a subset of more important technical competences: wireless operation on the one hand and problem-solving skills on the other.

The problematics of 'foreignness', of how national authorities assure themselves of the loyalty of people who have close associations with the enemy culture, revolved around what might be seen as the acceptable compensatory limits within which difference can be safely and securely accommodated. Women serving in Y stations, civilian academics working at Bletchley Park, non-British-born refugee Jews, were all acceptable security-risks in 1940–5, largely because of the relative stability of their shared class structures. Nevertheless, the fact that those recruited had to have a developed understanding of the language and culture of the enemy meant that they could still be seen as slightly anomalous members of these same middle-class networks. Unease about quasi-foreigners certainly existed in some official quarters, with a spectrum of suspicion ranging from slight disquiet in the case of linguists like Y station listeners who were able to speak the colloquial language of the enemy to traces of condescension towards academics employed in translation and problem-solving: 'I am sure that...too much will not be expected from these enthusiastic and clever men.'[47]

Linguists in intelligence appeared to accommodate the multiple positionings in which they were placed in a variety of ways. For those in direct contact with the foreign culture, the likelihood of personal stress could be high. Y station listeners, exposed to the voices of individual German combatants, were clearly sometimes ambivalent about the present situation in which they found themselves, secretly listening in to enemies who might just a few months previously have been the sort of people they knew in Germany. In both the Y stations and Bletchley Park, language specialists constructed their own group identity within the intelligence structure in which they were placed. In the listening posts, those with foreign language skills seemed to bond together, operating in effect as a secret and largely invisible band of linguists inside the secret service. At Bletchley Park, linguists were subsumed into a wider grouping of academic researchers or female sections of ancillary language assistants. Loyalty to a broader ideal – the pursuit of knowledge – and to professional standards of working were key elements in the identities they constructed.

The practice of translating foreign intelligence texts into English led linguists at Bletchley Park to challenge notions about the sanctity and separateness of each piece of intelligence and the extent to which individual texts could be allowed to relate to or contaminate others. Translation and analysis were rapidly seen by them as indistinguishable. They argued that accurate intelligence could not be derived without a sophisticated linguistic infrastructure and that each piece of raw intelligence had to be related to its overall cultural background in order to be understood and properly analysed. Translators at Bletchley Park maintained that divorcing the analysis of a foreign language text from its producing culture, and from other texts related to it, could lead to misinterpretations, with potentially critical consequences: 'a translation linguistically sound, but without background knowledge is worse than no translation at all ... it may be dangerous'.[48]

Arguably, the continued invisibility of foreign languages within contemporary discussions of intelligence-gathering and evaluation may relate in part to these broader issues of how we understand the whole process of translation. Failing to recognize and problematize the role of foreign languages in intelligence – the illusion that the exercise of translation itself is an automatic and transparent one – carries with it particular security dangers. It can, for example, serve to mask the extent to which translating might domesticate a foreign text, screening out key aspects of its essential foreignness and allowing recipients of such translated intelligence to maintain a type of cultural parochialism (see Venuti 2008) in which information from foreign sources is compared only with what is known – similar texts and situations in English – rather than provoking radical speculation on what may be unknown and as yet, in intelligence terms, unthinkable.

Notes

1. NA, HW 50/15, GC&CS European Naval Section.
2. NA, HW 3/137, The History of NS VI, 16 (original document numbering used throughout).

3. IWM, 660 91/4/1, Ackroyd Papers, Testimony, Lt Commander F. Marshall.
4. IWM, 660 91/4/1, Ackroyd Papers, Testimony, S. Welch (Russell).
5. IWM, 660 91/4/1, Ackroyd Papers, Testimony, M. Gray (Woodhouse).
6. IWM, 660 91/4/1, Ackroyd Papers, Testimony.
7. IWM, Testimony, 660 91/4/1, Ackroyd Papers, Testimony, Shirley Gadaby (Cannicott).
8. IWM, 660 91/4/1, Ackroyd Papers, Testimonies.
9. IWM, 660 91/4/1, Ackroyd Papers, Testimony, Joy Hale (Banham).
10. Selwyn College Archive, Cambridge, SEPP/FOR Forster, 'Reminiscences of Selwyn College 1938–1950, Seen from 1993'.
11. Churchill College Archive, Cambridge, papers of Sir Stuart Milner-Barry, GBR/004/MNBY, Box 3, Denniston to Wilson, 3 September 1939.
12. NA, ADM 223/472, 'Development and Organisation of the Naval Intelligence Division September 1939–April 1944'.
13. NA, HW3/119, 'History of Hut 3, 1940–45', vol. I, 49 (original document numbering used throughout).
14. NA, HW3/119, 21.
15. NA, HW3/137, 12.
16. NA, HW 50/15.
17. NA HW3/119, 168.
18. IWM, 660 91/4/1, Ackroyd Papers, Testimony, Lt Commander F. Marshall.
19. IWM, 660 91/4/1, Ackroyd Papers, Testimony.
20. IWM, 660 91/4/1, Ackroyd Papers, Testimony.
21. NA, HW 3/119, 214.
22. NA, HW3/119, 11.
23. NA, HW3/120, 'History of Hut 3, 1940–45', Vol. II, 357 (original document numbering used throughout).
24. NA, HW3/119, 24.
25. NA, HW 3/137, 3.
26. NA, HW 3/120, 437.
27. NA, HW 50/15.
28. NA, HW3/119, 357.
29. NA, HW3/119, 44, 45.
30. For an analysis of the indexes from an Information Science perspective, see Brunt (2006).
31. NA, HW3/119, 68.
32. NA, HW3/137, 68.
33. NA, HW3/137,70.
34. NA, HW3/137, 57.
35. NA, HW3/120, 441.
36. NA, HW 3/120, 379.
37. NA, HW 3/120, 441, 442.
38. NA, HW 3/120, 358.
39. NA, HW 3/137, 35.
40. NA, HW 3/137, 34.
41. NA, HW 3/137, 26.
42. NA, HW 3/137, 30.
43. NA, HW 3/137, 37.
44. NA, HW3/119, 54.

45. NA, ADM 223/469.
46. NA, HW 3/119, 139; HW 3/120, 356.
47. NA, ADM 223/472, Memo J. H. Godfrey, Director of Naval Intelligence, 7 November 1942.
48. NA, HW 50/15, discussion 5 April 1943.

2
Frameworks for Understanding

'I wanted to do Russian originally, but couldn't get on the course, so they said do something unusual that nobody else wants to do and then switch over once you're here.'[1]

Intelligence depends on past and present knowledge about 'the other', but knowledge is never produced in a vacuum and our understanding of the other is constructed in varying ways at different times. States, governments and intelligence services and the individuals who constitute these organizations rely on and develop discourses of the organizational and national self and its corresponding others: frameworks of understanding that fill the categories of 'domestic' and 'foreign' with meaning. These become applied to places, people(s), languages and even fields of knowledge to construct them as more or less appropriate objects of scrutiny and study. Though these constructions themselves change over time, the persistent nature of the frameworks means that intelligence perceptions do not always keep pace with intelligence needs.

The intelligence failures discussed in the introduction to this Part, where agencies have proved unable to anticipate attacks that led to thousands of deaths and to fundamental shifts in a state's foreign policy, suggest that intelligence services also prioritize certain types of foreignness over others as focuses for the gathering of knowledge. A cultural perspective on British readiness during the internationalization of the Yugoslav crisis in 1992 exemplifies the effects of hierarchies of foreignness in intelligence and military preparation. As scholarly research on British perceptions of South-East Europe has made clear, Bosnia-Herzegovina belonged to the symbolic complex of 'the Balkans' which British writers, travellers and politicians had been investing with historical and civilizational meanings since at least the nineteenth century. During the Cold War, however, the foreignness of Serbo-Croat-speaking regions had not required such urgent action as the foreignness of the Soviet Union, which had been constructed by the British state and the West as a systemic threat that required a permanent intelligence response. This chapter shows how the urgent need for knowledge of former Yugoslavia and the accompanying need for language knowledge to underpin British operational and intelligence needs inverted the calculations of necessity that Britain had made about Slavonic languages in the Cold War world.

Language capabilities in a moment of crisis are contingent on years of education- and defence-related language policy and funding, which determine whether or not a society or organization will be able to bring to bear sufficient capacity in a particular language. Such policies are in turn embedded in longer-term perceptions that influence how central or otherwise a language is seen to be to the interests of the state and the individuals who comprise its public. The disintegration of Yugoslavia which resulted in full-scale war in 1991 and urgent plans for international intervention in 1992 was the paradigmatic military, humanitarian and diplomatic crisis of the 1990s: conflict develops in a strategically marginal location, media urge governments to act, politicians determine a rapid response is necessary, international organizations and agencies prepare to send teams to the region at short notice, and militaries are similarly forced to gather intelligence on regions where they have not needed expertise for decades or at all. To carry out the thousands of tasks on the ground which comprise an intervention requires the capability to interact with local civilians, soldiers and power-holders in languages they understand. Even to gain an advanced understanding of conditions in the sites of intervention requires personnel within these foreign entities to be able to read or translate from local media and scholarship.

Sites of humanitarian and military intervention are often remote and the languages spoken often little-known; yet the remoteness of the places and the unfamiliarity of the local languages are relative concepts, given meaning by experts and interested parties. In the case of Bosnia, the discourse of bloodshed and genocide on the 'doorstep' or in the 'back yard' of Europe brought the conflict close enough to Western European publics to legitimize military involvement yet set the country just outside the imagined peaceful European homestead itself. The intellectual history of these images dated back to nineteenth-century travel narratives that constructed the Balkans, then part of the Ottoman Empire, as a space for civilizationally and technologically superior Europeans to display mastery over nature and disorder. Andrew Hammond's Foucauldian discussion of Anglo-American travel writing on the Balkans thus argues that 'properties of chaos, backwardness, savagery and obfuscation' construct the Balkans as incapable of self-governance and therefore 'fit for political manipulation' by imperial and post-imperial powers (Hammond 2007: 3, 29). Compounded images of distance and unfamiliarity are less obviously denigratory but still have an exclusionary effect, enabling perceptions of the Balkans as conceptually non-European and encouraging 'self-congratulatory definitions of the West as modern, progressive and rational' (Bracewell 2009: 2). These constructions in turn, as seen in Chapter 8, may facilitate the exploitative exercise of privilege in foreigners' interactions with the Othered region.

Imperial Britain's military, political and economic priorities nonetheless meant that knowledge of the Balkans was produced on a far smaller scale than the paradigmatic example of linguistic and area studies in the service of power (Said 1985), knowledge of the Middle East. In order to defend its routes to India, Britain governed the emirates of the Gulf coast as a protectorate and, after the collapse of the Ottoman Empire, exerted mandates over Palestine and Iraq. James Craig, a principal instructor at the Middle East Centre for Arab Studies (MECAS) in the 1950s, understood that diplomatic and military language instruction had been conceived as part of a system of domination during the planning process that gave rise to the language school:

> It was assumed that the empire would continue after the war and that we should therefore need a pool of men equipped with a knowledge and an understanding of the people who were going to enjoy the benefit of our rule. If you accept the premise (and of course it was mistaken) the intention was good. (Craig 2006: 2)

The languages of South-East Europe had no equivalent to MECAS, though Russian, the most critical language of the Cold War, had been taught to more than 5000 National Service conscripts in 1950s Britain. The fondly-remembered 'secret classrooms' (Elliott and Shukman 2003) pump-primed the UK with emergency linguists and – as it turned out, more significantly – a generation of Russian teachers in secondary and tertiary education. A snapshot of British attitudes to Serbo-Croat in the late 1980s shows that this and other Slavonic languages existed in the shadow of Russian, the strategic language asset: though Yugoslavia enjoyed a certain profile as the European motor of the Non-Aligned

Movement, the host country of the 1984 Winter Olympics and a slightly unusual destination for beach holidays, this did not extend to widespread awareness of, let alone familiarity with, its most widely spoken language. A post-colonial perspective on military language provision would see it as embedded in an impulse to know and rationalize foreign space, the better to exert power (see M. Baker 2006). In the case of Serbo-Croat, however, this impulse was constrained by previous decisions that left the British military needing to acquire rapid competence almost from a standing start.

'Je li Miroslav Antić Jugoslaven?' ('Is Miroslav Antić a Yugoslav?'):[2] politics, crisis and the demand for knowledge[3]

Information pertaining to attitudes towards Serbo-Croat in 1980s Britain is itself difficult to find. A resource guide published in 1982 by the Centre for Information on Language Teaching and Research stated that Cambridge, Nottingham and the School of Slavonic and East European Studies (SSEES) at the University of London were the only UK universities to offer degree courses in Serbo-Croat, with ten other universities offering non-degree instruction.[4] Readers in search of a degree course were advised to consult the Hobsons *Degree Course Guides* and – symptomatically – to 'see the "Russian" section which includes information on Serbo-Croat courses' (CILT 1982: 30–1). Those in search of private tutors were directed to the British-Yugoslav Society, the Institute of Linguists or the Yugoslav embassy. By 1992, according to a handbook of educational institutions teaching Russian in the UK, Serbo-Croat was being taught with Russian at Durham (to what level is unclear), SSEES and Nottingham, while three other universities (Cambridge, Exeter and Sheffield) taught unspecified Eastern European languages which might or might not have included Serbo-Croat. This compared to six universities teaching Polish, five offering Czech and 21 universities and polytechnics where Russian could be studied with Western European languages (Muckle 1992).

Clearly, Serbo-Croat was considered no more than an adjunct to Russian, and an even more marginalized adjunct than Polish or Czech at that – a status to which Yugoslavia's membership of the Non-Aligned Movement rather than the Warsaw Pact may well have contributed. In 1989, the Wooding Report into Soviet and East European studies in the UK recommended an increase in government funding for studies of that area, including the creation of ten new lectureships. The response of Lord Peston, the opposition spokesperson for education and science, during a House of Lords debate in 1990 suggests that even Wooding tended to subsume the other Slavonic languages into Russian:

> Does the noble Baroness [Blatch] not recognise that ten new lecture-ships hardly represents one per East European country? ... To take an obvious example, Czechoslovakia alone is a country for which we need ten lectureships. (HL Deb 26 July 1990 vol. 521 c. 1615)

Language priorities in the military, as in civilian life, made Russian by far the most privileged Slavonic language. Between 1951 and 1960, the Joint Services School for Linguists (JSSL) had trained more than 5000 National Service conscripts as Russian-speaking translators and inter-preters at its facilities in Bodmin, Caterham, Coulsdon and Crail. The initiative deliberately aimed to create a long-term 'pool of excellent linguists for use in a future military emergency' (Muckle 2008: 130): indeed, students on the more advanced ('interpreters') course spent so much of their National Service in training that they were never deployed for other military functions. Less proficient students on the 'translators' course were used as signals intelligence operators who listened in on Russian radio transmissions. James Muckle, the historian of Russian lan-guage teaching in the UK, suggests that this injection of Russian into the national language capacity facilitated a growth of area studies in British higher education which would serve the country well throughout the Cold War:

> For two decades from 1945, services Russian, now including the Royal Air Force, was the backbone of the Russian-speaking profession in Britain, on which the universities and schools fed until they were in a position themselves to contribute to the pool of experts. (Muckle 2008: 125)

The military need for Arabic after 1945 was more modest but still constant, with defence attachés required in the Gulf and officers involved in the protectorate over the Trucial States (now the United Arab Emirates) or seconded to the Omani armed forces. Until 1976, students from all three services attended the Foreign Office language school, MECAS, in the Lebanese village of Chemlane along with diplo-matic and private industry students from the UK and its allies. The generic MECAS word list was tailored to military as well as civilian students – 'where else in those more peaceful times', remembered a US Arabist, Benjamin Foster (2006: 188), 'would I learn Arabic for "mine

sweeper" and "land mine"?' – but military students were taught separately and each service supplied its own language exams. Both JSSL
and MECAS relied on émigré instructors (largely White Russians and
Poles at JSSL and Palestinian Christians at MECAS) for imparting the
spoken language, exposing students to colloquial Levantine Arabic and
pre-revolutionary Russian which could only serve as a baseline for further proficiency. At least one JSSL instructor also participated in 1990s
Serbo-Croat training: one Serbo-Croat tutor of Russian and Serb origin
in 1992 was the daughter of a post-war Russian instructor, who in
the MOD's urgent search for language capacity and teaching experience was also approached to teach Serbo-Croat, but one of her students
recalled she was so elderly that 'she kept talking to us in Russian'.[5] The
émigrés' students also drew on the instructors' own life stories in constructing their expectations of the societies where their languages were
used:

> For many *kursanty* [a nickname in Russian for JSSL students] these
> refugee Slavs and Balts represented their first substantive contact with
> 'foreigners', and their memories and adventures were glimpses of a
> harsh, alien world beyond most British middle-class comprehension.
> (Elliott and Shukman 2003: 74).

The dependence on émigré instructors combined with a lack of first-
or second-hand contact with contemporary Soviet life created 'a Russia
which had, by the 1950s, largely been lost' and a collective imagi-
nary that students and ex-students constructed around exoticized exile
experiences (Footitt 2011: 115).

Something of this classroom dynamic also existed in military Serbo-
Croat instruction during the 1990s, where learners of this language
likewise drew inferences from instructors' stories of leaving former
Yugoslavia as refugees and from observed classroom behaviour they perceived as foreign. Thus one learner's remark on a classroom argument
between two instructors at the Defence School of Languages (DSL) in
1998:

> [T]hey absolutely hated each other. And none of them, the pair of
> them would not give an inch. You know what I mean. They was
> proper at each other's throats. And I thought, if that's typical of their
> behaviour here, you know, what's it going to be like when we got
> into operational theatre? And it was exactly the same, the whole
> behaviour. They hated each other.... [T]hat was the only real big

argument. They always used to snipe at each other. Yeah. It was just typical of what we experienced out in theatre, in Bosnia.[6]

The Yugoslav crisis did not just create a sudden demand for the teaching and learning of Serbo-Croat but also altered its visibility in the UK as a source of translated writing, injecting the language into the textual practices of readers who considered themselves discerning and cosmopolitan in consuming translated fiction. As one of the lesser-known east European languages, Serbo-Croat had been hardly present on the mainstream translation fiction market until the violence during and after the collapse of the Yugoslav state created public awareness of ethnic cleansing, civilian suffering and the emergence of new nationalist regimes. Recent research by the anthropologist and novelist Andrea Pisac suggests that the literary market favoured exiled writers such as Dubravka Ugrešić and Slavenka Drakulić whose authorial brands combined the personal authenticity of an exile narrative with the authority of representing a national literature and the liberal appeal of standing for free speech (Pisac 2011).[7] Older novels, such as those by Ivo Andrić, were also marketed and read as insights into the historical and ethnic causes of the war in Bosnia. Readers' tendency to use translated fiction as a source of and substitute for ethnographic knowledge, facilitated by booksellers (including the specialist travel bookseller Daunt Books in London) marketing novels alongside histories and travel guides, made high street paperbacks one of the first sources through which aspiring language learners gained knowledge of 'the Region' (Pisac 2011).[8] Recognizing and interrogating the perceptions students form through independent study remains a challenge for academic language teachers today.

'Mora da je tamo lijepo!' ('It must be lovely there!'):[9] a 1980s Serbo-Croat textbook

Britons who decided to learn Serbo-Croat in the late 1980s or found themselves studying it when Yugoslavia collapsed had the benefit of a new self-study course, *Colloquial Serbo-Croat*, developed by the prominent translator and SSEES language lecturer Celia Hawkesworth for Routledge and Kegan Paul. Undergoing several changes as politics and language policy in former Yugoslavia disintegrated and transformed, Hawkesworth's course has remained in print until the present day (and was joined in 1993 by David Norris's competing 'teach yourself' book for Hodder and Stoughton). From the opening page, learners were left in no doubt that their study of Serbo-Croat would not fit the normative conception of a single language for a single nation where political and ethnic boundaries were fully congruent:

> The history of the Yugoslav lands has been turbulent and complex. Something of this complexity is reflected in the name of its main language. Present-day Yugoslavia is a federation of peoples living in six republics. Each of these peoples has undergone a more or less separate cultural development. The southern and eastern areas of the Yugoslav lands came initially into the Byzantine, Orthodox sphere and use the Cyrillic alphabet, while the northern and western areas are traditionally Catholic, and use the Latin script. With the Ottoman advance and occupation of the southern and eastern regions, the situation was further complicated on the one hand by several centuries of virtually complete separation, and on the other by the growth of a substantial Moslem population, concentrated largely in the republic of Bosnia and Hercegovina. Each of the republics thus has its own identity and its own distinct cultural tradition reflected in the language of the various groups.
>
> Despite several centuries of separation, the majority of the people, who may be loosely divided into Serbs and Croats (largely according to their traditional religious allegiance), speak the same language. In Yugoslavia, this language is referred to by Croats as Croato-Serb (hrvatskosrpski) and by Serbs as Serbo-Croat (srpskohrvatski), as well as several other variations (Serbian *and* Croatian, Croatian *or* Serbian, etc.). In practice, as all the variations on this name are somewhat cumbersome, the language is generally referred to by Croats as Croatian and by Serbs as Serbian. Potential learners should not be alarmed by this apparent profusion: all these various designations refer to the same language, known in English as Serbo-Croat. (Hawkesworth 1986: xvii).

In practice, the course simplified the task of learning by concentrating on the western variant, '[b]ecause the majority of tourists from Britain visit Western areas and notably the Dalmatian coast'. A few reading passages in the eastern variant and an appendix of texts in Cyrillic aimed to show 'that the differences are slight and amount to something approaching those between British and American English' (Hawkesworth 1986: xvii), a typical explanation used by native English-speakers (at least in the UK). Many of Hawkesworth's exercises, short texts about love letters or business travellers, have survived into post-Yugoslav editions of the course. Other contents, adding a Cold War layer to the Yugoslav regime, would suddenly have become outdated for learners using the coursebook in 1992, such as a reading passage about a young worker arrested by militiamen while travelling to visit his fiancée or a set of 'krimić' ('thriller') passages where an English-speaking businessman is kidnapped from a train at the Yugoslav border by a gang seeking to commit industrial espionage.

Writing shortly after the Sarajevo Winter Olympics, Hawkesworth constructed a Bosnia of touristic beauty, cultural wonders and socialist industry. A long reading passage about Yugoslavia's six republics referenced Bosnia and Herzegovina's cultural heritage and architecture, the setting of Ivo Andrić's novel *The Bridge over the Drina* (*Na Drini ćuprija*), old monuments in Herzegovina, Sarajevo's experimental cultural scene, the Jajce Declaration of 1943 (a turning-point in the establishment of Partisan authority in Yugoslavia), forestry, mining, hydroelectricity, Herzegovinan tobacco and wine production, and the republic's largest industrial plants (Hawkesworth 1986: 226). 'Idem u Bosnu, u malo selo blizu Sarajeva' ('I'm going to Bosnia, to a small village near Sarajevo'), confided one train passenger in an early dialogue. 'Mora da je tamo lijepo!' his interlocutor replied ('It must be lovely there!') (Hawkesworth 1986: 37). Yugoslavs were 'well known for their spontaneous generosity and hospitality', Hawkesworth reassured the traveller, and 'calculating and egotistical behaviour is regarded as eccentric' (Hawkesworth 1986: 85). Westerners' all too common cynical and relativistic view during the post-Yugoslav conflict that all Bosnians were simply out for what they could get was certainly not supported in the coursebook's attractive landscape. The book did, however, support (or, for new learners, introduce) a perception of Serbo-Croat as difficult, with its instructorial voice apologizing for the language's complexity ('Adjectives have three genders, singular and plural forms and case endings which, unfortunately, differ somewhat from those of the nouns' (Hawkesworth 1986: 50)). Hawkesworth anticipated but would not be complicit in students' (and soldiers') fascination with Serbo-Croat's capacity for profanity:

Serbo-Croat is rich in imaginative slang expressions, particularly in the speech of the young. This includes a large number of colourful oaths which are extensively used by many Serbo-Croat speakers and are consequently not as offensive as their literal translation would be in English. One group of such expressions involves a certain verb, which may be omitted, and a highly emotive noun, such as majka [mother] or Bog (God). Learners should be aware of this vocabulary, and with experience they will learn to distinguish between its use as the equivalent of punctuation marks and genuine abuse. (Hawkesworth 1986: 228–9)

For all that had changed in the politics of teaching Serbo-Croat, this problem had not gone away when a Bosnian woman working as a civilian language instructor for the Ministry of Defence started teaching her first courses in Colchester, using the Hawkesworth course as the class grammar. 'We had a student who was pretty good in the language, and he would collect the swear words', she remembered. 'I wasn't happy to write down the swear words.'[10]

After the fall of Yugoslavia, the publishing histories of both the Routledge and Hodder and Stoughton Serbo-Croat courses would themselves become a story of fragmentation, with both books splitting into separate Croatian and Serbian courses in the 2000s. Hawkesworth's book was first retitled *Colloquial Croatian and Serbian* in 1998 and then, drawing on input from Croatian and Serbian language teachers at SSEES, became *Colloquial Croatian* and (with Jelena Čalić) *Colloquial Serbian* in 2005. In 2003 the Norris course became *Teach Yourself Croatian* by Norris and *Teach Yourself Serbian* by Norris and Vladislava Ribnikar. The publishers added a *Teach Yourself Croatian Conversation* audiobook in 2008 and reissued the packages as *Teach Yourself Complete Croatian/Complete Serbian* in 2010. As tourist travel to Croatia returned to and exceeded Yugoslav-era levels, the travel publishers Berlitz, Collins, Rough Guides and Lonely Planet also entered the market with Croatian (but no Bosnian or Serbian) phrase books in 2005–8. As of 2011, no UK publisher had offered a self-study Bosnian course, though Ellen Elias-Bursać and Ronelle Alexander's comprehensive grammar and textbook *Bosnian, Croatian, Serbian* for the University of Wisconsin Press recognized a need to discuss all three as official languages of former Yugoslav states.

'Zar učiš hrvatski?' ('You don't really mean you're learning Serbo-Croat, do you?'):[11] Serbo-Croat and the British military

Pressures of cost and time in the British military created a demand for language training to deliver a precisely targeted skill set and no more. Until 1991, no need was foreseen for the military to acquire a pool of capacity in Serbo-Croat, a sharp contrast to languages of permanent need such as Russian and (to a lesser extent) Arabic. Instruction in Serbo-Croat, if necessary for a particular post such as a defence attaché, would have been delivered by arranging one-to-one private tuition. The number of available British military Serbo-Croat speakers in 1992 (one graduate from Nottingham and three Anglo-Serb heritage speakers) suggests that this system had not produced any larger cadre of uniformed personnel with relevant language knowledge. The cadre of personnel who had or might have acquired Serbo-Croat during Special Operations Executive (SOE) work during the Second World War and while administering the Trieste area until 1954 had long since retired, though the traveller and SOE agent Fitzroy Maclean (the author of *Eastern Approaches* and a British liaison officer to Tito's Partisans) was invited to brief an Army reconnaissance party before it entered Bosnia-Herzegovina in 1992.[12]

British preparations for troops entering Yugoslavia and other parts of formerly occupied Europe in 1945 had included the production of Foreign Office pocket guides for every country. The wartime Pocket Guide Sub-Committee's draft for Yugoslavia had acknowledged Serbo-Croat as 'not easy for us' but did more to familiarize the Yugoslav linguistic landscape in English-speakers' eyes than 1980s/1990s teaching materials would generally attempt:

A good many Yugoslavs, particularly Slovenes and Croats, know German and, in Dalmatia, Italian too. If you happen to know German or Italian, don't start talking these languages until you are sure that the Yugoslav, who may not recognise your uniform, will not mistake you for a German or Italian and 'see you off' accordingly.

Some people speak French and a few English, but only in the bigger towns. It is not always the chap who knows foreign languages who is your best friend, so learn a bit of their own language for yourself. Serbo-Croat is not easy for us. The grammar is complicated and to make matters worse two alphabets are used. But in its favour, and unlike English, it is pronounced just as it is written, so that once you have mastered the sounds made by the individual letters, it is easy to read. The Cyrillic alphabet is used in Serbia and Montenegro, the Latin in Croatia, Slovenia and the west generally. Remember that the Slovenes have their own Slovene language and a flourishing literature of which they are justly proud. Slovene is closely akin to Serbo-Croat which most Slovenes can understand.

When the letter r comes between two consonants it is rolled to take the place of a vowel, so that krv (blood) becomes krrv: this is easy for a Scot. In general there is no marked accentuation in Serbo-Croat, but in pronouncing long words, emphasise either the first or second syllables.[13]

Bosnia was not even included in this overview of western and eastern variants, suggesting that the complexities of dialect distribution there were considered unnecessary or disruptive in a pocket guide.

The neglect of Slavonic languages other than Russian in UK language policy for education and defence between the Second World War and 1991 forced staff at the Defence School of Languages into fast-reacting and iterative improvisations. DSL's ab initio and conversion Serbo-Croat courses, naturally part of the School's Russian Language Wing, depended on Russian-speaking instructors from the Royal Army Educational Corps who had themselves taken conversion courses (or in the case of the first instructor, Nick Stansfield, relied on language skills acquired while studying for a joint degree at Nottingham) then served in Bosnia-Herzegovina as military interpreters. As with military Russian and Arabic, grammar teaching by military educators was supplemented by conversation lessons with native-speaker civilian instructors. The head of Russian Language Wing between 1994 and 1997 (who himself took a conversion course and served two tours in Bosnia) had realized while operating as a Russian linguist in the 1970s and 1980s that military language teaching at that time had not equipped learners with sufficient speaking skills:

> I have to say that the [1970s] language course, though good in its way, was much stronger at instilling the rules of grammar than in encouraging spoken communication. For fairly obvious reasons, I suppose, particularly with Russian in those days, the opportunities for speaking to Russians were somewhat limited, and the teaching staff, though hard-working, actually contained very few Russians (laughs). They came from many parts of what you might term the Soviet empire. And it was very much the grammar translation method of language teaching. And when I left the language training and started work using the language, it was still being used in a very passive way. There was very little spoken language. And indeed, I have to say, it wasn't really until very many years later, when I started working for the Joint Arms Control Implementation Group in UK, when by that time we had the Conventional Forces in Europe Treaty and were doing all sorts of work with the Russian forces and the forces from the former Warsaw Pact countries, that ... I, and my colleagues in fact, who had a knowledge of Russian, actually spoke Russian to Russians, and had to listen to Russians speaking Russian. And I think one of the things that struck me then, and still I find now, is that the language of the classroom is in many ways quite different to the language 'as she

is spoke' (laughs), I think. And though I rarely got my case endings wrong, I did very often find it difficult to have an ordinary conversation with Russians, because it was not what we were used to.[14]

In-theatre experience in Bosnia-Herzegovina, compounded by longer-term experience of interpreting Russian for the Joint Arms Control Implementation Group (JACIG) and military liaison missions, encouraged DSL's Serbo-Croat team to base their course around scenario-based methods better suited to, and grounded in, the tasks that military interpreters and 'colloquial speakers' (the term for those who had passed a short three-month language course) could be expected to perform.

Conclusions

Just as the British Foreign Office pocket guide to Yugoslavia had warned during the Second World War, excessive language competence was still thought to spell trouble for a British soldier five decades later. The context for understanding this risk, however, had changed. In the 1990s, the likely cause for suspicion in Croatia and Bosnia-Herzegovina was not a foreign soldier's knowledge of a convenient lingua franca such as German or Italian but inexplicably detailed knowledge of the local language itself. This could lead to rumours that soldiers with obviously foreign names were concealing a local ethnicity or even create a presumption that the soldier was a spy, especially if s/he transgressed the fast-changing linguistic norms that were emerging from the ethno-politicized separation of Serbo-Croat into three languages. The shifting of this linguistic field just as planners were beginning to comprehend a need for extra competence in a language they had comfortably known as 'Serbo-Croat' introduced extra confusion into forecasting future language needs. Britons with hands-on involvement in delivering and using the language on the ground adopted a pragmatic attitude, adapting to interlocutors' expectations in order to achieve the practical objective of the interaction. Soldiers who had served in the late 1990s or later tended to refer to the local language as 'Serbian' (if they had been stationed in the RS) rather than Serbo-Croat. The institutional boundaries would finally harden in the next decade when the languages returned to their pre-1991 state as a rarely needed asset delivered through outsourced one-to-one instruction and were certified separately under their new names.

Impressions that Serbo-Croat provision in the UK had been insufficient to meet the demands of the early 1990s were confirmed by a 1995 report by the Higher Education Funding Council for England (HEFCE), which noted that the Foreign and Commonwealth Office, the British Council and several universities had all identified gaps in Eastern European area studies provision in higher education. HEFCE adopted the FCO's five levels of priority for Eastern European and ex-Soviet languages, in which 'Serb' and 'Croat' were placed among seven 'second order' languages 'given the UK's prominent role in seeking solutions to regional disputes'; 'the FCO would like to see these languages available in several universities, which should also offer area studies' (HEFCE 1995: 13).[15] The working group did not include a Ministry of Defence representative, consider military language needs, or, it seems, draw on the Army's recent experience of delivering short functional language courses, even though one of the report's objectives was to increase the availability of tailored courses for particular professional groups. The military's collective memory, in short, had not been tapped, leading to a deficiency in the collective memory of the state.

Even civilian experiences of the impact of the lack of provision in languages other than Russian were, however, sufficient for the report to recommend that HEFCE should break its practice of avoiding hypothecated subject-specific initiatives and should fund 40 new full-time academic posts in institutions or consortia prepared to triangulate area-, language- and discipline-specific expertise (HEFCE 1995: 35–7). What the Wooding Report had not been able to implement, the extended crisis in former Yugoslavia began – but only began – to achieve. By 2010, the University of London contained three research centres for South-East European area studies, though Serbian and Croatian language degrees were still only available at Nottingham and SSEES. Former Yugoslavia's other two official languages still fared even worse. Slovene was available as a second language in Slavonic language degrees at Nottingham and on request at SSEES (if sufficient students signed up to make hiring a tutor cost-effective), which also offered Macedonian on the same basis. Bosnian as a named language was not available at any UK university.

Every urgent language need throws up particular obstacles based on the language and its social and cultural contexts. Teachers of Serbo-Croat had to decide how and to what extent to represent the different variants and their changing political meanings; instructors at MECAS, and at DSL when British troops returned to the Middle East in 2003, had to choose between teaching a literary Arabic or one of its many spoken dialects.[16] The unique characteristics of each language further complicate planning for the unexpected. Besides not knowing which languages will be required in several years' time, one cannot even be certain how long ought to be allowed for training new speakers to an acceptable standard. Serbo-Croat did not have the profile of Russian or Arabic at the end of the Cold War, nor had it had the profile of German or French during the Second World War. As a result, individuals responsible for assessing and fulfilling language needs when Britain became heavily involved in the Yugoslav crisis were forced into often desperate and often creative strategies of improvisation that resulted from the previous institutional neglect of Serbo-Croat and the construction of all other Eastern European languages as a supplement to Russian. They were simultaneously called on to resolve and explain the confusion arising from Serbo-Croat's politicized fragmentation into 'Serbian' and 'Croatian' and later 'Bosnian', which complicated 1990s language teaching as instructors as well as students struggled to keep up with the emerging norms.

UN and NATO soldiers' general level of cultural awareness in Bosnia-Herzegovina has been criticized on several grounds: soldiers and other foreigners fell back on long-running historical myths of the Balkans as a site of insurmountable ethnic difference and violent wishes for revenge (Duffey 2000: 152–3); simplistic understandings of the roles ethnic groups had played in the Second World War were transferred into the very different historical context of the 1990s (Simms 2002: 178–80); some forces' training scenarios assumed an antagonistic relationship between soldiers and locals and invoked inaccurate stereotypes (NIOD 2002: 2.8.3.1); briefings had been based on fixed concepts of own and other cultures which inhibited reflection (Rubinstein 2008). The servicemen and women who contributed their experiences to the *Languages at War* project often came forward because they believed they had worked exceptionally hard to understand or (sometimes literally) to interpret. These individual initiatives were able to alter practices in a particular area of the military establishment (the Defence School for Languages) and in units where deployed DSL staff and graduates could exert influence. On a structural level, however, they were outweighed by a legacy of public underinvestment in Serbo-Croat and expectations that military language needs would consist of large-scale requirements for a few well-rehearsed languages. This framework for understanding was grounded in the relative certainties of Cold War contingency planning and intelligence and, when applied to the post-Cold War world of rapid response to short-term crises, turned out to be fundamentally insufficient.

With this perspective, the domestication of foreignness in intelligence appears as a process of path dependency, conditioned by the legacy of decisions taken in previous years or decades and affected by longer-term historical constructions of foreign sites and cultures. A state's capability to act in international affairs will be structured by the intelligence it has been able to acquire and to bring to the attention of politicians: this will have required a commitment to expertise including to translation capacity from the intelligence target's source language(s). In the case of military deployments under Chapter VII of the United Nations Charter, collective security treaties or ad hoc coalition agreements, the state's capability to operate effectively on the ground will depend on a certain amount of language knowledge among its own military personnel. The presence or absence of these capacities, which cannot be instantly trained, will be determined by prior policies and priorities that derive from the collective meanings generated in state organizations. This reading is supported by the work of the constructivist International Relations scholar Alexander Wendt, who views the production and sustenance of collective meanings as the motor of international politics: institutions such as states or militaries 'are … a function of what actors collectively "know"' and conduct their affairs in an intersubjective relationship between themselves and others (Wendt 1992: 399). One result of this intersubjectivity can be discerned in Britain's sudden need to deploy knowledge of Bosnia-Herzegovina – and to deploy linguistic expertise to gather further knowledge – after the Cold War. Serbo-Croat knowledge in the UK had been conceived as an adjunct to Russian, the prioritized language of the systemic enemy. Russian linguists were available for retraining into Serbo-Croat, but the effects of language policy and intelligence-gathering in a two-superpower world could not be reassigned so easily. The Yugoslav crisis produced its own crisis of understanding in the British state as politicians, diplomats, soldiers and the intelligence services struggled to construct a replacement frame of global humanitarianism and intervention over the remnants of their Cold War knowledge.

Notes

1. Interview with Serbo-Croat graduate from the University of Nottingham, 25 February 2009.
2. Hawkesworth 1986: 3.
3. Each sub-heading in this chapter contains a line from a language exercise and its translation as given in Celia Hawkesworth's Serbo-Croat textbook. The sentence in this heading, a simple factual question in 1986, would turn into a fraught enquiry into Mr Antić's sense of identity only a few years later when the term 'Yugoslav' became politically but not culturally meaningless.

4. Of these ten, one (Lancaster) was no longer accepting new students.
5. Interview, 26 February 2009.
6. Interview, 27 July 2009.
7. Ugrešić and Drakulić had both been criticized in Croatia for urging the writers' organization International PEN not to hold its 1993 congress there as a protest against the state's treatment of Serb and non-nationalist writers.
8. 32 post-1991 works (including 20 works of fiction) by 6 former Yugoslav authors have been translated and published in the UK, and a further 13 works (10 fiction) by 11 further authors translated in other English-speaking countries (Pisac 2011). These figures do not include reprints of pre-1990 works.
9. Hawkesworth 1986: 7.
10. Interview, 17 April 2009.
11. Hawkesworth 1986: 7.
12. 'There was a reconnaissance trip in August. Sir Fitzroy Maclean came out to Zagreb, he was about 80 years old then, and he was part of the briefing setup for the officers that came out from United Kingdom Land Forces.' Interview with a member of the reconnaissance party, 17 September 2009. *Eastern Approaches*, the most famous SOE memoir, was republished by Penguin in 1991. Andrew Hammond characterizes it as one of many British texts which depict the Balkan region as an arena for the travelling military man to develop masculine virtues, in this case 'competence, simplicity, masculinist flair and active participation in "gallant struggle" and "comradeship"' (Hammond 2007: 201–2).
13. NA, FO 898/483.
14. Interview, 24 July 2009.
15. The other five second-order languages were Bulgarian, Czech, Hungarian, Polish and Romanian, with the only first-order language being Russian: 'The sheer size of Russia, its huge population, and its economic and military potential, put it in a class of its own' (HEFCE 1995: 15).
16. Craig's response: 'we teach a modified colloquial, the dialect of the Levant with the extreme local peculiarities involved. But that, you will say, is not proper Arabic at all. No, but it will provide a base on which the student can build when he gets to his first new post' (Craig 2006: 6). One alternative method, currently for instance in use at the Royal Danish Defence College, is to teach Egyptian Arabic on the grounds that Egyptian film is so widely consumed across the contemporary Arab world that speakers will be able to make themselves understood even in other countries.

3
The Human in Human Intelligence

'We didn't rely on interpreters at all. They were there to help non-linguist officers. The interpreters were looked down upon by German speaking officers. We were one step above the interpreters.'

(Interview, 18 August 2009)

Among the many tasks of Allied troops on the ground in the liberation and occupation of Europe, the need to find information about the enemy was of paramount importance: interrogating those who might hold this information, in other words obtaining 'human intelligence' (Humint), was a key necessity throughout the whole conflict. Humint refers to the gathering of intelligence through interpersonal contact. According to the NATO *Glossary of Terms and Definitions*, it is 'a category of intelligence derived from information collected and provided by human sources' (NATO 2010: 2H5), as opposed to intelligence-gathering through technical means such as 'Sigint' (signal intelligence). Humint therefore involves 'the human', highly-charged face-to-face encounters with 'the other', at different stages of the conflict, and generally in the context of interrogations. The quality and strategic usefulness of human intelligence are markedly dependent on the way the foreign is domesticated in these first-contact encounters with the other and on the ability of the mediator, namely the interrogator, to 'translate' the message in such a way that it becomes intelligible and assessable for strategic purposes. Humint is radically language-dependent. The material collected is foreign precisely because it is usually expressed in a different language and belongs to a different culture, so that those who can mediate through multiple cultures and languages inevitably become invaluable intelligence operatives. Tens of thousands of interrogations and interviews were performed during and after the Second World War in Europe. The conflict also represents one of the very few cases in which it is possible to find a range of sources and personal narratives with which to glimpse the experiences of those working in human intelligence as language mediators.

This chapter examines some of the language issues relating to human intelligence. To what extent were languages involved in the recruitment and training of interrogators? How did the roles of those involved as language mediators differ in different human intelligence situations – at the front line, investigating crimes, in military interrogation centres? What was the effect of working in such highly-charged situations on those who were involved and on the frameworks of perception they used in order to make sense of the war itself and of 'the other'? Languages have thus far been hidden from our histories of intelligence, but this human element is vital in war in general (Bourke 1999: 369–75) and in interrogation in particular: without languages, 'human intelligence' is not accessible.

Requisites for 'British' interrogators

During discussions on the establishment of an interrogation camp in the Western European Area in early 1945, Lieutenant-Colonel Robin 'Tin Eye' Stephens showed himself to be very keen on the idea of becoming the commanding officer of the new centre: 'The burden upon a Commandant of a CSDIC [Combined Services Detailed Interrogation Centre] of this nature is extremely heavy if he is expected to be both an Intelligence officer and a soldier. I venture to think I am qualified to give an opinion on this subject.'[1] He had dedicated his life to interrogation and certainly considered himself to be one of those 'breaker' interrogators who are born and not made, able to establish guilt and obtain a confession (Hoare 2000: 18). Well known at MI5 as temperamental and authoritarian, Stephens had intimidating manners and 'with his glinting monocle and cigarette holder, he looked exactly like the caricature Gestapo interrogator who has "ways of making you talk" ' (Macintyre 2006). His most important feature, however, was his obsessive abhorrence of the enemy, an abhorrence which he regarded as the most important characteristic for any interrogator in the field: 'First and foremost there must be certain inherent qualities. There must be an implacable hatred of the enemy...the interrogator must treat each spy as a very individual case for that matter, a very personal enemy' (Hoare 2000: 7). In Stephens's case, this hatred was combined with a linguistic background considerably broader than that of the average Briton at that time. He had been born in Alexandria, had travelled extensively and could speak a number of languages with different degrees of proficiency: French, German and Italian as well as Urdu, Arabic, Somali and Amharic. Once at MI5, Stephens was instrumental in establishing a dedicated permanent interrogation camp and worked for the creation of Camp 020, which became operative in July 1940 under his command. Whilst, as we shall see, the duties and skills of intelligence operatives varied, there appeared to be two essential requirements for all those who would become military interrogators: proven loyalty and foreign language competence.

Some of the British nationals who came to work in human intelligence already had a well-established language background. John,[2] for example, was a linguist almost 'by birth' and in the Second World War became an intelligence officer whose duty was to interrogate prisoners of war. He was born in Germany, where his father had been working, and had married a German woman during his internment in the First World War. John and his family returned to England when he was four years old; besides German, he very soon learned Latin, French and Spanish. Before the war, he had worked as a professional linguist, a technical translator in a pattern specifications agency. When he joined the forces in 1940, John was soon recruited into the Intelligence Corps. While training to be commissioned in the Artillery, an officer had found out that he was born in Germany so 'they had me have a language test and I was commissioned in the Intelligence Corps'.[3] Already possessing the requisite language skills, he then embarked on the process of training for intelligence and interrogation which consisted mainly of specific courses, work observation and practical training 'on the job'. When John followed this training, the intelligence course was held in various premises[4] (MI5 and MI6 were also part of it) and included learning all about German armed forces, uniforms and ranks, as well as field security and dealing with enemy and foreign civilians. This part of the course, based at the Intelligence Training Centre in Cambridge,[5] was called the 'War Intelligence Course'. Besides an Interrogation Course, it included for German-speakers a German Language Refresher Course[6] in which trainees would be given different sets of long glossaries of German keywords, with English translations or explanations, on specific topics relating to issues they might come across in the course of their work as officers of the Intelligence Corps or as interrogators. The interrogation part of the training was held at the London District Cage, also known as the Prisoner of War Interrogation Section (PWIS), and headed by Lieutenant-Colonel Alexander Scotland. For the practical part of his training, in 1943, John was sent to the CSDIC facility in Cairo: 'A group of 15 of us interrogated the whole Afrika Corps and that was an excellent exercise. We were there for about a week, it was a terrific training exercise.'[7]

Others recruited to intelligence, however, had a much less well-developed languages background. Jim, for example, had joined the Army (Infantry) in 1943 but stayed in England until the conflict had ended and was posted to Germany in the first months of the occupation. There, he developed a self-taught basic knowledge of the language, through a relationship with a 'young lady',[8] and although 'the authorities didn't do much to help the people speak the language',[9] he was asked to teach some German to his comrades, which allowed him to improve. After a while, he learned that the Intelligence Corps were recruiting German speakers to initiate an intelligence course, so he applied and was subsequently hired together with a group of about 30 people. All he could remember about the course was that 'they taught that the threat from the Nazis was not necessarily over, that Nazis were hiding under false names ... they just accepted you spoke German, there was no test'.[10] Jim was trained for fieldwork, and his task was to work on assignments from CSDIC, mainly to interview or arrest specific people and to provide CSDIC with interview reports in English.

Both John and Jim recall that they were working closely together with people of non-British nationality, especially towards the end of the war: 'Not only British officers were in this training exercise. There were two Poles, two or three Norwegian officers, South Africans ... some of the British officers were not necessarily British ... a lot of German Jews ... and of course their language skills were probably better than those of most British officers.'[11] These recruits, most often German or Austrian Jewish refugees, were a vital source of language-competent interrogation officers. In the Second World War, the very nature of the conflict provided intelligence chiefs with a solution to their problem of recruiting staff who were both loyal to the Allied cause and able to communicate in the foreign language. Many of these refugees had joined the British war effort to defeat the Nazis and after the end of the conflict some of the 'King's most loyal enemy aliens', the estimated 10,000 German and Austrian Jewish refugees who had fought with the British armed forces against Nazism (Fry 2007: 199–223), became available to contribute to the denazification effort back in their countries of origin. It is interesting to note that, when British policy towards Zionism changed in the post-war period, MI5 decided that it could no longer recruit Jews for the Security Service, precisely because of their probable dual loyalty, to Israel and to Britain (Andrew 2010: 363–4). War and occupation, however, were very different times.

Fred Pelican, for example, was a German Jew, originally from Upper Silesia, who had been in Dachau before he managed to reach England and join the Pioneer Corps. In May 1945 he was posted to an Army Interpreters' Pool in Brussels where he was told, together with about a dozen other interpreters like himself, 'to keep in a state of readiness for partaking in the first peace negotiations'.[12] At this stage, the interpreters' training seemed to consist of little more than attending a motorcycle course. Pelican was fluent in Polish, French and English as well as German, and was selected to proceed to Bad Oeynhausen. There he was interviewed by Lord Russell of Liverpool and Lieutenant-Colonel Alan Nightingale. He was then sent back to England to attend an intensive intelligence and legal course which covered legal procedures on how to obtain sworn depositions usable in courts, how to interrogate people and basic investigation training.

> I was flown back to England and landed at Stansted airport to attend an intensive intelligence and legal course. The location of it was kept secret, in some place out in the wild. I was received by various officers. First of all it covered the legal procedure for how to obtain a sworn deposition from arrested persons that could then be used in court. There was a certain format to be followed: every interrogation had to start with the swearing on the Bible (Sworn before me, Staff Sergeant Fred Pelican of the War Crimes Special Investigation Branch, BAOR...). When the deposition finished, the same sentence had to be repeated. I was also taught how to cross-examine people. I went to a course of investigation, where I learnt to consider small details of vital importance which had to be considered during interrogations, such as interrogating by using only a lamp, never with a ceiling lamp. You can instantly see the reflection on the person's face and you can instantly tell whether he is telling the truth or if he is a bloody liar. They were very kind to me because they realized my potential. I was given a camera for taking photographs. The use of force was not addressed directly.[13]

At the front line: debriefing prisoners of war

Linguistic requirements and the importance of languages for operational effectiveness varied at different stages of the conflict, in relation to the particular strategic and operational needs. One of the most typical settings for interrogation during hot or shooting war was the interrogation of captured enemies, prisoners of war, which took place immediately behind the front line during advances in the North West European and Mediterranean theatres. This exercise required the ability to collect information and assess it very rapidly, to produce strategically useful reports and then to process the groups of POWs. The work was done both by trained and specially-recruited officers of the Intelligence Corps and occasionally by soldiers (mainly infantry soldiers) who might have the necessary skills to interrogate, although this would not be their primary task. In open warfare, interrogation duties were performed mainly at Intelligence Corps level, and roles were carefully planned centrally. Those to be employed in these capacities were recruited and trained with care, as seen above, and language skills were an essential part of the recruitment and training of British officers, although always paired with other military skills.

Such officers operated at the front line and were the first contact for newly-captured prisoners of war. Their primary task was specific and military: they had to find out any possibly useful strategic information regarding the enemy. In addition, however, they also screened captured enemy officers for potential war criminals who were then separated from the rest of the prisoners and sent to special units for further interrogation. In each case, it was vital to work quickly and assess the information provided in the foreign language in as short a time as possible. Speed in finding out information was key on the front line. In this situation, languages were conceived of mainly as technical skills: intelligence officers had to master technical and military terms in both languages, with cultural knowledge requirements limited to the structure of the enemy armed forces.

John's experience on the front line is an example of this rapid on-the-spot type of interrogation. John had followed the front line to Italy, and after the last battle of Cassino in May 1944 he was sent to Rome to an interrogation centre with 19th Division:

> I was based at Divisional HQ but my interrogation base was a little forward, a mile behind the actual frontline. When POWs were captured, they were brought straight to me and I kept them in a little cage and interrogated them one at a time.
>
> My prime motive was to find out what German units were on the other side, we were actually fighting against. The name of the unit was easy because the pay book had a code and I had a solution to the code, which they thought was secret. I had to find out their officers'

names, whether they were going there a long/short time, what units they would be waiting for. They didn't like to tell me where they were going to go.... As soon as they were interrogated, I asked for a truck to take them to Corps HQ where they would be interrogated again. The other intelligence officer had my interrogation reports and would interrogate them again.[14]

As the war went on, John was moved further north, and near Rimini he dealt with more senior officers:

I interrogated senior officers who were in a camp outside Riccione, they were field officers, colonels, some generals. My job there was finding war criminals, people who had taken part or witnessed war crimes.... The length of the interrogation depended on how well the prisoner and I went on together. Usually the interrogation report was only one page because we were looking for precise information.[15]

Both there and later on in Austria, where John had to interview people in prisoner of war camps and at a CSDIC interrogation centre in Graz, the first task was to find out if the interviewees were high-ranking Nazis:

The first thing they had to find out was if they were ever SS. This was easy because the SS were elite troops and they had their blood group tattooed on top of underarm. Some of them burned it with cigarette, very painful, but again if there was a scar, SS.[16]

Investigating war crimes

The importance of languages and multicultural mediation in interrogations was increasingly recognized towards the end of the war and in the post-war period because, on the one hand, contacts with the enemy became more and more frequent and, on the other hand, institutions were increasingly aware of the vast reservoir of native German-speakers available in the armed forces. At this stage, the tasks German-speaking interrogators had to perform were very different from those performed by wartime front-line interrogators. It was no longer a case of asking questions, gathering information and assessing it quickly in order to produce strategically useful reports. Foreign language speakers now had to perform the much more complex role of investigator, a role which involved a much deeper familiarity with the foreign culture as well as the ability to carry out an investigation, collect evidence and prepare cases which could be brought to war crimes trials.

The investigation, prosecution and trial of war crimes was carried out by bodies such as the War Crimes Investigation Unit (WCIU) at Bad Oeynhausen in the British zone of occupation of Germany, which was part of the British Army of the Rhine (BAOR) and was active until 1948. Group Captain Anthony Somerhough, a barrister by training and 'a big, jolly man with razor-sharp intellect and a cynical wit' (Helm 2005: 218–19) was its commander, and together with his unit he reported to the Deputy Judge Advocate General (DJAG) of the BAOR. The WCIU was in charge of the investigations and cooperated with the Judge Advocate General (JAG) in the preparation of evidence and charges as well as in the setting-up of trials. It was organized into separate branches: the Legal Section, headed by Lieutenant-Colonel Leicester-Warren with Captain Gerald Draper, 'a qualified solicitor who was later to become a leading human rights jurist', and 'had become hardened to war crimes by 1946, having already prosecuted the Belsen case' (Helm 2005: 218); the Investigation Section; the Haystack (or Search) Section, which was 'a group of highly motivated Nazi hunters, mostly volunteer German or Austrian exiles, usually Jewish, who were capable of finding a needle in a haystack' (Helm 2005: 202–3), and was headed by Somerhough's deputy Lieutenant-Colonel Nightingale.

Foreign language speakers working in WCIU might carry a higher status than those on the front line, but they also bore an arguably greater personal and emotional burden. Vera Atkins, a Romanian-born woman who had spent part of her life in France studying modern languages before emigrating to England, was the former leader of SOE F Section and after the war attached herself to the WCIU in the British zone to investigate the fate of some of the agents she had sent to France who had never come back. While she was there, Rudolf Höss was captured and kept in a small prison in Minden (not far from Bad Oeynhausen). Vera was asked to act as interpreter at his interrogation because she was the only trustworthy person who could speak good enough German. Despite her many years of intelligence work, this experience was not without emotional consequences for her.

> He was disguised as a local countryman, with big moustache disguise. The interrogation started as: 'So you are Blinky Blonk – the assumed name', and he said 'Yes!' 'and you've been on the farm, working on the farm?' 'Yes' 'and you had the lack of feeling to steal a bike from one of the farmers'. That was what we pretended to accuse him

of, and he claimed that that was absolutely wrong. 'Well possibly, possibly, possibly that's true. But we know that you are not X X, because we know that you are Rudolph Höss, former commandant of Auschwitz'. Höss was taken outside to the courtyard, and the sergeant removed his moustache. He no longer denied who he was. 1 million 500 thousand people killed under his surveillance was the accusation, but he claimed that that was their own figure, but the correct one was over 2 million, about 2 million 300 thousand. We were all stuck silent for a moment.[17]

Later on, Vera had to go to Landsberg prison, where Hitler had written his *Mein Kampf*, in order to interrogate some of the people who were being kept there. Among them was Bruno Tesch, the man who tested, created and produced Zyklon B, the gas that was used in all the concentration camps. Again, despite being an experienced 38-year-old woman, this face-to-face meeting left a mark on her:

> This was a regretful experience; when I went to his cell I felt like I was fainting to reach the door of this chap. He discussed the technical details of Zyklon B, and the disposal of the bodies. He had this vast amount of human ashes and decided to experiment with these ashes to try and grow tobacco.[18]

In January 1946, the number of known crimes had reached a figure of 3678, and the unit had 1281 prisoners suspected of war crimes in custody, although cases against them were still incomplete (Bower 1995: 205–29). However, despite the ongoing importance of the work, it was clear that the WCIU had relatively low priority in terms of manpower and equipment. Language was one of the major problems in tracking down war criminals, and having struggled to obtain investigators and interrogators from the War Office since its beginning in July 1945 the unit was in great need of German-speaking officers of suitable rank and with appropriate experience. The presence of former refugees of German or Austrian Jewish background soon became invaluable in this environment.

Less than a fortnight after his training as an investigator and interrogation officer was over, for example, Fred was already back in Bad Oeynhausen. At the beginning he worked with a more qualified investigator who did not have language skills, so his tasks were mainly confined to interpreting. After a few weeks, he was sent on investigations alone and was given almost unlimited power. His duties covered both the investigation and the interrogation of alleged war criminals. Between cases, he usually remained in the office in Bad Oeynhausen for a couple of weeks, where he had to translate documents needed to prepare the documentation for the trials. His role thus shifted from that of investigator to that of interrogator and translator.[19] In Bad Oeynhausen, Fred took part in the investigation leading to the arrest of Bruno Tesch, and in the course of the investigation he found Tesch's private diary:

> The diary was kept meticulously. It showed that he was not faithful to his wife. In Berlin he had a girlfriend named Ruth, and he recorded meticulously every aspect of his sexual life, the roll of film was photographs illustrating sexual activities of Tesch and his wife, taken in the garden, probably taken by a third person. They were sickening pictures, especially for that time when the standard of decency was very different from today. The man was sick in his head in my opinion, and I was shocked because that man probably had the destinies of hundreds of thousands of my brothers and sisters in his grasp.[20]

War crimes investigations clearly imposed particular strains and emotional burdens on those involved, most particularly as they were able to access the words of those they were investigating directly, in the original language in which they had been written or spoken.

Interrogation centres

As well as interrogations conducted on the front line and in war crimes investigations, there were also specific interrogation facilities set up to deal with prisoners of war or suspected spies. These facilities included the (in)famous London District Cage based at Kensington Palace Gardens; Camp 020, the centre established in 1940 by Stephens at Latchmere House, near Ham Common on the outskirts of West London; and, of course, the various CSDICs. The charter that created CSDIC stated that its purpose was 'to submit selected prisoners of war, either Naval, Military or Air Force, or internees, to a comprehensive interrogation by specially qualified officers'.[21] In 1944, the military authorities had started to think about preliminary plans for the organization of prisoners of war and, more generally, for enemy interrogation during the invasion of Europe. At the end of the hostilities in Europe, the centre, which had been in operation in the UK since 1942, continued to work with selected prisoners, including high-ranking enemy officers.

Besides the home facilities of CSDIC (UK), during the course of the conflict the structure had also established various other centres overseas, together with a number of mobile units: in the North African theatre (Cairo) and in the Mediterranean theatre (at first in Naples and then in Rome, following the advance towards the north), and later on in the invasion of Europe, near Graz in Austria and in Diest, Belgium. After the hostilities had ended, another detailed interrogation centre was finally established in Bad Nenndorf, in the British zone of occupation of Germany, which was run by the War Office in collaboration with MI5 until 1947. The centre was modelled on MI5's Camp 020. In fact, Camp 020's commandant, 'Tin Eye' Stephens, was transferred to Bad Nenndorf together with some of his staff in order to run the new facility.

These interrogation centres provided a very different context for human intelligence than either frontline encounters or war crimes investigations. As John, posted to the CSDIC facility in Austria at Lassnitzhöhe near Graz, described it:

> At Lassnitzhöhe, we were fed dubious characters, most of whom had been picked up in camps for displaced persons. Many of these turned out to be soldiers attempting to get back home under their own steam, probably having become tired of waiting for an official transport. Some had been resorting to crime to fund their passages. Some of them were former members of the SS, scared of being picked up and detained indefinitely. (Oswald 2004)[22]

Wherever they came from and whatever their rank or involvement in the Nazi crimes, John was still convinced that the only way to get human intelligence was to be friendly to prisoners: 'Interrogation skills are skills in getting on with other people, making them feel that you are a good guy ... I can only think of four prisoners who didn't tell me what I wanted to know in my entire career.'[23]

Together with officers from the Intelligence Corps, those who were more likely to be employed in interrogation facilities because of their fluency in the language, their knowledge of the enemy culture and their hatred for the enemy were again German or Austrian Jewish refugees who had already proven their loyalty to Britain: 'I can only think of one or two of my fellows at the course who were not native German speakers, and they might have had little trouble in interrogation', John admitted, 'but even so, if you are nice to the person, you can get what you want'.[24] The borderline between interrogation and mistreatment in these intelligence situations, however, could clearly be problematic. Lieutenant Richard Oliver Langham, interrogating officer at Bad Nenndorf, who had been born in Munich in 1921, was court-martialled in 1948, accused of ill-treatment of prisoners and 'disgraceful conduct of a cruel kind' (*The Times*, 3 March 1948) at CSDIC, although he was later acquitted on all counts (*The Times*, 1 April 1948). Langham was only 25 years old when he had to face former SS officers in Bad Nenndorf in 1946, and, when he was interviewed by the court of inquiry during the investigations, he described the way he performed his job:

> Instructions are that the actual approach to an interrogation is left to the interrogator within definitely laid down rules. I am not permitted to use any physical violence whatsoever. I can not interfere with the man's rations in any way because that is quite outside my job. I am not permitted to award any punishments to a prisoner. Anything in that line must be done through the Officer in Charge of the Section.[25]

The actual reality of life in the camp, however, seemed to be quite different. During the investigation, the inspector from Scotland Yard found that conditions in the CSDIC centre were very different from those described in official papers and by Langham, who in his witness statement seemed to be reciting the prison's standing orders by heart.

Another particular feature of the CSDIC interrogation system, widely used throughout the following decades, was that of bugging – each cell was bugged so that the detainees' conversations could be carefully screened in search of valuable intelligence. The ideal candidate for this type of job, which in effect consisted of eavesdropping, listening to the prisoners' private conversations through microphones hidden in the light fittings, was undoubtedly a native speaker. Only a native German or Austrian could pick up the differences of accents and dialects and identify where each prisoner was actually from. This was one of the most effective ways to gather useful intelligence because prisoners were more likely to talk frankly to each other than to an interrogator, and this system became the signature feature of CSDIC and of its strategic effectiveness.

Bugging required mediators who were in effect 'domesticated' aliens, but whose role was quite different from that of interrogators and investigators, since it did not involve the same emotionally-charged face-to-face encounters with an enemy. Bugging cells required the ability to mediate instantly between two cultures, listening in one language and drafting reports directly in another language, but the assessment of intelligence involved a more complex process: information was assessed only partially by these multicultural mediators, who had to choose relevant pieces of information about which they produced reports. A second step was the monitoring of transcriptions and records of conversations, which was carried out by a more experienced 'eavesdropper' who became a supervisor. Intelligence collected was then assessed by the Centre's officers who took decisions as to the fate of particular prisoners and which pieces of information were to be sent out to higher authorities.

Each operator monitored two or three cells at a time and recorded anything interesting they heard at once. Fritz, originally from Berlin, was among those refugees who later became one of the 'King's most loyal aliens', and was recruited by the War Office and MI5 precisely to do this type of work firstly at the CSDIC (UK) centres in Latimer and Wilton Park, and then in Germany, at the Bad Nenndorf centre:

> There was no training... he told me what I would be doing, listening to prisoners of war... [My colleagues] were all ex-refugees whose mother tongue was German.... before that wave of new recruits in 1943 the previous people who had been doing the job had not necessarily been native speakers of German, they had been officers who spoke... British officers who spoke German, but then in 1943 they realized that there was a vast reservoir of native German-speakers in the Army from whom they could recruit people who could understand German much better than the English people.... we only listened to them when they came out of the interrogation and of course this was particularly fruitful because they would tell their cell mates what they had been asked and what they had told them and what they had not told them.[26]

When Fritz was made a sergeant, his job became that of checking the work of his colleagues, monitoring the transcriptions, the records taken of conversations which were transcribed and then checked by a senior ranking officer. Anything which was not important was deleted, any mistakes were corrected and only what was useful to British intelligence was retained, deciding 'well, from one's knowledge, you got the knowledge on the job, and only the people who were considered capable of the job were promoted'.[27] If a person mentioned war crimes, the record was specially marked and went in a special registry: 'The other records of ordinary military intelligence were scrapped afterwards, but any record which contained information about atrocities were kept.'[28] For Fritz, going back to Germany proved to be quite an experience, and he was glad to be able to do 'something important and useful' to fight the Nazis. Germany, however, did not feel like home anymore and Fritz interestingly used his language skills to detach himself from the Germans, publicly assuming his British-assimilated identity:

> In September 1945, we were sent to Germany and there the prisoners were political prisoners...to Bad Nenndorf. Certain parts of the little town had been surrounded by barbed wire and the people of the houses which were taken over had been moved, had to leave their furniture behind and we were living in those houses.... again listening in to the prisoners...same as in England....we were allowed to go out of camp, at first it was forbidden to fraternize with the Germans, but it didn't last very long...it was quite strange talking to the Germans, because they pretended that there had been no Nazis....When we talked to the German population we talked in English accent, because we didn't want to give away our identity.[29]

Conclusions

Human intelligence required three common features in those who promoted the process of mediation: interrogators had to be of proven loyalty, they had to speak the enemy's language and they had to have the best possible knowledge of the enemy's culture. As seen above, languages played a very great role in the process of interrogating the enemy during and after the Second World War: without language intermediaries, it would have been impossible to conduct business smoothly. The quality and strategic usefulness of human intelligence depended on the way in which the foreign was domesticated in first-contact encounters with the Other and on the ability of the intermediary to translate the message and render it intelligible for strategic purposes.

On the ground, human intelligence operations were framed by the context in which they operated: on the front line, speed and specific information was needed; in war crimes investigations, evidence had to be collected and criminal cases built up; in interrogation centres, face-to-face interrogations or covert bugging established the enemy as a potential spy or criminal. In each of these situations, the linguistic skills required were slightly different: technical/military vocabulary on the front line, a broad cultural/historical background on the country for war crimes investigations and excellent listening and speaking skills for interrogation and bugging. In each situation, too, the likely effect on the linguist mediator involved was different: on the front line, a hurried, largely technical exchange made the one-to-one contact brief and impersonal. In war crimes investigations, the nature of the material revealed often made it difficult for those who accessed it directly to divorce their emotional responses from the enemy whom they were investigating. In interrogation centres, the prison context and the expectation that interrogators were expected to extract information by a variety of means could bring with it an atmosphere of physical danger and harm.

Besides language, the other essential requirement for an interrogator was loyalty. This issue posed a complex problem for military institutions which had to assess the loyalty of individuals who, as language intermediaries, were clearly linked to the enemy culture. In the Second World War, this problem was dealt with at least in part by exploiting the very particular nature of the conflict, those German or Austrian Jewish refugees who had a deep knowledge of German culture and language but who had also proved their loyalty to Britain by joining the British forces in the war against the Nazis. It is a paradox of human intelligence in the Second World War that speaking the language of the enemy in Britain stood proxy as loyalty to the country to which the refugees had come. The voices of linguists employed in human intelligence show us the variety of one-to-one situations in which they can be placed, and the effects that these can have on the intelligence encounter and on the linguists themselves.

Notes

1. National Archives, KV 4/327, 14 April 1945.
2. Interview, 18 August 2009.
3. Interview, 18 August 2009.
4. Interview, 18 August 2009.
5. IWM, Department of Documents, 2686 Con Shelf.
6. This material is based on the papers of Lieutenant-Colonel Prentice, who left a large collection of documents in the IWM archive, including his materials and notes for the Intelligence Course he attended between June and November 1940 and between March and November 1941. IWM, Department of Documents, 2686 Con Shelf.
7. Interview, 18 August 2009.
8. Interview, 2 June 2009.
9. Interview, 2 June 2009.
10. Interview, 2 June 2009.
11. Interview, 18 August 2009.

12. IWMSA 9222.
13. IWMSA 9222.
14. Interview, 18 August 2009.
15. Interview, 18 August 2009.
16. Interview, 18 August 2009.
17. IWMSA 9551.
18. IWMSA 9551.
19. IWMSA 9222. See also Pelican 1993: 112–93.
20. IWMSA 9222.
21. National Archives 2010.
22. This testimony is drawn from *WW2 People's War*, an online archive of wartime memories contributed by members of the public and gathered by the BBC: http://bbc.co.uk/ww2peopleswar (accessed 4 May 2010).
23. Interview, 18 August 2009.
24. Interview, 18 August 2009.
25. NA, FO 1005/1744, statement by witness, 7 April 1947.
26. Interview, 3 December 2009.
27. Interview, 3 December 2009.
28. Interview, 3 December 2009.
29. Interview, 3 December 2009.

Part II
Preparation and Support

Preparations for the linguistic and cultural challenges of conflict are a key factor in the success of any intervention. This was just as important in the lengthy and detailed preparations for the liberation and occupation of continental Europe as in the hurried arrangements to launch the first stages of the UN/NATO intervention in Bosnia-Herzegovina. Where the Allies were able to prepare systematically for the battles to come and their longer-term presence, NATO battalions had little specific preparation and no certainty about their future role.

What remains common to both the cases is an underlying conception of the value of preparation in language and culture. Planners wished to ensure that their forces had the capability required for the operation. In both cases, planners saw that relationship-building was a major priority for making peace and rebuilding the societies affected and that language and culture would play a key role. However, they were also aware of the need to balance costs against benefits, particularly with the long timescales needed to achieve high levels of language proficiency. They recognized that cultural briefing is in contrast comparatively inexpensive.

The following chapters in this Part explore the ways in which the armed forces prepared for conflict and the impact they could have on the society in which they were operating. Chapter 4 explores the ways in which the problematic relationship between language and culture was developed in preparation for deployment in a large number of countries in occupied Europe. Allied planners were particularly concerned that young conscript soldiers should behave well with foreign populations who were unarmed, grateful and highly vulnerable. They were confident about winning the war but aware that winning the peace might not be so easy. Chapter 5 examines the ways in which British forces were prepared to meet the challenges of peace support operations in Bosnia-Herzegovina from March 1992. They had little preparation initially but rapidly developed a more concerted approach to preparing for their involvement. They learned the value of meta-language, helping troops to use language resources so as to make themselves understood. They also learned to be specific in identifying the language needs for groups of speakers with whom they were preparing to engage.

Chapter 6 examines the language policy of the international military force in peace-building in Bosnia-Herzegovina. It explores the interaction between the force's language policy and the wider social and societal circumstances outside it. It argues that even though the language policy of the international military force can be seen as a purely institutional policy – concerned with translation and interpretation policies and the production of official documents – it nevertheless forms part of the linguistic landscape of present-day Bosnia-Herzegovina and has an impact on the wider peace-building concerns of the international community.

In practice, it proved difficult to learn the lessons of language preparation and support identified through these experiences. No conflict precisely resembles its predecessors, and the regular rotation of troops tends to erase institutional memory from one deployment to the next. Nonetheless, clear lessons can be drawn which could improve the preparations of later cohorts.

4
Preparing to Liberate

> It is never very easy to make yourself understood at first in a foreign language, and it may be even less easy to understand a Frenchman's reply[.][1]

In recent times, the importance of troops undertaking some form of cultural preparation before they deploy to foreign countries has become of considerable relevance, as shown in the Ministry of Defence's 2009 Joint Doctrine paper 'The Significance of Culture to the Military', which devoted 508 closely-argued paragraphs to the ways in which soldiers' cultural understanding pre-deployment could be strengthened by using cultural analysis templates and frameworks of cultural capability (Ministry of Defence, Development Concepts and Doctrine Centre 2009). The relationship between cultural preparation on the one hand and linguistic preparation on the other, has, however, always seemed more problematic. An epistemological uncertainty about how language and culture relate in pre-deployment preparations tends to position languages as an addendum to cultural training (only three paragraphs in the 2009 MOD document), a high-level competence area which is necessarily restricted to a minority of servicemen and women: 'Whilst all personnel can benefit from enhanced cultural capability, language capability will remain a specialisation' (Ministry of Defence, Development Concepts and Doctrine Centre 2009: 1/5–1/6).

This chapter seeks to explore how the problematic relationship between language and culture was developed in one particular pre-deployment situation (in 1944–5) in which the Allied Command had the benefit of a considerable lead-in time before operations were due to begin and where they could establish centralized procedures with which to train and prepare their soldiers. Whereas peace support operations in Bosnia-Herzegovina (see Chapter 5) engaged a small professional army in one specific albeit highly complex area, the liberation of Western Europe would see millions of conscript soldiers deploying to a huge range of continental countries: as General Grasset explained at a press conference in May 1944, 'We have Norway, Denmark, Netherlands, Belgium, Luxembourg, France, Germany, and perhaps Austria.'[2] In addition, units were already operating in Italy, Greece, Albania and Yugoslavia and were expected to enter Romania. It was clear that some form of cultural preparation would be urgently needed to cope with all this. Beyond immediate military and tactical considerations, what most concerned Allied planners at this stage was the question of how their young conscript soldiers would actually behave when they reached continental Europe, faced with foreign populations who were unarmed, grateful and above all highly vulnerable.

In the summer of 1943, Colonel Buckmaster from the Special Operations Executive (SOE) was warning that: 'From the first day of occupation German troops have behaved towards the French population with the greatest courtesy... It would have the worst possible effect if the French population were to draw a disparaging comparison between the German army and ours.'[3] The consequences of large-scale army misbehaviour in this situation, it was thought, could well create political problems for the Allies, and affect their standing in the crucial months and years of post-Liberation reconstruction. A confidential War Office note pointed out that, whilst Europeans might initially greet their liberators with enthusiasm, there was every likelihood that disillusion would set in quite speedily: 'There is no need to stress the point that our behaviour will have to be exemplary..., especially when the first delirium of liberation is over, when our troops are becoming a bit bored with things.... We shall undoubtedly win the war. But winning the peace... mayn't be so easy.'[4] For political reasons, as well as in the general interests of military discipline, it was vital that soldiers should be instructed to act as good ambassadors of their country when liberating continental Europe. This chapter examines the approach which Allied planners took to the relationship between language and culture in their detailed pre-deployment preparations, firstly for the mass of troops passing through liberated Europe on their way to Germany and secondly for that cadre of soldiers, Civil Affairs officers, who would, for operational reasons, have a longer and more sustained relationship with the foreign civilians they would be meeting.

Troops

As far as cultural preparation for the troops was concerned, two major considerations were to influence planning: firstly the sheer volume of soldiers involved and secondly the number of countries that they would potentially be visiting. By 1 September 1944, approximately 2 million men had been landed, and an estimated 3.5 million were to be in continental Europe in the seven months after the projected 'D' Day. Without knowing exactly how operations on the ground would develop, planners had to work within a scenario in which their soldiers would be moving through Europe at some speed and hence finding themselves deployed to a variety of formerly occupied non-Anglophone countries.

In order to meet this situation, the decision was taken to mass-produce cultural information which would be targeted at soldiers, produced on the same model for each country, and specifically designed to address the public relations implications of liberator/liberated meetings. Significantly, the responsibility for this cultural preparation for troops was rapidly taken away from the War Office and placed within the Foreign Office's political propaganda section, the Political Warfare Executive. A special Foreign Office sub-committee, the 'ABC', and subsequently 'Pocket Guides Education Sub-Committee', was set up in order to develop a suite of guides which would cover every country which troops might enter. Huge numbers of the guides would be printed, so that relevant copies could be issued to all soldiers. In order to encourage troops to read the guides and take them to continental Europe, the format agreed upon was a pocket-book one, with the booklets designed to be small enough to be carried in a soldier's kitbag or uniform. The aim was to influence soldiers' behaviour by giving them background information about the countries they were visiting and offering them specific advice on how they should behave once they were there.

The Sub-Committee began by developing an overall template for the whole suite of guides and then proceeded to fill in the detail for each country: France, Holland, Norway, Denmark, Romania, Belgium/Luxembourg, Albania, Greece, Italy and Yugoslavia, as well as Germany and Austria, with the Americans producing separate guides to Syria, Iraq and China. The template had an introductory section on the country itself, followed by a brief contemporary history, what the inhabitants thought of the British, and then practical information – Do's and Don'ts, money, weights and measures, road signs and so on. Accessibility was paramount, both in terms of the format of the guide and of its content. At all times the projected audience, soldiers themselves, had to be considered, with Sub-Committee members suggesting that priority should be given to such subjects as currency, weights and measures, cafés, restaurants and women, 'since...from experience...these are more or less the only subjects in which the British soldier is directly interested'.[5] It was agreed that guides should be written in a straightforward style, with a simple continuous narrative, and early drafts which did not conform to this requirement received short shrift: 'might have been drafted for the benefit of a posse of political students or a gaggle of bank clerks'.[6]

From the beginning, foreign languages were expected to form a part of this cultural material, and a specific Vocabulary Sub-Committee was established to address the whole language issue. One early option considered was that of separating language from culture by issuing a phrase book for each language, entirely separate from the pocket guide itself. Quite soon, however, members of the Sub-Committee decided to integrate the language within the original guide, putting foreign language phrases towards the end of the booklet, directly after 'Do's and Don'ts', and before 'weights and measures'. Across the suite of guides, an identical standard vocabulary was developed, together with a standard system (Hugo's) of phonetics. A careful check was kept on the amount and type of vocabulary to be included, with large lists of purely military words rejected in favour of the sort of phrases which soldiers in a mobile/transitory relationship with locals might conceivably need to use. Seven standard sections were agreed for the template: 'Meeting Someone', 'Difficulties and Enquiries', 'Travelling by Road'; 'Car Repairs', 'Accommodation, Baths', 'Food, Drink', and 'Accidents'.

Filling in the actual foreign phrases for each country was normally the job of the Political Warfare Executive, although on occasions representatives of recognized exile governments in London were given an opportunity to read and comment on drafts. The Dutch, for example, deplored elements in the original Dutch language section, arguing that it contained a great many errors and that its tone, 'threats and peremptory demands', appeared to have been taken over wholesale from booklets designed for German and Italian enemies.[7]

The way in which languages were to be translated into these cultural preparations did not, however, stop at a brief standard selection of disparate phrases, placed in an annexed limbo. Instead, in a section, 'Making Yourself Understood', which prefaced the foreign phrases, the guides deliberately positioned the foreign language as an integral part of that attentive troop/civilian relationship which the Sub-Committee had been advocating throughout the whole exercise. Even in those countries where English might be widely spoken (Norway, for example), it was explained, the soldier could well find himself among people 'who do not understand a word of English, and it is to help you to cope with that sort of situation that the following list of words and phrases has been included in this guide'. Rather than aiming to develop levels of proficiency in a specific foreign language, what the guides were giving soldiers was in effect a meta-language on how to speak to foreigners, with practical tips, and reminders of linguistic etiquette. The 'Making Yourself Understood' sections presented the soldier with an imagined space of encounter which he could negotiate with courtesy and under-standing: 'Don't shout when you are talking to a Dane. This won't help him to understand!' The expected Anglophone/foreigner meeting was portrayed as one which could be successfully managed if certain easy strategies, both in the foreign language and in English, were adopted by the troops. Thus soldiers going to France were told: 'If you find someone who knows a little English, speak very slowly and distinctly. If you are trying to understand French, get the speaker to say the words slowly, or (if that will help) to write them down clearly.' Those being deployed to Romania were advised that open questions would be unhelpful in their encounters with locals: 'Never ask a question which requires a long answer: you won't understand the answer. So don't say "Which is the way to...?" but point and say "Is this the road to...?" and then if the answer is negative, you can make another shot.'[8]

Above all, the guides placed the foreign language within the frame-work of accessibility which marked both the booklets' format and their narrative. Learning a little of the foreign language, they argued, was a skill which any soldier could acquire: 'It is quite easy to learn to read Danish...'; 'Norwegian is not a very difficult language for English-speaking people to pick up... If you follow the phonetic rendering you cannot go far wrong'; '(Italian) pronunciation... is not really difficult, once you have memorised a few simple rules.' The expected mobility of the soldier once on operations was presented to him as a further oppor-tunity to learn something more about the language as he passed through a country: 'Use your eyes and ears. You will pick up a lot by reading notices in the streets and shops, and headlines in newspapers.'

Foreign languages were thus embedded in cultural preparations for troops, an integral part of attempts to influence and moderate expected military behaviour on the ground. Rather than aiming for soldiers to actually learn a great deal of the relevant foreign language, the plan-ners' efforts were concentrated on arguing that what was important was the nature of the relationship which troops would have with liberated peoples, and this, it was suggested, could be negotiated and managed with linguistic courtesy and respect, whatever the foreign language spoken.

This understanding of language as an element which might foster positive experiences in liberated Europe contrasted strongly with the positioning of the enemy language, German. In Germany, it was expected that Allied soldiers were going to be distanced and hostile visitors rather than co-operating and courteous guests. Early on, the Sub-Committee recommended that the German booklet for troops should include a foreword, preferably signed by the Prime Minister, 'which would emphasise the unprecedented scale and nature of Germany's crimes and so offset the feelings of pity on the part of our men likely to be aroused by the spectacle of the suffering and devastation in Germany.'[9] By the end of 1943, one of the key concerns surrounding the creation of the German booklet was indeed whether it was still too lenient in tone.[10] Care had to be taken, it was thought, to ensure that there was a clear separation between Allied soldier and German national: the Sub-Committee wondered whether an injunction to '[k]eep every German at a distance until his trustworthiness is proved beyond doubt'[11] was already going too far by implying that some of the enemy might ultimately manage to make themselves acceptable. Overall, the German guide to troops sought to emphasize the distance between Allied troops and the Germans they would encounter: 'Don't be taken in by surface resemblances between the Germans and ourselves. Underneath they are very different.'[12]

In this situation, the self-reflexive attitude and the meta-language of linguistic good behaviour which had been prime characteristics of the other guides were replaced by a narrative which started from English, progressed through sign language, and only then finally permitted a terse version of German: 'English is taught in all German secondary schools . . . so that many Germans have at least a smattering of English . . . in the depths of the country or in working class districts, you may have to speak German if you cannot get through with the language of signs . . . If you speak plainly, your meaning should be quite clear, and that is all that matters at this stage.'[13] The language itself was understood to be a symbol of the enemy's hostility. Under a photograph of Allied soldiers, for example under the heading 'Hier Spricht man Deutsch', the American troop newspaper *Stars and Stripes* explained that '[t]he boys in the picture are talking the German too. They're talking the language the Germans understand better than any other . . . now we're giving the German a little backtalk – in his own lingo – in the harsh, guttural, growling, deadly syllables the Teuton respects and heeds.' In this representation, gunfire was at least as effective in communicating as the foreign language: 'It won't make much difference how we spricht the Deutsch... Our accent may be lousy. Our words may be wrong. Our grammar may stink. But the German will understand.'[14]

To some extent, the pre-deployment language/culture preparation for liberated Europe spilled on into the early stages of the deployment itself. Thus, the American soldiers liberating Normandy were urged to become aware of the linguistic element in the landscape through which they were passing, noting the 'église' and the 'mairie', as well as 'a sample list of the signs you see over French shops in any town where you happen to be... Two other signs you run into wherever you go in France... are "RF" and "Liberté, Egalité, Fraternité". RF stands for République Française.'[15] A light-hearted reinforcement of pre-deployment preparation was provided by the daily foreign phrase printed on the front page of *Stars and Stripes* in the first nine months of the operation on the continent. From 7 September 1944 until 17 May 1945, the newspaper regularly carried a daily phrase in French, on its front page, next to the banner title. From 4 October 1944 until 17 May 1945, a daily phrase in German was also given on the other side of the page. The contrast in the phrases taught in the two languages could not have been greater. In the case of French, the vocabulary narrated a developing soap opera of amorous relationships between the American soldier and French female civilians: 'je suis américain' (7 September 1944); 'Vous avez des yeux charmants' (15 September 1944); 'Voulez-vous promener avec moi?'(19 September 1944); 'Non, je ne suis pas marié' (21 September 1944); 'Où est votre mère?' (22 September 1944); 'Il faut que je vous quitte maintenant' (25 September 1944); 'Vous allez beaucoup me manquer' (26 September 1944); 'ne manquez pas de m'écrire' (27 September 1944).[16] In comparison, the daily German phrases depicted a staccato hostile relationship formed in war: 'Ergeben sie sich!' (4 October 1944); 'Zur Seite treten!' (7 October 1944); 'Sie die tür' (18 October 1944); 'Wo ist der scharfschutze verstect?' (30 October 1944). Troops were clearly expected to be meeting German civilians only to give them harsh and explicit orders: 'Waschen sie meine sachen' (10 October 1944); 'Räumen sie die strasse' (27 October 1944); 'Melden sie sich morgen früh' (1 November 1944).[17]

In the extraordinary situation of 1944 in which millions of troops were going to deploy to a bewilderingly wide range of European countries, the Allied Command adopted a policy of cultural preparation which focused on producing accessible and portable information on each country, given to the individual soldier. The foreign language was embedded in these preparations as an attitudinal shaper, as part of the means by which troops would be encouraged to behave to liberated peoples (as opposed to the enemy) with respect and courtesy. What was important was not the achievement of a particular level of language competence but rather the transmission of a meta-language of good communication foreigner to foreigner – respecting the other's language, speaking both English and the foreign language in ways which would assist communication and understanding. Once in theatre, these pre-deployment approaches continued to be stressed, with encouragement to the soldier to be aware of the linguistic landscape he was in and to remember the presence and importance of the foreign language.

Civil Affairs officers

The cultural preparation of Civil Affairs officers brought into play a far more complex set of networks and issues. The War Office had defined Civil Affairs as having four functions: 'Ensuring the security of the occupying forces; maintaining good order; conserving fighting troops for active operations; and developing the economic resources of the occupied territory.' All of these were intended to serve one overriding purpose: 'to further present and future military operations' (Donnison 1961: 456). The job of a Civil Affairs officer had clear cultural implications, since he was supposed to be the interface between the Allied Army and local civilians, dealing with the interim administration of the country and generally smoothing out relationships so that combat troops could be released for future operations. Although it was originally expected that Civil Affairs officers would operate only for a temporary and interim stage, as events unfolded in liberated Europe it became evident that this phase might well last longer, at least until the newly installed national governments could actually resume power. In this situation, officers would have to deal with a range of issues relating to the country and its people: the restoration of services, the provision of food, the relaunching of economic activity and the early conduct of legal and judicial processes.

As it was framed, therefore, Civil Affairs was a multifaceted job, with military obligations (ensuring security requirements were met), functional duties (contributing to the repair of the country's infrastructure) and cultural implications (maintaining good relations with local civilians). Before Allied structures came together in early 1944, the British and Americans had developed slightly different conceptions of how Civil Affairs officers should be prepared. For the British, Civil Affairs was always understood to be primarily responding to military needs, so that training for it had been kept firmly under the control of the War Office. For the Americans, on the other hand, there was a split between the military role of Civil Affairs, working primarily alongside other Allied forces, and what was perceived as a more cultural aspect of the job, meeting and dealing with local civilians. Reflecting this division, authorities in the USA had initially run a dual training system. Courses based at Charlottesville, and held under the aegis of the Army, taught students to address what were anticipated to be the generic problems of Civil Affairs. Other courses, located on a network of university campuses – Harvard, Yale, Michigan, Chicago, Boston, Pittsburgh, Wisconsin, Northwestern, Western Reserve, and Stanford – concentrated on preparing men to operate in specific countries, and placed a greater emphasis on providing them with background information about the places to which they would be deployed. When the joint Allied Supreme Headquarters (SHAEF) was established in London, however, these American and British training operations effectively merged, and were centred on premises in the UK controlled by the military, originally at Shrivenham and afterwards at Eastbourne and Manchester.

The curricula of Civil Affairs trainers, and the position they accorded to the teaching of foreign languages, developed as the concept of Civil Affairs itself changed. In the US, the syllabus at the Civil Affairs School at Charlottesville had given very little weight to language instruction. As Zink suggested about officers trained for Germany, 'trainees who had entered with only a smattering of knowledge of German history, politics, economics, social institutions and psychology left with not a great deal more' (Zink 1957: 13). The stress in Charlottesville was on military governmental problems and solutions, and the tendency of the curriculum was to take a broad generic perspective which implied that occupying Burma or occupying Bulgaria would be much the same, 'in that they involved an occupying army and an indigenous enemy – or allied population' (Brown Mason 1950: 184). In this context, it was unsurprising that foreign language teaching was not provided at all to begin with and, when given later, was allotted very little time.

A British observer, reporting on what was happening in Civil Affairs training in the US, noted how very different the Charlottesville approach was from the university programmes. Civil Affairs students in universities were allocated a great deal of language tuition – 75 per cent of the course at Yale was said to be given over to languages.[18] They were taught largely by civilian professors who were experts in the countries concerned, with 15 hours of language teaching provided every week.

The curriculum, modelled on the intensive language programme of the American Council of Learned Societies, emphasized communicative methods, with students drilled in small language groups (Brown Mason 1950: 186).

In the British War Office model, languages had been included from the beginning. The proposed syllabus for Wimbledon courses in November 1943 included 60 hours of language teaching out of 360 contact hours over a nine-week course, a programme which also included: 'Functions and Regions' (144 hours), 'Military' (36 hours), 'MT [Motor Transport] Driving and Maintenance' (18 hours), 'Outdoor Exercises' (72 hours), 'Arrival/Dispersal/Inoculations' (30 hours). Language groups were expected to be a maximum of eight in size, with the aim of providing instruction on a 'refresher' course basis in one language (French, German, Flemish, Dutch, Norwegian or Danish), 'plus an elementary course in German for all students designed to give a vocabulary of 800/1000 words and phrases in common use in Germany. In all cases concentrating upon vocabulary applicable to Civil Affairs.'[19]

When the British and American systems were brought together in early 1944, languages were supposed to form about 185 hours of a four-week, six-days-a-week course. There were to be 34 hours of 'intensive drill in French and German at 3 levels, elementary, intermediate, advanced', as well as approximately 38 hours of 'study and supplemental language'.[20] As the courses developed, however, it soon became evident that the foreign languages element of the programme was often a good deal less important than the original syllabuses had suggested. To begin with, it was sometimes difficult to find adequate language teachers. At the Eastbourne centre, for example, a visiting colonel claimed that 'no proper arrangements have been made for language classes and (I think) the only language instruction available is that for which the officers themselves are prepared to pay'. Whilst this criticism was vehemently denied, it was certainly the case that the centre was having to request an extra six German or Austrian nationals in order to strengthen its language teaching.[21] In addition, the sheer quantity of material which had to be covered in Civil Affairs courses could easily mean that language elements were squeezed out. With the range of military and functional information which students had to assimilate, normally over a four-week intensive course, it often appeared to be foreign language classes which were sacrificed both by the staff organizing the training and the students attending it. Progress reports on Civil Affairs courses for Norway, for example, raised serious concerns about the language element: 'It is felt that the present system of language instruction...is not achieving the desired results....Frequent change of instructors and spasmodic attendance.'[22]

One approach to dealing with this, of course, was to seek to recruit Civil Affairs officers who were already qualified linguists, either native speakers of the languages required or else Englishmen who possessed language qualifications. As far as foreign nationals were concerned, the Allied Command made a clear distinction between employing native speakers as language instructors, which they felt was acceptable, and actually recruiting them as Civil Affairs officers in the field, which was deemed to be impossible. Apart from employing French Canadians in France, there was a general fear that using other foreign nationals 'born in the occupied country might create difficult political situations and might', in fact, react very unfavourably in the...officer himself [sic]'.[23] As an alternative, foreign language qualifications were built into the desired profile of all candidates for Civil Affairs posts, although, in practice, foreign language competence tended to be seen as relatively unimportant in comparison with the military and functional aspects of Civil Affairs. Thus, only around a quarter of recruits who arrived at training courses already had prior qualifications in languages. An early British course in February 1943 recorded 41 attendees out of 154 (27 per cent) as having language competence, and in a later joint syllabus in June 1944 the proportion had shrunk to 20 per cent.[24] Part of the problem was that it was clearly difficult to find enough Anglophone soldiers who already possessed language skills. In addition, however, there appeared to be some slight suspicion about the military suitability of those candidates who did present themselves with attested language qualifications. Donnison, the official historian of British Civil Affairs, argued that traditional military competences were often sadly lacking amongst good linguists:

> knowledge of the country in which they were to work, and of the language spoken there, were clearly desirable. But linguistic experts tended to be poor risks from a security point of view, and were frequently not persons who could gain the confidence of soldiers. The conclusion was early reached that...'it is better to have a really good man who is not a linguist rather than a doubtful man who possesses outstanding linguistic qualifications'. (Donnison 1966: 292)

In practice, as Civil Affairs preparation developed, the presence of foreign languages was given meaning not through the more traditional routes of prior qualifications or language classes but rather through particular aspects of pre-deployment preparation which were seen to be much more central to the operational requirements and competence of a Civil Affairs officer. The major focus of all Civil Affairs training was to give officers as much information as possible about the particular countries to which they would be going, with a series of background lectures on the relevant history, geography and politics, provided by outside experts. Central to this approach was the Civil Affairs Handbook which had been developed for each region within countries which were to be liberated. These books were extraordinarily detailed. The Belgian Zone Handbook for East and West Flanders, for instance, included a local directory of personalities, plus lists, down to commune level, of police stations, hospitals, hotels, garages and schools. Information was included on market days in each town and on where radio dealers and printers were located. That this knowledge was assumed to be vital to the officers in operational terms was evidenced by the caveat at the front of the handbooks: 'the reader is cautioned against regarding it as infallible. Due to the conditions under which the books were prepared, often without access to recent sources or adequate means of checking available data, a large percentage of error should be expected and allowed for.'[25]

Training courses sought as far as possible to recreate the situations which the men would have to deal with in continental Europe. Syndicate-based exercises enacted scenarios of what probable tasks might be, with trainees role-playing how they would set up food distribution systems for civilians or how they would interact with local officials like the station-master, the post-master or the manager of the water supply company. Students were given advanced material, a précis of relevant contextual issues and then a problem to solve. The 11th course, for example, had as its object to give students practice in a first interview with a German official: 'Students will be prepared to discuss...a) outline policy for the administration of the area...b) an agenda for the second conference, c) whom, if anyone (the officer in charge) would take with him to the two conferences. After discussion, the second conference will be enacted by students.'[26]

On occasions, members of the courses even moved outside the training rooms in order to gain some understanding of the possible physical conditions they would meet. Civil Affairs officers preparing to go to Norway, for instance, were made to cook and sleep out in the open in Aberdeenshire: 'A blizzard at the end of the first week...vitally assisted the instructors in producing realistic conditions',[27] and a cohort about to land in Holland were taken to Wolverhampton for a full-scale 'rehearsal of the steps which would be taken for dealing with the thousands of

Dutchmen and other nationals who would make their way to the Dutch frontier on the cessation of hostilities'.[28]

In all this operational information, foreign languages were present inter-textually – in the lectures delivered, in the handbooks prepared about each country, in the syndicate exercises, and in the regular updates which officers were given about the contemporary situation in the particular country for which they were being trained. The Norwegian Unit, for example, mounted a five day intensive workshop for its officers, Exercise Percy, attended by Crown Prince Olav and representatives of the exile Norwegian government. After each session, questions raised by the trainees were referred to the official Norwegian guests who sought to supply relevant answers.

In addition, a mass of foreign language material was produced to assist the officers when they actually landed in the country, with bilingual police arrest reports, oaths in the appropriate language for use in legal court processes, and specific glossaries of useful terms. The Field Handbook for Belgium, for example, had a 26-page glossary of relevant medical terms in English, French, Flemish and German for use in hospitals and medical centres. Feedback from Civil Affairs officers who were already operating in the field, after the landings in Sicily, emphasized how crucial it was for operational effectiveness to take in material written in the local language: 'This obviates the extreme difficulty in endeavouring to "put across" technical terms to local officials who are often not well educated, through indifferent interpreters, which invariably results in queries which the Civil Affairs officer is unable to answer.'[29] By the time Civil Affairs officers arrived in Belgium in September 1944, they brought in with them 500 copies of proclamations, 25 Directives and 1800 police armbands, all in the appropriate languages, and were expecting to receive another 7600 copies of foreign language material, including forms for police arrests in English, French, Flemish and German.

In the field, active skills in a foreign language were regarded as additional extras, of psychological rather than of operational importance: 'from a psychological standpoint, it is advantageous to have the officers and men possess at least a small knowledge of the Norwegian language.'[30] This, incidentally, was supported in early feedback reports from Civil Affairs officers in Sicily who noted that a little language knowledge would be useful in order to keep a check on locally-recruited interpreters.[31] Overall, however, what was important to Civil Affairs was the operational material which would enable the officer to do his job. Within this, the foreign language was fully integrated, present in informative lectures, in the detailed preparatory handbooks, in syndicate discussions, and in the operational material – posters, glossaries, and legal procedures – which the officers would be taking with them into liberated Europe. Foreign languages were embedded in the operational material on which the success of Civil Affairs was to depend.

Conclusions

Cultural preparations for the Liberation of Western Europe involved the Allies in producing pre-deployment material for soldiers and for Civil Affairs officers. In the case of troops, the Foreign Office Political Warfare Department took responsibility for promoting a model of positive military behaviour in liberated Europe. The need to provide relevant information for a massive number of troops and ensure that it was accessible and comprehensible resulted in a suite of pocket guides for each country. In these booklets, the foreign language was positioned as much more than a series of annexed language phrases. Languages were presented as part of an imagined encounter between soldiers and civilians which would need to be handled with courtesy and care, and for which useful and accessible strategies could be developed. The generic – the meta-language of good linguistic manners – was of a great deal more importance than the particular – basic competence in a specific language.

The smaller specialist cadre of Civil Affairs officers were expected to have a more sustained relationship with local populations than was envisaged for the troops. Whilst language qualifications and foreign language teaching were considered to be important for these officers, linguistic fluency was of much less relevance to them than understanding how language was related to what would be their key operational procedures. In practice, the major place of foreign languages in Civil Affairs was within the material produced by planners to train future officers, to inform them about the country, and to make them operationally effective when they landed. Whereas separating the foreign language into an area of distinct qualifications and specialist tuition appeared to lessen both its visibility and its relevance, integrating foreign languages within the contemporary material to be used in future operational deployment seemed to make a great deal of practical sense.

The long-standing dilemma of the relationship between language and culture was addressed in Second World War preparations by eschewing any sense that there was in practice a language/culture division, refusing, as it were, to ghettoize languages as a minority capability. Foreign languages were embedded in cultural preparations for all troops by con-centrating not on the specific language itself but on the generic, the meta-language of good linguistic manners. Although foreign languages were present as separate components in the syllabus for Civil Affairs, they appeared to be most successfully integrated into the curriculum when they were subsumed within the operational material and training exercises which men received. Rather than the goal of particular language competences, seen as one of several aptitudes to be acquired, Civil Affairs training integrated languages inter-textually within the pressing operational necessities of the job officers were being called upon to do.

Overall, the evidence of the 1944–5 case study suggests that difficult language-policy questions necessarily raised by any essentialized notion of 'language capability' (which language? what level of fluency? how much language?), could be changed into broader and arguably more operationally relevant questions like 'how do we communicate politely as a foreigner with other foreigners?' and 'What language material is needed in relation to the particular tasks that will have to be performed?' In this scenario, language is not a minority interest of high achievers, separate from the cultural concerns of the majority of military participants. Instead, it becomes an integral part of overall strategic and operational objectives.

Notes

1. NA, FO 898/478, Pocket Guides Education Sub-Committee, 1943.
2. NA, WO 219/3700, 10 May 1944.
3. NA, FO 898/478, memo, 25 August 1943.
4. NA, WO 219/896, 11 May 1944.
5. NA, FO 898/478, Fairlie memo, 31 August 1943.
6. NA, FO 898/478, 11 November 1943.
7. NA, FO 898/483, 9 September 1943.
8. All quotations from Guides, NA, FO 898/478, Pocket Guides Education Sub-Committee.
9. NA, FO 898/478, Pocket Guides Education Sub-Committee, 30 October 1943.
10. NA, FO 898/478, Pocket Guides Education Sub-Committee, 6 December 1943.
11. NA, FO 898/478, Pocket Guides Education Sub-Committee, 9 November 1943.
12. NA, FO 898/478, Pocket Guides Education Sub-Committee, 9 November 1943.
13. NA, FO 898/478, Pocket Guides Education Sub-Committee, draft guide, 18 November 1943.
14. *Stars and Stripes*, 4 October 1944.
15. *Stars and Stripes*, 17 August 1944.

16. 'I'm American'; 'You have lovely eyes'; 'Will you come for a walk with me?'; 'No, I'm not married'; 'Where is your Mother?'; 'I'm going to have to leave you'; 'I'll miss you a lot'; 'Don't forget to write to me'.
17. 'Surrender'; 'Step aside'; 'Open the door'; 'Where is the sniper hiding?'; 'Wash my clothes'; 'Get off the street'; 'Report tomorrow morning'.
18. NA, FO 371/40434, Lt Col Rowe, 5 February 1944.
19. NA, WO 219/3687, Proposed syllabus, 5 November 1943.
20. NA, WO219/3700, Activities of CAC, 18 January 1944.
21. NA, WO 219/3849, Memo Colonel Bridge, 25 July 1944; Memo Colonel Bruce, 29 July 1944.
22. NA, WO 171/3827, CA Progress Report no. 17, 17 October 1944.
23. NA, WO 32/10764, 'Interim Report of the Sub-Committee on politico-military training AT(E)/P (42) 30', 26 September 1942.
24. NA, WO 32/10764, 20 May 1943.
25. NA, WO 220/101, *Belgium Zone Handbook, No. 1*, October 1943.
26. NA, WO 219/3689, 11th course issued to students, 17 August 1944.
27. NA, WO 171/8445, Historical Report, 1–31 January 1945.
28. NA, FO 898/368, Report on visit, 9/10 July 1944.
29. NA, WO 220/273, Captain Dyer, 29 March 1944.
30. NA, WO 171/3827, CA weekly conference, 13 October 1944.
31. NA, WO 220/273, Captain Dyer, 29 March 1944.

5
Languages and Peace Operations

'There was very little thought or planning done to how to organize linguistic support for an operation of that kind before it actually took place. And there was a lot of improvisation on the ground.'[1]

NATO forces were initially unprepared for the armed conflict in Bosnia-Herzegovina from March 1992, and struggled to meet the challenges of bringing peace in an environment that was foreign in language and culture (Malcolm 2002; Bose 2002). The first units were deployed in November of that year, as part of Operation Grapple, and included some 2400 British military personnel. Most of the fighting was ended by the Dayton Peace Agreement of December 1995. Following that agreement, a series of NATO and EU interventions supervised the ending of the conflicts and the reconstruction efforts of the next decade.[2] British contingents were deployed as part of the UN peacekeeping force (UNPROFOR) from an early stage and continued to serve through successive phases of the intervention until they withdrew in 2007. This chapter examines how, although the British forces initially had little preparation for the linguistic and cultural conditions they would encounter. they quickly developed a more concerted approach to preparing for their involvement.

Being prepared

The issue of preparedness was a difficult one, especially in the early stages of the operation. NATO was fundamentally unprepared for involvement in the events surrounding the disintegration of Yugoslavia. For the previous 40 years, its preparations had focused on the requirements of the Cold War, and the grand strategy that governed the manoeuvrings of the two military blocs. The more complex conflicts that emerged after the end of the Cold War were of a different order, and for a long time were not regarded as 'proper war' (Frantzen 2005). The idea of 'military operations other than war' (OOTW) was developed in the mid-1990s to accommodate this (Stech 1995; Stofft and Guertner 1995), but has been gradually replaced by a recognition that the nature of warfare has changed into more complex forms. In this context, it becomes even clearer that the concept of preparedness itself is an aspect of warfare, where preparations may easily be construed as a hostile act.

Nor was NATO prepared for the kind of operation it was undertaking. As a non-war operation, peacekeeping has been a well-established practice under the auspices of the United Nations since 1948. It aims to create the conditions for lasting peace in situations of conflict, and generally works by consent of the opposed forces in conditions of ceasefire. Although many NATO countries have participated in some of the 60 or more UN missions,[3] NATO itself was not involved in peace support before the intervention in Bosnia-Herzegovina. On the contrary, it was a warfighting organization, even if the war in question was a cold one. As an illustration, several British commanders commented ruefully that, whereas the Cold War had been cold in the metaphorical sense, the operations in Bosnia-Herzegovina were 'cold' in the very literal sense of operations taking place in wintry conditions on the ground (Barry 2008; Howard 2006). Their experience was that, in the metaphorical sense, this conflict was at times extremely hot.

The entry of NATO into the Yugoslav crisis also coincided with significant changes in the nature of peace support operations. These were extended beyond the traditional mission of UN-style peacekeeping, which depended on the consent of the parties, strict impartiality and the non-use of force except in self-defence. The new missions included peace-making, which aims to secure a ceasefire or peaceful settlement in a continuing conflict; peace enforcement, which aims to maintain a ceasefire or peace agreement which has uncertain levels of support and is likely to be breached; and peace-building, a longer-term process in which the military work alongside diplomatic and civil initiatives to address the underlying causes of conflict. Whereas peacekeeping was well defined, the strategic importance and military implications of other kinds of peace support were only beginning to be understood in the 1990s (Dandeker and Gow 1997; Johnston 2007; Fortna and Howard 2008).

The Bosnian conflict was NATO's first active deployment of troops, though not the first time Britain or other member countries had sent troops into active service over the previous half-century. NATO's raison d'être was the prolonged military stand-off of the Cold War, and at the time of the Yugoslav crisis it was only beginning to define a role for itself in the 'new world order' of the 1990s. In many respects, the Bosnian operation was a learning experience for the new context. It emerged as a conflict that had not been expected, and the intervention was an operation for which NATO was scarcely prepared. This unpreparedness was reflected in the language sphere, where little or no linguistic preparation was in place in 1992. As Nick Stansfield, a military interpreter and instructor, put it: 'There was very little thought or planning done to how to organize linguistic support for an operation of that kind before it actually took place.'[4]

At NATO level, language preparations in general were largely aimed at ensuring interoperability, and focused on the ability of NATO forces to communicate effectively with one another (Crossey 2005). The principal concern was to maintain an effective policy on working languages. Since 1949, NATO policy has been that 'English and French shall be the official languages for the entire North Atlantic Treaty Organization' (NATO 1949). This has been maintained in official documents, though English tended to predominate in other contexts, and, as Nick Stansfield pointed out, 'the decline of French as a working language was considerably accelerated when France withdrew from the military structure'.[5] France formally withdrew from NATO military command in 1966, lasting until 2009. As a result, the use of French had largely been abandoned in practice for communication between military contingents, and English had become the de facto working language. Policy in this area was therefore primarily directed to enhancing the ability of different NATO forces to achieve an adequate level of competence in English. In the case of Britain, the main impact of this policy was that British services provided a significant amount of English language instruction for partner countries.

NATO also provides a framework for language testing, whether in English or in other languages. Since 1976, the Organization has used a Standardization Agreement (STANAG), which defines language proficiency levels in a scale entitled STANAG 6001.[6] This provides a six point scale (0–5) for competence in Listening, Speaking, Reading and Writing. It is now mapped against the scale of the Common European Framework of Reference, which has gained international acceptance since its publication in 2001 (Council for Cultural Cooperation 2001).[7] Policy in this area is primarily concerned with the dissemination and implementation of good practice.

The provision of language teaching, and its assessment, remained firmly the responsibility of individual NATO member countries. Some 40 different countries provided contingents in Bosnia-Herzegovina. Each had a different approach to their mission in general, and, in consequence, different responses to the language issues involved. These could lead to very divergent approaches to communication with other units, communication with the local population, translation of documents or use of interpreters, for example. And as a result they had different views of their operational language needs. Some countries provided different types and levels of language preparation for their personnel. Others, by contrast, undertook no language preparation for their forces, preferring to rely on civilians with the requisite skills, who were either contracted or enlisted. However, all forces relied to some degree on locally-employed staff to meet at least some of their language requirements.

Meeting language needs

The language needs of the British forces changed over the course of the 15 years of their deployment. The range of activities assigned to the UN and NATO forces remained a good deal narrower than those carried out by the Allied forces in Europe after 1945. In particular, most of the legal and administrative tasks undertaken by the international community were undertaken by other agencies. These included the Office of the High Representative, which oversaw the civilian implementation of the Dayton Agreement; the International Criminal Tribunal for the Former Yugoslavia, which dealt with war crimes; UN and EU civilian agencies; and an expanding range of non-governmental organizations, concerned with human rights, health, safety, education, infrastructure and many other issues. Initially, the needs of the military centred on communicating effectively with the different armed groups in the Bosnian conflict. The focus subsequently moved to wider communication with the civilian population as the number of civilian/military cooperation (CIMIC) projects increased. And, as time passed, more and more of the forces' requirements were met through the use of locally-employed interpreters as key intermediaries. The British response to language needs in the early stages of the conflict is of particular interest, since key decisions taken in haste often had longer-lasting consequences. But, as the conflict and its aftermath developed, lessons were learned which established a more stable pattern of language preparation for the future.

In the first stage of language preparation, following the outbreak of hostilities in 1992, the British forces were caught largely unawares. The availability of language preparation at the beginning of the conflict was still largely based on the conditions of the Cold War and oriented towards increasing competence in Russian. The realization that this no longer corresponded to strategic needs emerged in the early 1990s. In addition, language preparation was mainly designed for combat with opposing forces and for intelligence-gathering. It was not designed to enable close and detailed engagement with local populations in order to build peaceful relations.

The British forces scrambled to devise a response to the needs of the Bosnian intervention. As Nick Stansfield put it, 'there was a lot of improvisation on the ground'.[8] This approach, which might be described as 'bricolage' (Lévi-Strauss 1966), mobilized whatever resources were to hand. Although service personnel might state their language expertise in their personal file, no systematic records were held that would have revealed which service personnel possessed relevant language skills. Commanders initially fell back on the traditional mustering procedure of phoning around their friends to see if anyone knew of anyone who could speak Serbo-Croat, as the language was then known. The frustrations caused by this chaotic lack of system did eventually lead to the establishment of a more effective database of language competences.

In the event, in 1992, four soldiers were identified as being able to speak the language. All of them were eventually deployed. Three of them had a family background from the area, while a fourth officer had a degree in Slavonic Studies from the University of Nottingham, which had included Serbo-Croat. The latter was given five or six weeks of intensive refresher tuition in Serbo-Croat and deployed as the interpreter to a field ambulance unit in Croatia, where, as he said, 'I was all they had'.[9] He was joined a few weeks later by an Intelligence Corps captain, who had only a very basic grasp of the language. It was at this point that the Royal Army Educational Corps (RAEC) and others recognized that there was a language issue and began working to develop training programmes.

When the conflict broke out in 1992, Serbo-Croat was not taught at the Defence School of Languages (DSL), Beaconsfield. Nick Stansfield, who had graduated in Slavonic Studies, played a key role in reinstating it. Knowing he was due to be deployed to Croatia, he was invited to the RAEC headquarters at Eltham Palace. He realized that no plans had been put in place to address the longer-term language needs of the campaign in former Yugoslavia and commented forcefully on this. His comments, and perhaps comments from other officers, led to the decision to develop teaching from within the Russian department of DSL, as he described:

> [T]here was a fantastic Russian course at Beaconsfield. At that point there was no Serbo-Croat course. There was a lovely lady who was extremely good, who spoke Russian and Serbian. Her father was a Serbian pilot in the Yugoslav air force, and around that time, probably just a bit later, whilst I was actually serving in Yugoslavia, she set up, or she was instructed to set up at Beaconsfield Defence School of Languages the first Serbo-Croat training course, which she did very well.[10]

The high quality of the Russian programme may not be surprising after more than 40 years of experience, and the Serbo-Croat programme was an organic development from it, based on an existing member of staff who had an appropriate language background. On his return from Croatia, Nick Stansfield was appointed as the officer commanding Serbo-Croat training within DSL's Russian department. From that point onwards, linguistic preparation for the Bosnian operation was given a higher priority. As deployments became more predictable, language learning featured as part of the programmes of military preparation for those due to serve in the region. The programmes at Beaconsfield initially drew on native-speaker Serbs, who provided the earliest instructors, though they were soon joined by instructors from Britain and from other parts of former Yugoslavia. It echoes the case of the first four Serbo-Croat speakers in the military, three of whom were from Serbian family backgrounds. Considering the widespread feeling in Britain that the Serbs were the principal instigators of the conflict, the contact of British forces with people of Serbian origin in the language context may well have broadened their perspectives. Some commentators have suggested that British policy in general was excessively favourable to the Serbian cause (Simms 2002), but this is not reflected in the comments of military participants, who were at pains to be even-handed.

Other parts of the military also made rapid ad hoc arrangements to supply their language needs. Alma Kovač described how she was engaged by Military Intelligence to initiate training in the language in the autumn of 1992. She was Bosnian and had fled from Sarajevo in July 1992 with her husband, who secured a post as Visiting Professor at the University of Essex. She was approached to set up a language programme at the Army Education Centre in Colchester. A well-educated woman, she had taught English at primary school, though had never taught her own language and nor had she taught adults. Starting with no learning materials apart from a small grammar book, she developed the first course for a group of a dozen officers from the Regular and Territorial Army, who expected to be deployed to Bosnia or to gather intelligence from refugees.[11] The first course lasted four to six weeks and provided only a very basic level of competence. Subsequent courses were longer, typically three months for 'colloquial' level, roughly equivalent to a British GSCE school qualification (B1 in CEF). A further course of three months was required for the more advanced so-called 'linguist' level, roughly a British 'A level' qualification (B2 in CEF). The number of teachers was increased, and later cohorts included ambassadors and defence attachés. In this case, too, a very ad hoc approach at the beginning was quickly transformed into an organized programme, delivered to professional standards. It was noticeable, however, that there was little contact between DSL and the Military Intelligence initiative. Opportunities were clearly lost to develop a more coordinated and more effective service.

Pedagogical issues in language training

Many of the military personnel to attend these early courses were already trained in Russian and were therefore able to make rapid progress in Serbo-Croat, which the US military later referred to as 'Turbo Serbo' (Quinn-Judge 1995: 21). Fred Whitaker, a military linguist who took a 15-week course in early 1993, commented:

> At least for me and some of my colleagues, with a background in Russian, that was at least a help, because you understood the way the language behaved, even though sometimes it could mislead you, because [there are] quite a lot of false friends, things that you think are the same word are not the same word. But nevertheless it was an advantage.[12]

Conversely, those who did not have a background in Russian found it difficult to achieve even a basic level of competence. There was frequently disappointment when apparently trained 'linguists' were not able to meet the expectations of commanders on the ground. Over time, this provided a stimulus to increase the amount of language training offered, to reduce the language deficit. It was also a key factor in increasing the use of locally-employed interpreters on the ground.

The modestly-trained British troops were unable to provide linguistic, cultural or political expertise comparable to that offered by local people, who had often acquired a sophisticated grasp of the English language and Anglo-American culture to complement their awareness of the local situation. This was compounded by the relatively short deployments, which did not give British personnel time to develop and consolidate their knowledge of the local language and culture.

At a lower level of language function, troops who had little or no training in languages were issued with vocabulary lists. These were not available in the early stages of the conflict and Nick Stansfield recalls being asked to produce the first one:

> I was the one in Croatia, in Zagreb, at the airport, asked by my people to actually write a vocabulary, a basic vocabulary for soldiers, because it hadn't been done. Now, to ask a Brit to write a vocabulary in Serbo-Croat is a bit of a challenge, because normally you get a native speaker to do that task, but anyway it was done, and it was handed out as what they call an aide-memoire, for the pocket. I'm not sure how useful it was. They could probably order coffee, and pay the bill, maybe (laughs). And say 'Don't shoot me, I'm British' (laughs).

This ad hoc solution was better than nothing. But, as the experience of operations developed, further versions were produced, reflecting the emerging needs of troops on the ground. They drew on a wider range of expertise and incorporated lessons from practical experience.

By December 1995, some assistance with language preparation was included in the *Country Handbook*, produced by the US Department of Defense and issued to NATO troops in the Peace Implementation Force, IFOR (Department of Defense 1995). A component of the same length and scope was included in the British *Aide-Memoire*, a ring-bound handbook of similar content and purpose (Murray 1997). In a dozen pages, these manuals provided a guide to pronunciation, basic phrases and expressions, and more specialist vocabulary for military purposes. Similar guides were also produced in card form, which troops could keep in a pocket, or in many cases in their helmet. The approach was to provide a list of words and phrases in three columns, comprising the English phrase, the Serbo-Croat equivalent and an approximate pronunciation guide. This was modelled on the familiar format for holiday phrase books (see Table 5.1).

From the use of capitals, diacritics, font and phonetic rendering, it is clear that the two phrase lists quoted here were produced independently

Table 5.1 Greetings in American and British phrase lists

US Handbook	Good day	Dobar dan	*dobahr dahn*
UK aide-memoire	good-day	dobar dan	doh-bar dan
US Handbook	Good night	Laku noč	*lahkoo nohtch*
UK aide-memoire	good-night	laku noc	lak-oo notch
US Handbook	Hello	Zdravo	*zdrahvo*
UK aide-memoire	hello	bok (Croat)	bok
		zdravo (Serb)	zdra-voh

of each other. The American version may show Slovenian influences, such as the accent on 'noč', which is not used in the Serbo-Croat 'noć'. There are also cultural differences in choice of words and tone of voice. In both cases, the lists refer to differences between Serbian and Croatian but do not differentiate between them in vocabulary, with the sole exception of the Serbian and Croatian words for 'hello', shown above from the UK aide-memoire. The difference was almost entirely identified with the use of Latin or Cyrillic script. The American handbook gave a warning, however:

> *Special caution*: Only Croatian script and usage are presented to save space. Be sensitive to this if attempting to communicate with people of Serbian or Montenegran extraction. You could, by employing Croatian usage, seem biased towards the Croat cause. (Department of Defense 1995: 3–1)

The note goes on to outline some differences in the pronunciation of vowels, but does not otherwise offer any guidance on how 'Croatian usage' might be avoided or handled sensitively.

Cultural sensitivity was certainly on the training agenda for troops deploying after the Dayton agreement, focusing mainly on the political and ethnic division revealed in recent history. In addition, troops received advice on their behaviour in the context of local attitudes. The British 'DO's and DON'Ts' were broadly based and focused on the importance of appropriate behaviour to the success of the mission. They also included, among other things, advice on respecting women, reciprocating hospitality, avoiding discussion of religion and politics and acknowledging greetings. The latter point was accompanied by a warning not to attempt to mimic specifically Croatian or Serbian hand-waves. The rather precise nature of this advice reflected the experience of British troops during earlier deployments. They had learned to avoid trouble by offering their usual style of wave.

Building capacity for language support

The preparation in linguistic and cultural matters was essentially functional in nature. It was concerned with getting the job done. This was certainly the case in the earlier part of the campaign, where the conflicts were at their most dangerous and where immediate military objectives took overriding priority. After the Dayton agreement, the profile of activity shifted to building the peace and rebuilding the country. In those circumstances, a broader conception of the culture of the region emerged, informed by the experience of people who had spent longer getting to know the place and the people, often in several tours of duty there.

After the initial scramble to develop linguistic competence, language learning settled into a more orderly pattern, aimed at preparing troops who now had longer advance notice that they would be deployed to the region. Courses in Serbo-Croat were established by a number of military and civilian providers, including DSL, the Military Intelligence training centre and the Foreign Office Language School (which was closed in 2007). Vocational language courses were developed at universities, most notably the Ministry of Defence Languages Examination Board (MODLEB) programme, based at the University of Westminster, which provided accreditation and quality assurance for military language courses.

The precise nature of language training provided was defined in response to demand from military clients. During the Bosnian intervention, most of the decisions remained firmly at operational level: what language capacity was required, how it would be achieved and how it would be deployed. It was principally the responsibility of battalion or company commanders, who decided what their operational requirements were and set about fulfilling them. They took a pragmatic view and acquired the resources needed wherever they could find them. Hence, alongside general-purpose language training for all services, there were special programmes for particular units or missions. The Special Air or Boat Services, for example, were generally taught in separate groups. The intelligence services had their own programme. Courses varied in length but might typically consist of 10–12 weeks of intensive training as part of a wider training programme, or up to 18 months of more advanced training for the most specialized linguists.

As the Bosnian intervention progressed, the provision of suitable language support services improved and commanders were able to develop correspondingly greater language capacity in their units. In the early stages, the total capacity on which they could draw was limited to a handful of native or near-native speakers and a small number of soldiers with a few weeks of language training. Later on, they were able to call on linguists with more experience of the region and a higher level of linguistic and cultural skills.

Initially, the course design and materials used were often ad hoc. Alma Kovač, who established the language course for intelligence services, was quite candid about the limited resources on which she could draw.[13] Not only was she herself not specifically qualified for the task but she was also confronted by an almost complete absence of learning materials. Like many teachers before and since, she used her initiative to compile a programme, drawing on her own experience in other areas and on the resources that her learners brought to the class. As a teacher of English at primary school, she drew on the methodologies she had used there, modulating them to suit her adult learners of Serbo-Croat. She had access to a small grammar book, which she used to good effect, and encouraged the learners to develop role-play exercises, drawing on their own experiences and using their limited knowledge of the target language. After the first course, she was able to develop her methods. However, the driving force behind these enhancements was the needs of her learners, as they articulated them. No doubt this highlights a characteristic of language preparation, which can become increasingly effective over time as the needs of the learners are more clearly defined.

Languages for military purposes

In a broad sense, linguistic preparation for military service is an example of languages for specific purpose. This is an area of second or foreign language teaching and learning, in which teaching is designed to meet the specific needs of learners who require the language in order to carry out particular tasks in their education or work (Gollin and Hall 2011; Mayer 2001). Driven primarily by the needs of learners, it typically focuses on teaching language competence, using materials and situations which the learners are likely to encounter. British linguistic preparation for the Bosnian operations developed organically from the needs of learners. The largest institution in the field, DSL, rapidly generated Serbo-Croat courses, using expertise in its existing courses. In doing so it demonstrated its 'tailored-to-task' approach, which a more recent commanding officer described in brief:

> We react to operational requirements. There are certain organisations that can only come to see us at certain times and the training will then be quick and dirty. (Morrison 2009)

For the most part, such training was assembled by existing instructors from resources and materials which were already being used on other courses. But, in the case of the Bosnian operation, the requirement was for a language that was no longer taught at DSL, posing a more general challenge, to which it responded by redeploying an existing instructor and rapidly developing relevant resources and materials. As the longer-term nature of the engagement became clearer, the 'quick and dirty' approach was correspondingly replaced by a more robust programme which accumulated the necessary expertise and resources.

The teaching methods employed for Serbo-Croat in Beaconsfield, Colchester and elsewhere were recognizably similar to learning in other languages, though with some distinctive features. There was a relative lack of learning tools for the language, in the form of grammar books, dictionaries, course manuals and audiovisual aids. There were some commercial courses. The Routledge guide to colloquial Serbo-Croat (Hawkesworth 1986) formed the basis of the first six-week course in Colchester, in which learners with Russian were able to advance at a chapter a day.[14] Hodder and Stoughton published a Serbo-Croat guide in their 'Teach Yourself' series in 1993, which was widely used (Norris 1993). However, teachers were required to produce many of their own materials. They did this, drawing on an eclectic range of approaches.

The traditional grammar-translation method contributed a legacy of grammatical tables, showing the inflections of root stems in different grammatical positions. One of the most complex examples was a handwritten matrix in 14 rows and 30 columns to represent the inflection of six different types of noun, adjective and pronoun in three different genders and seven different cases, in singular and plural.[15] This grammar-translation method also involved vocabulary learning, with long lists of words to be memorized, comparable to the vocabulary cards that were distributed to soldiers. As with the cards, the vocabulary lists were aimed at relevant contexts, and as Eric Wilson, an intelligence linguist, put it: 'the vocabulary was very much geared, not to your holidays in Dubrovnik, but very much to what was happening in Banja Luka'.[16] At the more advanced levels, this approach contributed some sophistication in translation. In most European countries, the language training programmes were likely to be based on the grammar-translation method, at least in the early stages of the conflict. This was still the dominant methodology, which continued to dominate in the 'philological' tradition of language education. One Danish language learning manual, for example, worked systematically through successive grammatical categories. The first lesson of the *Serbokroatisk grundundervisning* focused on phonetics, the second focused on personal pronouns, three families of verb, and word order. Successive lessons progressed through the tenses and conjugations of verbs, declensions of nouns and different categories of pronouns and adjectives. Each lesson was accompanied with an apparatus of word lists, exercises and passages for comprehension and translation. It is a model of the grammar-translation approach.[17]

The behavioural model of language learning was less in evidence, though it contributed drills and mimicry to establish good linguistic habits, and a technology of repetition, of which 'flash cards' were the most familiar tool. However, much of the teaching practice was based on the communicative approach, sometimes referred to as the functional-notional approach, which had established itself as the most widely accepted framework for language teaching (Brumfit and Johnson 1979; Finocchiaro and Brumfit 1983).

This approach focused on the needs of the learner rather than the teacher, and encouraged a high level of initiative from the learners. It attached great importance to effective communication, encouraged maximum use of the target language and emphasized task-based activities, preferably related to a relevant socio-cultural context and using authentic materials as far as possible. In many ways, this matched the situation in which military personnel had a strong sense of the purpose for which the language was required and were accustomed to using their initiative to solve problems. Nick Stansfield, who ran a small team of UK-resident ex-Yugoslav local staff in the Serbo-Croat courses at Beaconsfield, explained that he simplified existing courses, avoiding detailed grammatical explanations but conveying grammatical points through practice, including simple conversations which exemplified them in operational situations. In his view, this made it 'manageable for soldiers, who had little time, and would not become great linguists in Serbo-Croat in ten weeks or 12 weeks or 14 weeks, whatever it might be'.[18] His most noticeable innovation was the extension of simple 'role-play' activities into more complex scenarios, where the learners were required to communicate effectively in the kind of situation they might encounter 'in theatre'. He explained this in detail:

A lot of the course would be based on scenarios, so we would write scenarios based upon what I remembered from Bosnia, being stopped at a checkpoint, meeting a Bosniak liaison officer or a Serbian liaison officer, coming together on the front line, doing a body exchange, and simply scenarios. And then they were told to act out those scenarios using the words that we would give them, and they would go ahead and do that.[19]

The scenario-based approach was well aligned with wider military practices in training. Scenarios and simulations were widely used, both for small-scale tasks and for larger operations, up to the level of military exercises. As the Bosnian conflict developed, more elaborate scenarios were developed, and some use was made of the village on Salisbury Plain that had been modified to simulate a Bosnian village. Similar exercises were also conducted in Germany. Whereas the use of these simulations was commonplace in military training, this was probably the first time that language issues had been incorporated in such a simulation.[20] Part of the purpose of the simulation was to train officers in the use of interpreters, and increasingly use was made of the locally-employed interpreters in Bosnia-Herzegovina, who were flown out to participate. Along with learning how to modulate their own use of English, personnel were given the experience of working in a context where Serbo-Croat was spoken and an opportunity to use the limited language knowledge they had acquired.

The results of preparation

It is difficult to assess the levels of proficiency achieved by those who received linguistic preparation. In the early stages of the conflict, relatively few soldiers had language training, perhaps a few from each unit. At most they would receive an awareness package, which would not qualify them for a STANAG qualification.[21] Certainly, for those who did receive language training, the expectations of their commanders was likely to be unrealistically high. Gregory Cook, an RAEC language instructor, explained:

> We were asked to produce interpreters with three weeks' training, and we had to inform the system that actually you can't become an interpreter in three weeks (laughs), and we were given six months. So the first people that went out got six months' training. And I think within about a year and a half something like 30 to 40 people had gone through six months' intensive training. But because they all knew that they were going to be deployed and they were going to be deployed as linguists, the standard reached in six months was surprisingly high, because they knew they were going to be used.[22]

The unrealistic expectation that people could be trained as interpreters in three weeks demonstrates the initial lack of understanding of language issues on the part of military planners. In part this may be accounted for by the unexpected nature of the conflict, which raised language issues that had not previously been encountered. In the following years, experience brought understanding, as commanders recognized what could realistically be expected from a period of language training. The remarkable success reported for trainees in the first year and a half suggests that strong motivation was an essential ingredient for language learning. It may also reflect the high number of trainees who already had a working knowledge of Russian, on which they could build for Serbo-Croat. It is perhaps a lesson learned from this experience that, when operations were undertaken in Iraq and Afghanistan a few years later, general service personnel were given a two-week course as part of their pre-deployment package and would be expected to achieve elementary speaking and listening, each to STANAG level 1.

A significant learning point was that language preparation needed to be specific in identifying the group of speakers with whom the military are preparing to engage. This now appears an obvious point, but until the early 1990s Russian had sufficed for many purposes, as the lingua franca of the Warsaw Pact countries. However, in the new situation, language requirements became much more localized and the implications of military training were correspondingly more focused. The 'localization' of language education also encouraged a 'cultural turn', where intercultural understanding became more important, as part of the process of understanding the language community (Ministry of Defence, Development Concepts and Doctrine Centre 2009). And this in turn has been accelerated by the changing nature of the military operations. 'Non-kinetic' operations such as peace support are in large measure a battle for hearts and minds, and therefore much more dependent on cultural understanding.

During the 1990s, there was little concerted action to develop a more general policy on language capacity in the British forces, even in the light of the issues raised by the Bosnian operation. It needed a much larger intervention to trigger change in this area. In 2006–7, after three years of war in Iraq, a new unit was created, the Defence Operational Language Support Unit (DOLSU), to generate, sustain and manage operational language capability.[23] This has extended the national level of policy, for example by establishing a database of language skills across the three services, made feasible by advances in information technology.

It also oversees a scheme of financial incentives to develop language skills.

Conclusions

It is clear that the outbreak of hostilities in Bosnia-Herzegovina caught the British forces unawares, and as a result their language preparation arrangements were in considerable disarray. In the scramble to respond, the military services adopted a series of ad hoc solutions which were later refined in the light of experience. These solutions were appropriate to a highly-focused professional army, and they may not have been scalable for a more extensive operation approaching the size and scope of the Allied forces in 1944. The Bosnian experience opened a new chapter in linguistic and cultural preparations to engage with the theatre of conflict.

However, the lessons identified at this time were not easily learned. In many respects, Bosnia appeared as an exceptional 'one-off' conflict, very much in contrast to the settled certainties of the Cold War. With the benefit of hindsight, it may appear as the first in a new breed of conflicts in which NATO and Britain would become involved. In the following decade, the operations in Iraq and Afghanistan encountered a remarkably similar range of military, linguistic and cultural issues. They also provided a strong stimulus to improve the quality of language preparations, and sparked the introduction of systems and institutions which could be expected to reduce the disarray experienced at the outbreak of the Bosnia conflict.

Notes

1. Interview, 31 March 2009. This and other notes refer to a series of 52 interviews carried out by Catherine Baker with participants of different nationalities in the Bosnian conflict and peace operations. The interviews were conducted on different dates during 2009–10. The quotations are extracted with permission from the transcripts, which are not at present in the public domain. Where the interviewee's name is given, this is an agreed pseudonym, except where otherwise stated.
2. IFOR, the Implementation Force, 1995–6; SFOR, the Stabilization Force, 1996–2004; EUFOR, the EU Force, 2004 to the present.
3. See the UN Peacekeeping website at: http://www.un.org/en/peacekeeping/operations/past.shtml (accessed 19 August 2011).
4. Interview, 31 March 2009. Nick Stansfield has agreed that his name can be quoted without the use of a pseudonym.
5. Interview, 31 March 2009.

6. The most recent version of STANAG 6001 is the third edition, 20 February 2009, which is available at: http://www.bilc.forces.gc.ca/stanag/doc/STANAG_6001_Edition_3-eng.pdf (accessed 19 August 2011).

7. See: http://www.campaignmilitaryenglish.com/Course/teacher.htm (accessed 13 January 2011), which provides a link to a comparison chart. The STANAG levels 0–3 map closely against CEFR levels A1–B2. Level 4 (Full Professional) maps against CEFR levels C1–C2. STANAG level 5 is a further level described as Native/Bilingual.

8. Interview, 31 March 2009.

9. Interview, 17 September 2009.

10. Interview, 17 September 2009.

11. Interview, 17 April 2009.

12. Interview, 24 July 2009.

13. Interview, 17 April 2009.

14. Interview, 5 June 2009.

15. A photocopy of this handwritten table was provided by Eric Wilson, interviewed on 5 June 2009. At the time referred to, early 1993, word processing and other forms of computer based text handling were at an early stage of development, and the training course concerned was not provided with equipment then available.

16. Interview, 5 June 2009.

17. A photocopy of this manual was provided by Thomas Nielsen, interviewed on 5 May 2009.

18. Interview, 17 September 2009.

19. Interview, 17 September 2009.

20. Interview, 2 March 2009.

21. Interview, 2 March 2009.

22. Interview, 2 March 2009.

23. See: http://www.mod.uk/ DefenceInternet/AboutDefence/WhatWeDo/TrainingandExercises/DOLSU/ (accessed 19 August 2011).

6
Language Policy and Peace-Building

'It turns out not to be an insignificant thing because it entrenches the differences. You know, it is a physical representation of the difference, it is as much as a barbed wire fence between them. Something that they hold on to and because it's there they cling on to it even harder.'[1]

The previous chapter demonstrated how British forces were initially unprepared for meeting the very specific language needs occasioned by their involvement in NATO's operations in Bosnia-Herzegovina and how, as a result, their responses to the linguistic challenges were marked by improvisation and adhoc-ery. These were also characteristics of the language policy decisions of other national contingents involved in NATO's initial operations, and of those at the HQ level where the military personnel in the individual elements of the HQ were left to make these decisions on their own and according to the specific needs of their particular locality. This approach facilitated operations on a day-to-day basis in a peacekeeping context, but once the conflict had been brought to an end with the signing of the Dayton Peace Agreement on 14 December 1995 the nature of NATO's mandate changed to one of longer-term peace-building and reconciliation. At the same time, the linguistic environment was altered with the de facto recognition of three official languages in the Dayton Peace Agreement. Both these changes had implications for the language policy decisions of the international military force. This chapter examines the interaction between the force's language policy and the wider peace-building environment and argues that although at one level the force's language policy can be seen as a purely institutional policy – concerned with translation and interpretation policies and the production of official documents – it nevertheless forms part of the linguistic landscape of present-day Bosnia-Herzegovina and as such clearly interacts with the wider peace-building concerns of the international community. The focus therefore switches from the language policy of a national contingent to that of the NATO force HQ, based in Sarajevo, where senior officers conducted negotiations with the representatives of all three former warring sides after the peace was signed. This is the level at which there is the most obvious interaction between the force HQ's language policy and the changed ethno-linguistic situation on the ground.

In this analysis, peace-building is seen in terms of an external peace-building process, that is to say, one led by outside organizations and actors.[2] Dayton provided for the extensive presence of international organizations; NATO was given responsibility for overseeing the implementation of the military aspects of the agreement while the civilian aspects were entrusted to organizations such as the United Nations, the Organization for Security and Cooperation in Europe and the European Union, all of which were to be coordinated by a High Representative. It is appropriate, therefore, to consider the start of the external peace-building process to be the negotiation and signing of Dayton.[3]

Although primarily a peace agreement which consolidated the previously-established ceasefire, Dayton's state-building elements included a blueprint for the constitutional organization and future institutional structure of the post-war state.[4] These state-building provisions of the agreement were intended to reconcile the three main ethnic groups which had fought the war and to create a viable and stable state. Instead, in the years since the end of the conflict ethnic differences have become only more entrenched, largely because the complex system of power-sharing set out in the agreement gives primacy to ethnic identity. The political process is predicated on competition between the three constituent nations (the three former warring sides) – the Bosniaks, Croats and Serbs – and there is little room for a political party that would represent the interests of the whole of the population of Bosnia-Herzegovina rather than those of just one of the three constituent nations (see Bieber 1999; Bose 2002; Hansen 1997).

Another important element of peace-building is nation-building in the sense of creating a common identity tied to the new state so that different and formerly belligerent groups are integrated into it. Key areas in this process are the media and education, which can be utilized 'in order to establish a national political and cultural dialogue' (Kostić 2007: 40). As a marker of identity, language also has a role.

If more than one language is spoken in the new state, there is a need to decide how these languages will be treated and what the official language or languages will be. There may even be a need for a lingua franca to facilitate communication between groups speaking different languages throughout the state. This use of language for the purpose of creating loyalty to the integral state was evident, for example, in post-1945 Yugoslavia. The language of the Serbs and Croats, which were the nations that made up the bulk of the Yugoslav population, was known as Serbo-Croat or Croato-Serb, which represented a joint language that was flexible enough to accommodate the variant ways of speaking in the republics of Croatia, Serbia, Bosnia-Herzegovina and Montenegro. Thus the authorities hoped that a common linguistic identity would promote a feeling of loyalty to the common Yugoslav state. This approach was abandoned in post-conflict Bosnia-Herzegovina in favour of one linking linguistic loyalty with the ethnic group rather than the state.

In post-conflict Bosnia-Herzegovina, there is a basic disconnect between the state-building elements of the peace-building process and the nation-building elements. On the one hand, the state that has been created promotes the importance of ethnic identity over an identity linked to the common integral state. On the other, however, peace-building requires a sense of attachment to the common state in order to lock the former belligerent groups into the process and prevent renewed hostilities. As a marker of ethnic identity, language is used by the political and intellectual elites of the three constituent nations to claim linguistic distinctiveness as a way of legitimating separate ethnic identities for themselves; this is despite the fact that the official languages of Bosnian, Croatian and Serbian are mutually intelligible and were, as stated above, considered to be one language before the conflict. The emphasis on separate ethnic identities frustrates nation-building efforts at nurturing an integrative identity tied to the state. And even though the separate languages are also afforded minority language rights protection, there is still discrimination on an ethno-linguistic basis. This is the environment with which the language policy of the international military force interacts and which is examined further in the following discussion.

This chapter begins with a more detailed explanation of the political significance of the language issue in post-conflict Bosnia-Herzegovina before it moves on to consider two important decisions in the development of the language policy of the international military force HQ after Dayton. For the first decision, the discussion examines how an essentially institutional language policy feeds into wider divisive identity politics in Bosnia-Herzegovina and can frustrate external peace-building goals. For the second decision, the opposite view will be considered, and the chapter explains how the force's language policy can aid the peace-building process.

Language as a political question

The mutual intelligibility of the official languages in Bosnia-Herzegovina makes the question of language an essentially political one. The languages' communicative function is thus superseded by their symbolic function as a marker of ethnic identity, as each of the languages corresponds to one of the three main ethnic groups or constituent nations: Bosnian for the Bosniaks (formerly the Muslim Slavs), Croatian for the Croats and Serbian for the Serbs. In making this ethno-linguistic link, the politicians and elites of each of the groups use language to claim difference from the other two, thereby bolstering their own separate and distinct identity. Much has been written on the differences between the languages and whether they are in fact variants or dialects of just one language.[5] A detailed description of these differences is beyond the scope of this chapter, but it is necessary to note that these languages are all based on the ijekavian variant of the štokavian dialect. The differences between them are slight and concern mainly lexical differences,[6] which have been put at just 3 per cent of their lexicons (Bazdulj 2007). Aside from this, the Serbian written language can be distinguished by the use of the Cyrillic alphabet. Because of this mutual intelligibility, there are no barriers to communication between members of the three main ethnic groups. In this chapter, the variant speech of each of the constituent nations is described as a language because this is the term that is used both in the constitutions of the Federation and the Republika Srpska and in public discourse.

Each of the three languages provides for the three constituent nations what Joshua Fishman calls 'contrastive self-identification via language' (1972: 54). According to Fishman, language can be used to identify not only fellow members of the same group but also those who stand outside of it. It differentiates between 'Us' and 'Them'. Language is therefore one means by which each constituent nation in Bosnia-Herzegovina can claim an identity for itself that is distinct from the identities of the other two constituent nations. The linguistic feature that is most significant in this regard is the name of the language.[7] It is important that members of each constituent nation has a linguistic designation that is distinct from those of the other two constituent nations; the historian and commentator Ivan Lovrenović has even suggested that in Bosnia-Herzegovina when someone is asked what language they speak they are really being asked what ethnic group they belong to (Lovrenović 2002).

As mentioned in the Introduction, this self-identification according to ethnicity is important because ethnic affiliation is of overriding importance in society and in the political process. So, for example, political decision-making at the state level revolves around the equal representation of the three constituent nations: the three-member Presidency of Bosnia-Herzegovina consists of a representative of each of the constituent peoples elected by that respective people. The Bosniak and Croatian members are elected from the territory of the Federation and the Serbian member from the territory of the Republika Srpska. This means that anyone who is or does not identify as a member of a constituent people, such as a member of the Jewish community, is not politically represented in either the Presidency or the House of Peoples which is the second chamber of the Parliamentary Assembly.[8] As a consequence, politics is focused on the concerns of the three constituent nations and the power play between them without being mitigated by the interests and concerns of other groups. Moreover, this arrangement encourages the electorate to think about their voting choices solely in terms of their particular ethnic group and its interests rather than on an individual politician's merits or what is best for the country as a whole.[9] This is why it is crucial that members of the three nations have markers that enable them to identify as belonging to one of them.

These, then, are the language attitudes that all the main international organizations present in Bosnia-Herzegovina must take into account when formulating language policy. In producing translations, it must be considered which version would be more acceptable to the recipient of the translation; if the translation is to go to the representatives of all three constituent nations, three versions of the translation must be produced. Awareness of the need to differentiate between the three languages can also be seen in interpretation practice. Research (Askew 2012) has found that interpreters working for international organizations might adapt their speech depending on the ethnicity of the local interlocutor in a given encounter. As one Bosniak interpreter put it, during the conflict she spoke more 'Croatianly' during encounters with representatives of the Bosnian Croat forces (Askew 2012: 203). The recognition of the differences between the three languages therefore forms the basis of the language policy of the international military force.

This discussion focuses on translation policy because a three-language policy is more clearly manifested in translation than interpretation. It is possible to create three versions of a written text while it is almost impossible and totally impracticable to attempt to create three versions of an interpretation. During the interpretation process, attempting to give alternative versions of certain words is not only time-consuming but also almost impossible while trying to convey the meaning of the original utterance, and an interpreter can end up being tongue-tied. Such an eventuality is not worth the risk of failure to convey the meaning, especially considering that the three languages are mutually intelligible anyway. Furthermore, the three-language issue is more important with the written word because the different language versions are easier to identify when they are written down than when they are expressed verbally. For example, one way the international organizations distinguish the Serbian version of a translation is by automatically putting it in the Cyrillic alphabet, thus making it immediately obvious which language version is being used.[10] Moreover, interpreting as the oral transfer of meaning from one language to another possesses a certain impermanence or evanescence, which means that certain aspects of the language used may not be immediately recognized (and objected to) by the interlocutors. In contrast, three translated versions of a text are, as Lord (Paddy) Ashdown[11] put it in the epigram above, a physical representation of the differences between the languages and therefore of the supposed differences between the three ethnic groups. These differences can then be used as justification for withholding cooperation in the peace-building process.

The Dayton Peace Agreement, language rights and discrimination

The Dayton Peace Agreement says virtually nothing explicitly about language. Indirectly, the agreement specifies that the new state is required to sign up to the 1992 European Charter for European and Minority Languages and the 1994 Framework Convention for the Protection of National Minorities, both of which concern minorities and the protection of their language rights, but nowhere are the official languages of the new state stipulated. The only explicit mention of languages comes at the end of the agreement where it is stated that the agreement is '[d]one in Bosnian, Croatian, English and Serbian'. Although this wording may be perceived as a purely administrative instruction placed at the end of the agreement, it is nonetheless credited with giving international recognition for the first time to the Bosnian language and thereby to three separate official languages (Greenberg 2004: 136).

The de facto recognition of three official languages had an almost immediate effect on the language policy of the international military force, especially at the level of the HQ. During the negotiations that took place on the ground after the signing of the Dayton Peace Agreement, representatives of the former warring sides began to invoke their language rights and demand that they receive documents in their particular language version. This meant that the force was being asked to produce three language versions of every document that was submitted to the sides. The force's military personnel involved in the talks decided to agree to these demands and it became policy that three language versions of every document would be produced. Seen in practical operational terms, failure to provide these different versions not only risked complaints from the parties about disrespect for their language rights but also meant that any given document may not have been read or signed by them, thereby hindering or completely stalling the course of negotiations. This decision continued the approach of making an ad hoc decision to quickly solve an immediate problem. It is easy to understand why such a pragmatic decision was made in response to the demands of the local officials, because it facilitated smooth-running operations at a time of heightened tensions after the end of hostilities. This policy nevertheless continued for several years afterwards, even after the situation in the country had calmed down, and did not change significantly until defence reform was embarked upon in 2003.

Such an ad hoc decision failed to take account of its wider implication, the risk of reifying the slight linguistic differences that exist between the languages. In a purely linguistic sense, the translators and interpreters employed not just by the international military force but also by the other international organizations present in Bosnia-Herzegovina indirectly participate in efforts to mould the distinct standards. The Bosniak language planners especially have had to work hard to establish a norm that is distinguishable from the other two and have produced various grammars, orthographic manuals and dictionaries to this end.[12] This has, however, resulted in disagreement among them over the exact elements of this norm. For example, much of this disagreement revolves around the extent to which old Turkish, Arabic and Persian words should be present in it and the extent to which it is influenced by Croatian. In the absence of authoritative instruments of codification, the translators and interpreters of the international organizations must decide for themselves what constitutes a Bosnian version. Once a document goes into the public domain, it not only becomes part of the process of standardizing the Bosnian norm but it also contributes to the public discourse concerning three separate languages. In this sense, the reification of the linguistic differences feeds into wider identity politics in the country because it bolsters the efforts of local elites to claim difference between the ethnic groups and thereby distance themselves from each other. It could even be said that the production of three different language versions suggests that the international organizations in Bosnia-Herzegovina support these claims, thereby endowing them with a degree of acceptability.

The broader implications of the force's decision can be seen in the issue of language rights. The invocation of these rights by representatives of the former warring sides was in keeping with the provisions of the European Charter for Regional and Minority Languages (ECRML), the adoption of which was a requirement of the Dayton Peace Agreement, although Bosnia-Herzegovina has yet to ratify it. It also chimes with prevailing thinking on linguistic human rights where the recognition and preservation of a group's own language is considered automatically to be a good thing. As Vanessa Pupavac states: 'Identification with a specific language is treated as essential to a community's identity and self-esteem, which in turn is seen as crucial to securing a community's well-being, as well as fostering harmonious relations between communities and preventing violent conflict' (2006: 117). Although the Dayton Peace Agreement gave only de facto recognition to three official languages, the equal status of three distinct languages was verified in a 2000 ruling of the Constitutional Court.[13] The ruling refers to the ECRML (despite its non-adoption by Bosnia-Herzegovina), arguing that parts of the populations of the constituent nations had a minority position in certain parts of the country, and it explicitly linked linguistic pluralism with peace and the integration of state and society.[14]

One question arising from the ruling is whether this advocacy of linguistic human rights for minority groups really does develop harmonious relations between different groups and thereby contributes to the integration of the state of Bosnia-Herzegovina, especially given the fact that the languages are mutually intelligible. Linguistic rights legislation is clearly applicable to diglossic situations where two different languages are spoken by two different communities in the same area, as it allows the speakers of both languages to freely use each of their languages across the area they both inhabit. Allowing language rights for both groups essentially creates bilingualism, as the non-native speakers of each language would need to learn the other language in order for intercommunal communication to be facilitated. In the case of Bosnia-Herzegovina, however, there is no diglossic situation and therefore no bilingualism as the languages are mutually intelligible. The recognition of three separate languages which are mutually intelligible means that the communicative function of language has been superseded by its symbolic function but still makes possible discrimination on linguistic grounds. Discrimination does not occur on the basis of a failure to communicate between members of the ethnic groups because the mutual comprehensibility of the languages means that all the speakers of all the languages in a multi-ethnic community are able to communicate and socialize freely and easily.

Discrimination occurs, however, in more subtle ways. Vanessa Pupavac cites the example of members of a particular ethnic group having their teaching posts challenged because they supposedly did not speak the right language, although their colleagues with the same local accent but from a different ethnic group had no similar problems (2006: 124). In this example, supposed language difference is used as an excuse not to employ a member of a particular ethnic group, so the problem is not to do with how that person sounds but with the ethnic group they belong to. Similarly, in a 2006 report on discrimination in the workplace, Amnesty International found that vacancy announcements for one of the largest companies in Bosnia-Herzegovina, the Croat-owned Aluminij company in Mostar, were published in Croatian only and in media with a Croatian audience, thus tacitly discriminating against members of the population of Bosniak and Serbian ethnicity.[15] Prior to the war the Aluminij company had had an ethnically-mixed workforce, so there is no linguistic reason why only Croats should be employed now. Language in this case is being used to filter out the potential job candidates of Bosniak and Serbian ethnicity who would not now be welcome in a Croat-owned enterprise and appears to be a more palatable means of doing so than a more blatant advertisement specifying a requirement for workers of Croatian ethnicity only. More obvious discrimination soliciting applications from candidates of a specific ethnic group would most likely provoke a strong reaction from the international community.

The use of language as a discriminatory tool as detailed above has a twofold effect. First, it is exclusionary: it deprives the members of a minority ethnic group of the feeling of belonging to the wider ethnically mixed community and makes it more likely that the members of that particular group will nurture hostility to the majority ethnic group. This therefore undermines any efforts to nurture a sense of loyalty to the joint state. Secondly, it makes it more likely that the members of the minority ethnic group will nurture feelings of belonging not to the wider community but to their specific ethnic group where their particular language is recognized and respected. In the extreme case, this leads to segregation. Thus, linguistic pluralism in Bosnia-Herzegovina does not necessarily foster 'harmonious relations between communities' but is used to create animosity between the communities, thereby hindering overall reconciliation and integration. This strongly suggests that the linguistic pluralism–state integration link made in the Constitutional Court's decision is unrealistic and may indeed be counterproductive for broader peace-building aims.

This, then, is the wider environment in which the international military force's language policy operates. By meeting the language demands of the former warring sides, the force may have satisfied their representatives during post-conflict negotiations, but the force then became a participant in the wider language politics outside of it. As the above discussion shows, the bestowing of language rights in the context of Bosnia-Herzegovina has unforeseen negative consequences which the language policy of the international military force has helped make acceptable.

Language policy and defence reform

The above discussion has concentrated on the ways in which the three-language policy of the international military force feeds into divisive identity politics outside the force and thereby bolsters claims to ethnic distinctiveness by the constituent nations. It is, nevertheless, instructive to recall the view of Christina Bratt Paulston that '[t]he major point to understand about language as group behavior is that language is very rarely a causal factor that makes things happen; rather, language mirrors social conditions and human relationships' (1997:191). This suggests that, if attitudes to language outside the international military force changed, so too could its language policy. While generally in Bosnia-Herzegovina language attitudes remain rigid and implicated in efforts to frustrate the peace-building process, there is one area of post-conflict reform that is considered a success where inter-ethnic relations have relaxed and where language policy has also become more flexible. This is the area of defence reform.

Bosnia-Herzegovina came out of the conflict with three armed forces that numbered an estimated 430,000 troops.[16] The Dayton Agreement gave responsibility for the military aspects of the peace to an international military force headed by NATO. This Implementation Force (IFOR) was charged with ensuring that the military provisions of the agreement were adhered to by the former warring sides concerning such things as the separation of forces, demobilization and arms control. IFOR was succeeded after one year by the Stabilization Force (SFOR), but even after five years there were still three separate armed forces operating in the state. Impetus for reform came in 1999 when Bosnia-Herzegovina began to move towards integration into the EU and NATO. In 2003 the Bosnia-Herzegovina Presidency announced its intention for the state to join NATO's Partnership for Peace programme, and the armed forces embarked on a process to create a state-level command and control structure and a single state army which was led by SFOR Headquarters. The process ended in January 2006 when all competencies in the realm of defence were transferred to the state level and the number of active duty armed forces was set at 9000 to 10,000 troops. Bosnia-Herzegovina finally joined the Partnership for Peace in December 2006. SFOR was succeeded by the EU-led EUFOR force in 2004, but NATO retained a team (NAT) attached to the Ministry of Defence charged with promoting closer cooperation between Bosnia-Herzegovina defence structures and NATO.

The increased cooperation between the three armed forces was reflected in the language policy of SFOR HQ. Instead of the hitherto strict adherence to a three-language translation policy, the HQ moved after 2001 towards producing just one version of working documents that would be given to all three sides. This was a language policy decision instigated by the translators and interpreters working at the HQ who were involved in the defence reform process. This was another decision made for pragmatic reasons because it took less time to produce one language version, thereby speeding up the negotiation process. The single language version is not a separate language version that has been officially established as an alternative to an ethnically-hued version of a translation but a version produced by any given translator endeavouring to remove from the translated text any characteristic that they judge might be instantly identifiable with one of the ethnically-hued versions. In this process, they are doing the opposite to what they do when they produce a version for a specific ethnic group, which entails stressing the written markers that characterize each version, rather than minimizing them. This means that there is nothing in the text that would strike the reader as inappropriate to a version specific to their ethnicity and lead them to reject it as the 'wrong' language version. In this sense the importance of the communicative function of language is restored to the translation, because the meaning of the text then has greater significance than the actual language version it is written in.

This language policy decision was also in keeping with changing attitudes in the armed forces as they moved towards greater cooperation and collaboration. This spirit of cooperation therefore made the three-language policy untenable and, to a certain extent, anachronistic, because calls for separate language versions would have been at variance with efforts to move towards one armed force and membership of a multinational organization that requires a certain degree of linguistic tolerance from its members. This is another aspect to the interaction between language policy and the peace-building process. Even though the force's language policy was not a causal factor in the success of the defence reform, it nevertheless bolstered the increasingly cooperative environment of the reform process. Here, then, an international force is seen to look outwards beyond its own internal operations, reacting to changes in this outside environment and adapting its own policy accordingly without resorting to an ad hoc decision.[17]

Conclusions

The international military force, like the other international organizations in Bosnia-Herzegovina, does not operate in a hermetically-sealed linguistic environment. There is clear interaction between an institutional language policy and the socio-political linguistic circumstances outside the force. In a peace-building context, it is therefore to be expected that decisions regarding language taken inside the force will have ramifications for language issues in the wider society. The language policy of the NATO-led force in Bosnia-Herzegovina evolved on the basis of a pragmatic response to the language demands of the former warring sides. These demands were part of the broader peace-building context and this chapter argues that the force's language policy fed into the divisive post-conflict identity politics which was in fact an extension of the war but by other means. By accepting the ethno-linguistic link and therefore the idea of three distinct languages, the force contributed to the efforts of political and intellectual elites to keep the constituent nations apart and to use language as a tool of discrimination on an ethnic basis.

More positively, however, and seen in a narrower context of relations in the field of defence reform, it can be argued that the three-language policy facilitated the peace-building process, particularly after the end of the conflict, as it allowed for negotiations on the military aspects of Dayton between the NATO-led force and the former warring sides to proceed smoothly. Moreover, as attitudes in the Bosnia-Herzegovina militaries relaxed, particularly after 2003, language policy adapted to take account of a more tolerant approach to language. In this sense, language policy bolstered the positive trends in defence reform.

Language issues were not addressed in the Dayton Peace Agreement, which was concerned with more practical and immediate issues to do with the final cessation of hostilities, the division of territory and the constitutional set-up of the future state. This chapter shows, however, that language issues are nevertheless significant in a peace-building environment. A foreign military intervention force does not work in a vacuum and the case of post-Dayton Bosnia-Herzegovina demonstrates that language policy is not just a way of dealing with internal operations but also needs to look further afield at its impact on broader peace-building aims. In that case, NATO's experience in Bosnia-Herzegovina suggests that it is better to establish a well-thought-out and considered language policy from the outset of operations rather than rely on ad hoc and improvised decisions.

Notes

1. Lord (Paddy) Ashdown on the attitude of the former warring sides in Bosnia-Herzegovina to language. Interview, 21 October 2009.
2. This is in contrast to a peace-building process 'from below' in which 'solutions are derived and built from local resources' (Ramsbotham, Woodhouse and Miall 2005: 222) so that the focus is on the actions of local actors such as non-governmental and other community-based organizations.
3. The Dayton Peace Agreement is otherwise known as the General Framework Agreement for Peace in Bosnia and Herzegovina, available at: http://www.ohr.int/gfa/gfa-home.htm (accessed 20 November 2007).
4. The Dayton Peace Agreement created an asymmetric state, made up of the Federation of Bosnia-Herzegovina with a mixed population of Croats and Bosniaks and covering 51 per cent of the territory and the Serb-dominated Republika Srpska covering 49 per cent. The Bosniaks make up roughly 48 per cent of the population, the Serbs 37.1 per cent and the Croats 14.3 per cent. The Federation is highly decentralized, containing ten cantons with wide-ranging decision-making powers, while the Republika Srpska has a highly centralized structure. This asymmetry means that the entities can function virtually separately alongside each other.
5. See Greenberg (2004), Kordić (2010) and Gröschel (2009).
6. The extent of these differences is often compared to the extent of the difference between US and British English.
7. The Bosniaks' decision to call their language *bosanski* or Bosnian is challenged by the Croats and Serbs because the adjective *bosanski* refers to the whole of the territory of Bosnia and implies that all members of the population speak this language. They contend that a more appropriate designation would be *bošnjački* or Bosniak which relates to Bosniaks only and would

therefore imply the language of only this ethnic group. The Bosniaks, for their part, maintain that *bosanski* is the historical name of the language which they are entitled to use.

8. Elections to the first chamber, the House of Representatives, are based on a territorial principle and are free from ethnic considerations. The Constitutional Court is another state-level institution which has an ethnically-based composition.

9. This state of affairs came to the fore in December 2009 with a judgment by the European Court of Human Rights in response to a submission from Jakob Finci, a member of the Jewish community, and Dervo Sejdić, a member of the Roma community, regarding their ineligibility to stand for election to the House of Peoples and the Presidency of Bosnia-Herzegovina because they were not members of any of the three constituent nations. The court ruled that the relevant provisions of the Constitution of Bosnia-Herzegovina violated the European Convention on Human Rights and amounted to discrimination and breached their electoral rights.

10. Before the conflict, the Latin and Cyrillic alphabets were used throughout the former republic of Bosnia-Herzegovina. Now Croatian and Bosnian are never written in Cyrillic, while Serbian is generally written in Cyrillic but not always.

11. Lord Ashdown was the UN's High Representative in Bosnia-Herzegovina between 2002 and 2006. According to the Dayton Peace Agreement, the holder of the post has the role of coordinating the activities of the various international organizations which were to be engaged in carrying out the civilian aspects of the peace-building process. The Bonn Powers greatly enhanced his powers in 1997 and the High Representative is now entitled to impose legislation and sack officials.

12. The most influential Bosniak language planners are Senahid Halilović, Dževad Jahić, Josip Baotić and Ibrahim Čedić. The last of these authored *Osnovi gramatike bosanskog jezika* (*Basic Grammar of the Bosnian Language*) (2001).

13. The Constitutional Court ruling concerned a request made by Alija Izetbegović, the then presiding member of the Presidency of Bosnia-Herzegovina, in February 1998 to evaluate the consistency of the constitutions of the Republika Srpska and the Federation with the Constitution of Bosnia-Herzegovina, since the constitutions of the two entities had not been brought into line with the provisions of the Bosnia-Herzegovina Constitution after 1995. Izetbegović's request revolved around the question of whether all three constituent nations (Bosniaks, Croats and Serbs) had equal status throughout the state of Bosnia-Herzegovina. The provisions that Izetbegović regarded as inconsistent included, among other things, constitutional provisions on the official languages in the entity constitutions. The Federation Constitution named only Bosniak (which was the designation for the Bosnian language at that time) and Croatian as official languages and Latin as the official script, while the Republika Srpska Constitution specified only the Serbian language and the Cyrillic alphabet as official. The Court ruled that the contentious provisions were unconstitutional because they failed to provide equal rights in both entities for all three constituent nations and the nations risked being treated as minorities in certain parts of the state. As a consequence, the wording of the constitutions of both

entities was changed to ensure that all three languages had equal official status throughout the state.

14. See paragraph 57 of the decision available at: http://www.ohr.int/ohr-dept/legal/const/default.asp?content_id=5853 (accessed 12 September 2010).
15. Details of the report are available at: http://www.amnesty.org.uk/news_details.asp?NewsID=16770 (accessed 19 March 2010).
16. Figure from the *SFOR Informer Online* website available at: http://www.nato.int/SFOR/indexinf/127/p03a/t0103a.htm (accessed 9 March 2010).
17. It should be noted that the international military force still produces translations of official documents that go into the public domain in three language versions.

Part III
Soldier/Civilian Meetings

During the last decade, the way in which the military relates to local civilian populations has become of crucial, often overriding, importance in their operations. When the US general David Petraeus took over as the commander of US/NATO forces in Afghanistan in 2010, he announced that '[t]he human terrain is the decisive terrain' (Ackerman 2010). Military units are now often to be found engaged in what are termed 'Friendly Face' activities, where positive contacts with the local population are understood to be integral components of any final success and victory. Enabling soldiers to operate in this new environment has become a major concern of NATO high commands.

This section of the book examines the nature of soldier/civilian meetings 'on the ground', and the role that languages play in them. Languages, the chapters argue, cannot be discounted when setting the terms for putative soldier/civilian meetings in culturally complex environments of war. The important element here is not necessarily the ease and linguistic fluency of these exchanges, but rather the effect that military language policies, adopted either consciously or unconsciously, have upon the perceptions of those civilians in whose country the military has arrived and upon the efficacy of the operations themselves. Meetings between militaries and foreign civilians in any conflict situation bring with them, the chapters suggest, a set of assumptions about the languages of both parties which are as relevant to inter-cultural exchange as the histories, ideologies or beliefs of the two sides.

Chapter 7, 'Occupying a Foreign Country', explores the ways in which attitudes of an armed force towards its own first language can serve to frame relationships on the ground between military and civilians. Operational structures directly attributable to these language attitudes were one of the factors which conditioned the military/civilian encounter in the Second World War, creating autonomous armed forces communities which had different levels of openness to German civilians. The geography of meetings on the ground, the distance or proximity established between the separate groups, were at least partly a product of the military's native language, and of the status which they gave to it.

Chapter 8, 'Fraternization', brings the two case studies (1944–7 and 1995–2000) together in order to see the extent to which the 60 years between them have changed the nature of soldier/civilian relationships. Whilst there are clear differences between the two deployments, the chapter reveals some surprising continuities conditioned by those asymmetrical relationships which a military presence, whether in occupation or peace operations, almost inevitably fosters.

Languages are embodied, with communication dependent on the circumstances in which the physical entities involved, military personnel and local civilians, actually meet. However well-informed and friendly the 'Friendly Faces' of troops may be in these situations, the ways in which the military occupy the spaces they take over in a foreign country, and their naming of those spaces, create a landscape of war and conflict which will position speakers on all sides of the soldier/civilian encounter.

7
Occupying a Foreign Country

Because of their inability to speak German...officers have tended to put undue trust in Germans who could speak English.
(NA, FO 371/46971, Balfour Report, 10 August 1945)

The embodied meetings of war – when soldiers from the military physically encounter civilians from the local population – are radically dependent upon language exchange between the two groups. Rather than focusing on the role of potential intermediaries in these relationships, this chapter explores the ways in which the attitudes of military authorities towards language and the 'linguistic presence' of their forces in the foreign country serve to condition the framework of such encounters. Most military deployment involves, at least to some extent, the display of a form of power which is likely to be greater than that on offer in the indigenous community. A component in this power nexus is the attitude which the relevant occupier takes towards language, not in this case the foreign language of the local population but rather that of the army itself, the native language of the military who have arrived in the foreign country. The policies, implicit or explicit, around the use of the mother tongue of the army in these situations play a major role in how the two groups, military and civilian, meet and interact. This chapter examines these issues in relation to the early years of Allied occupation of Germany, looking particularly at how the first-language policies of two military forces, the British and the French, shaped the context in which relationships could be established between military occupiers and local civilians. The British approach to the use of English, and the attitude taken by the French to their own language, produced rather different settings for the military/civilian encounter in their respective zones of occupation.

Invasion

As they entered Germany in 1944, the Allies expected to meet sustained German resistance which would take the form of underground subversion and hostile propaganda. A major strategic goal was therefore to maintain the security and integrity of the military operation against the expected incursion of this enemy activity. SHAEF (Supreme Headquarters, Allied Expeditionary Force) argued that one of the ways in which a German resistance would seek to destabilize their operation would be through word of mouth, through language encounters on the ground between troops and civilians: 'word of mouth propaganda, under the direction of underground agencies ... Its methods will include attempts at fraternization by civilians (especially by children, women and old men); attempts at "soldier-to-soldier" fraternization; and social, official and religious contacts'.[1] French soldiers were explicitly told that '[a]ny German of any age and of both sexes is an enemy who will stop at nothing' (Hillel 1983: 76).[2]

Controlling this potentially dangerous language exchange in order to protect the Allied advance was thus understood as a key part of successfully managing the invasion of Germany. The overall approach to safeguarding security in an expected hostile territory was to refuse to have any communication at all with the Germans, a policy of non-encounter, non-fraternization, which aimed to segregate Allied troops completely from the German enemy, sealing them away from potentially harmful local resistance initiatives. Allied troops were told that they would incur punishments if they shook hands with Germans, allowed children to climb on their vehicles or socialized in any way. Meeting Germans, except on official business, would be regarded as a serious infringement of the rules – simply talking, for example, could attract a penalty of $10 for US servicemen (Ziemke 1975: 161).

In fact, of course, a total and complete ban on speaking was understood to be impractical in the context of an invading army. At the least, orders would have to be issued to captured Germans or civilians, either verbally or through sign language. In this case, a few words of German might have to be delivered by the conquering armies, and indeed the American Forces Radio network had prepared troops for this eventuality pre-deployment with a week's German language lesson, 'Combat German', which included suitably peremptory phrases and commands (see also Chapter 4).[3]

As part of the resistance struggle, it was expected that some Germans would also seek to delay the Allied operation by withholding communication themselves from the occupiers, refusing to speak English when they were perfectly well able to do so. One US war correspondent, for example, described working in a hospital for wounded German soldiers, explaining 'by gesture and pantomime' what he wanted them to do, only to find out that one of them could actually speak English: 'Perfect English! That made me madder than ever because for days I had been telling him what to do by gestures and a word or two of German, and all the while he could understand every word I said.'[4]

If some minor communication with German civilians was thought to be inevitable in the course of the invasion – 'Your Supreme Commander has issued an order forbidding fraternisation with Germans, but there will probably be occasions when you have to deal with them'[5] – the overwhelming message given to all Allied troops was that there should be a clear linguistic separation between them and any Germans they met: 'Keep Germans at a distance, even those with whom you have official dealings' (Bodleian Library 2007: 51). Limited and peremptory communication would be the only order of the day, and indeed French troops were explicitly instructed to jettison any linguistic softening devices: 'Coldly correct official relationships: no French politeness. Give orders and demand immediate obedience' (Hillel 1983: 74).

When soldiers actually entered Germany, however, the situation they found there was to radically challenge the messages on languages which they had thus far been given. To begin with, the landscape of war facing Allied troops was not the Manichean Allied/German one which they had been expecting. Invasion routes were thronged with Displaced People, natives of many different foreign countries, crowding along the roads, 'like nomads' as one British soldier described them.[6] Another recalled dense columns of weary refugees wherever he looked: 'huge crowds of miserable looking people ... wearing any sort of clothing they could get hold of, it looked like ... mostly grey'.[7] During his visit to Germany in early April 1945, First Lieutenant Daniel Lerner concluded that it was these foreign workers and refugees who represented the major problem facing Allied personnel in the course of the invasion: 'Everywhere in these areas the fact of "dislocation" dominates the surface of life ... The sheer numbers of foreign workers, and their apparently uncontrolled movement along every highway and byway of Germany, is staggering to the eye ... in every city and town, and especially on the roads, foreign workers dominate the scene.' In this situation, the small 'bewildered' units of tactical troops, left behind the main advance, were quite unable to cope: 'These units are doing nothing, for they have neither the training nor the mandate to do anything. Their mission,

they explain, is simply to hold on until competent authority arrives.'[8]
Basil Reckitt described arriving at one town hall in April 1945 to find
'an American captain on the verge of a nervous breakdown, trying to
cope with a long queue of people of every nationality...He was the
Military Government officer attached to one of the US forward battalions, and...Olpe was the twenty-seventh town he had tried to organise'
(Reckitt 1989: 26).

Secondly, the security imperative, based on a depiction of Germany as
hostile territory ripe for insurgency, seemed less and less relevant to soldiers who found themselves moving though a landscape from which
young and middle-aged German men appeared to be totally absent.
Most German males had been conscripted into the army and were either
fighting elsewhere or being held in prisoner of war compounds. What
greeted incoming Allied troops was thus a society largely composed of
women, the very young and the very old. Those German civilians whom
soldiers saw were in extreme need – desperately hungry, often homeless, and clearly very frightened. Children in particular broke through
the official non-communication barrier: 'even on that first day, even
then the soldiers were giving the kids chocolates and buns...and telling
them to take them to their Mother and come back for some more'.[9]
Increasingly, as it became evident that the blanket order to refuse all
communication with Germans could not be justified as a security measure, non-fraternization was hastily repositioned as being a necessary
prerequisite to the denazification of the country. Not communicating
with Germans was reframed as part and parcel of the justified punishment which Germans should be receiving for war crimes. Regular spot
announcements on the forces' radio stations repeated the message that
talking to Germans could make punishing them a good deal more difficult: 'The German must be taught that war doesn't pay. They must
learn the hard way. If you're friendly they'll think you're soft – don't
fraternize.'[10]

As the press reported, however, on the ground it was to prove
impossible to operate a non-fraternization policy. Quite apart from the
impossibility of enforcing and policing a ban on relationships between
soldiers and local women, it became clear in the first few months of
the invasion that a total linguistic segregation from the German people would, in practice, serve to impede Allied attempts to set up any
interim local administration: 'The policy of segregation will have the
effect of making us the prisoners and the Germans the free people.'[11]
If the Allies were to collect robust intelligence in these difficult early
days and gauge how hostile public opinion was towards them, they
would necessarily have to have some kind of communication with the

locals: 'Until Intelligence and other personnel ... are allowed to mix with Germans under relatively easy social conditions (e.g. being able to shake hands, exchange drinks, etc.) it will be extremely difficult to collect reliable information on what the real attitude of Germans is, and the success or failure of our policy towards them.'[12]

A policy framed to deal with enemy resistance, and then reframed as part of a preamble to denazification, gradually broke down in the light of experience on the ground. As Attlee reportedly pointed out, operationalizing any non-communication policy was always going to be fraught with difficulties: 'He himself favoured the policy of non-fraternization, but its interpretation in practice was a matter of great difficulty and with far-reaching consequences ... the carrying out of the non-fraternization order was a delicate matter.'[13] The sheer size of the occupation population and the social and economic problems that it now so acutely raised made the policy virtually unworkable. As Montgomery explained to the Prime Minister: 'I have some 20 million German civilians in the British zone. You cannot re-educate such a number of people if you never speak to them. The Germans have had their lesson; we have not spoken to them for two months.'[14]

In September 1945, the non-fraternization policy, then a year old, was officially relaxed. Controlled non-communication, refusing to acknowledge the existence of Germans, or communicating with them only in short bursts of 'Combat German', had proved unrealistic on the ground of war. Establishing an effective interim administration which might begin to address the social and economic problems of the country made it impossible to operate under a total ban on communication. In the words of the official rationale, what had happened on the ground had led to a rethink of the policy of non-communication: 'before the entry into and surrender of Germany it was absolutely necessary to have rigid rules, not only for reasons of security, but also because it was impossible to foresee the attitude of the Germans ... now that Germany has unconditionally surrendered ... it is absolutely necessary to get on with the job of restoring German civil life to the extent of preventing widespread famine and disease ... it is becoming increasingly difficult ... to ignore completely the existence of human beings that are seen and passed in the street daily under normal conditions of work.'[15]

Occupation

After an early period of interim administration, the Allies began to establish structures to govern their separate occupation zones.

The occupation of Germany was an unprecedented operation in its ambitious cultural aim, 'to remodel the traditional attitudes of the enemy' (Murray 1978: 64). As Torriani argues, the policies adopted to achieve this by British and French occupiers owed much to their distinctive colonial experiences (Torriani 2005). In both cases, the role they gave to their own language was a crucial element in the building of an occupation presence in Germany. British imperial history had been one of creating political structures and systems through which indirect British rule could be effected, with British political advisers, protectorates and trusteeships. For many of those charged with setting up the structures of occupation in the British zone, this colonial model came easily to mind: 'One feels rather like an administrative officer in a backward colony, and... it is in fact not easy to avoid having... the same paternal regard as a District Commissioner would feel for his native tribes, or an officer of a Gurkha regiment for his men.'[16] What characterized this approach was the maintenance of a clear social distance between governors and governed and a concern that the apparatus and structures of government should be created and expressed in the native language of the colonizers, English.

A briefing paper on 'The German Character' given to every new member of the British Control Commission, and to all British military units, provided a checklist of 'Do's and Don'ts' for personnel coming to Germany. It suggested that a clear separation should be maintained between the conquering power and the indigenous population (see Table 7.1).

Table 7.1 Checklist on 'The German Character'

Do *give orders*	**Don't** *make requests*
Do *be firm*	**Don't** *be weak*
Do *see orders are carried out promptly and ensure severe punishment if they are not*	**Don't** *try and be kind or conciliatory*
Do *drop immediately and heavily on any attempt to take charge or other forms of insolence*	**Don't** *be put off or led into arguments*
Do *play your part as a representative of a conquering power and keep the Germans in their place*	
Do *display cold, correct and dignified curtness and aloofness*	**Don't** *show hatred; the Germans will be flattered*

Source: NA, FO1032/1462, Documents on 'The German Character', 1 March 1945.

The sole language of government was expected to be English: 'Reports by Germans to any military authority shall...be in the national language of the authority to which such report is made. Forms, records of proceedings and other official documents should be in the national language of the units utilising...such documents.' Translating this machinery of government into German, except in the case of key public notices, was to be the job of the locals themselves, rather than of the British: 'The burden of accurately translating or interpreting...original and additional texts or other orders...of military authorities into German, or vice versa, is entirely up to the Germans.' The governed, the Germans, would thus take on the responsibility for understanding the messages given to them by the occupiers: 'It is felt that the onus of understanding orders and instructions issued to the Germans should rest with the Germans, and that error of translation or speech should provide no justification for the Germans in failing to carry out our requirements.'[17]

Some British officers had objected early on that such a rigid 'official language' policy would make any form of successful indirect rule extremely difficult to manage:

> Theoretically, it may be extremely desirable to speak one's own language to inhabitants and put the onus of understanding what is intended on them. Practically, though, the results of such a course would be delays and confusion. Every inhabitant will immediately excuse himself from complying with orders on the basis that he cannot find an interpreter or understand what you say in your own language. Indeed, if the ruling is rigidly enforced, the absurdity arises that no conversation will ever commence, because no officer will be entitled to tell an inhabitant in his own language that he must go and get an interpreter.[18]

Logistically, the point was an important one, as both sides in the argument recognized. A more flexible official language policy would necessarily have immediate implications for the number of interpreters and translators required by the British administration. In practice, the final position adopted was slightly more nuanced. The designation of English as an official language continued to be a vital part of the occupiers' public self-presentation, but it was recognized that British officers should be encouraged to learn a little German: 'Even if bilingual it is desirable always to speak in one's own language. Allied representatives should, however, learn the German language.'[19] The famous list of

Table 7.2 'Do's and Don'ts' for British personnel coming to work in Germany

Do *use English in your official dealings with the Germans*	**Don't** *try to air your knowledge of German*
Do *learn German and all you can about Germany and the Germans*	

Source: NA, FO1032/1462, Documents on 'The German Character', 1 March 1945.

'Do's and Don'ts' for all British personnel coming to work in Germany suggested a linguistic approach which differentiated between public presentation on the one hand and private understanding on the other (see Table 7.2).

Much as African or Indian languages had been traditionally considered by British colonizers, the German language, and knowledge about the country, were positioned as additional weapons in the armoury of the governing British official: not designed for direct communication with the locals, but rather seen as part of a private informational toolkit which might help the English occupiers to deliver a more effective administration by proxy.

For Victor Gollancz, visiting the British zone, the atmosphere he met was highly reminiscent of the British Empire:

> [T]he majority of officers and civilians of officer status...have practically no dealings at all with German males, except of a purely official kind; and this is not, on the whole, from 'bloody-mindedness', but simply because that's the atmosphere – that's the way ordinary daily life in an occupied country works out...the general attitude varies from a disgusting offensiveness, through indifference often identifiable with oblivion, to that humane and almost unconsciously superior paternalism which is characteristic of the 'white' attitude to the 'natives' at its best[.] (Gollancz 1947: 94–5)

Just as the ideology of occupation policies in the British zone was clearly influenced by Britain's imperial experiences, so the aims and attitudes of the French Occupation authorities reflected the colonial heritage of France. French planning for the occupation of Germany had necessarily been a hasty and somewhat last-minute exercise, with personnel assembled only in the winter of 1944–5 and given intensive four-week training courses at the Sorbonne. As Biddiscombe argues (2007: 156, 157), the resulting French occupation ideology was a mixture on the one hand of revanchism (the desire to neutralize the country's archetypal historical enemy) and on the other of the spirit of the Enlightenment, a wish, particularly emanating from the French Resistance, to bring what were seen as the traditional values of Republican France to those living in occupied Germany. In a sense, this latter impulse was a continuation of the long-standing Third Republic belief that any French colonial expansion had to be axiomatically linked to the civilizing mission of France. French soldiers entering Germany were told that they were to 'incarnate...what French civilization was: the Renaissance, classicism of the seventeenth century, the concept of the free man and of the French Revolution in the world' (Hillel 1983: 72–3). Officials argued that they intended to 'create a vast current of French and humanist thought which will result in all eyes being turned towards us' (Torriani 2005: 130). British observers noted that 'the French are...employing on an intensive scale the colonising methods which in the past they have used throughout the world'.[20] Rather than mainly prioritizing the establishment of new governmental and institutional structures as the British were doing, the French gave a key role to the spreading of French culture, represented as being synonymous with democratic values. As de Gaulle expressed it: 'Our action is designed to establish France here, in this country' (Mombert 1995: 19).

The exhibition on 'One Year of the French Occupation of Germany' held in Paris in the summer of 1946 to inform the French public about occupation policies presented cultural imperatives as a key component of denazification/democratization strategies (Heiser and Merz 2009). In this scenario, education would assume a central position in occupation policies. In post-First World War Alsace, the French had purged nearly a thousand teachers and school administrators, replacing them with personnel brought in from the rest of France. A similar approach was now to be pursued in occupied Germany (Biddiscombe 2007: 157). A key component of this educational and cultural colonization was inevitably the French language itself. In the British zone, the native language of the conquerors, English, was the language of government through which democracy would be passed on to the local population, via hand-picked local intermediaries. In the French zone, the language of the rulers was to be made available to everyone in the indigenous community so that the mass of Germans would come to have access to those democratic values said to be incarnated by France.

As the administration in the two zones developed, the radical difference between these two visions, and their linguistic consequences, became only too apparent. In the British zone, the goal of indirect rule through local elites rapidly mushroomed in practice into a defensive battlement of British bureaucracy which was then replicated in a second ring of German personnel, with some 30,584 locals working for the Commission:[21] '(we) muddle the whole principal of Military Government, which is to make the Germans do the work, by introducing controls which are not aimed at any particular purpose'.[22] High salaries, short-term contracts and arrangements which permitted families to accompany the employee made the Control Commission working environment extremely attractive to Britons who were struggling at home with rationing and the after effects of war. In this situation, the qualifications of some of the personnel who came to work in Germany were often problematic. R. G. Berensson, from the Economic Division, reported at the end of 1945 that: 'We have far too many high ranking officers who know nothing about Germany, nothing about economics, little about administration...I have never drawn as high a salary as I am getting here.'[23] The original Allied Civil Affairs operation which had been prepared for the invasion of Germany in 1944 had sought, not entirely successfully, to recruit officers who spoke some German, including in its training courses German language classes, detailed briefings on the history, background and political structure of the country, and role-play exercises, interviewing German officials (Chapter 4).[24] By the summer of 1945, however, reports were emphasizing how few of the incumbent occupation staff could actually speak German and how little interested they appeared to be in the environment in which they were now placed: 'they had had their lives made uncomfortable by the German love of war and...they now proposed to get their own back by achieving comfort at the expense of the Germans, and certainly were not going to inconvenience themselves merely in order to get Germany going again'.[25] A year later, one observer, billeted in a senior officers' mess, noted that: 'It was not done to speak German, still worse to learn it. "We have won the war, haven't we? Let the bastards learn English"' (Cooper 1979: 117–18).

British personnel increasingly operated in what was in effect a hermetically-sealed English-speaking community, deliberately distanced from the local population: 'At present foreigners live in a world separate from that of the Germans. It is inevitable that they are taken around by the apparatus of the military government. But this means that there are two widely different worlds in Germany.'[26] A draft paper in the autumn of 1945 on 'Symptoms of Leniency towards the Germans' argued that it was necessary to continually 'plug' the fact to all British personnel that the Germans would not change their character in a matter of months or even years.[27] In February 1946, the Deputy Military Governor issued instructions to all personnel to ensure that the distance between the

British authorities and the Germans was strictly kept: 'All ranks will be warned to be constantly on their guard against any action which might conceivably be construed by the Germans as the acceptance of a favour conferred by them, or as being in the nature of a "quid pro quo".'[28]

Positioned as they were in a large bureaucracy which was almost wholly Anglophone, members of the Control Commission necessarily found that most contacts with the world outside the British community had to be mediated by a third party. It was clear that interpreters and translators were going to be needed on the staff of the occupying authorities. Planning for this aspect of the linguistic requirements of occupation, however, had not originally given much weight to the need for qualified German military interpreters, compared with the more politically sensitive and higher-profile tasks of liaising with the other (non-Anglophone) occupying powers, Russia and France. Interpreting and translating from Russian and French were regarded as at least as important as German: 'work in three languages on documents of the highest-level-conferences, etc., as well as the full scale of routine responsibility, such as the Commission's negotiations with other members of the Quadripartite Organization and the translation of both highly technical as well as day-to-day orders to the Germans'.[29] By September 1945, the Control Commission's Interpreting Pool indeed provided for the same number of staff officers (four) for each of the German, Russian and French branches (see also Chapter 9).[30] Despite its dual purpose – as intermediary between the Germans and the British, and liaison between the occupiers – the cadre of official interpreters/translators was to be an infinitesimal percentage of the very large total of British personnel working in Germany. By the time that the Parliamentary Select Committee on Estimates reported on Control Commission activities (Berlin and the British zone) in mid-1946, the Interpreters' Pool had an establishment of only 760, out of a total of 26,000 British employees.[31]

During the invasion itself, the military approach had been to use the services of educated Germans who spoke and understood English, wherever such people could most readily be found (Reckitt 1989: 26). With the occupation of Germany and the recognition that there were not enough British military interpreters to fulfil all the tasks needed, it had been agreed that Germans could be employed as interpreters, provided that these were always security-checked.[32] As British administrators became more reliant on this cadre of educated Germans, however, it appeared that they were increasingly unlikely to look too closely at the political credentials of their German language employees. When Stephen Spender, for example, reported to one British officer that his interpreter was in fact an outspoken Nazi, the official seemed largely unmoved by the news: 'He (the British officer) was rather surprised, but not really at all shaken in his conviction that he was fortunate in having a remarkably intelligent interpreter' (Spender 1946: 44).

Messages between the bureaucracy which had been created, and the local population beyond the Anglophone community, were thus relayed by Germans often selected because of the quality of their English language, largely irrespective of whether or not they could reasonably be considered as natural and enthusiastic supporters of the policies espoused by the British:

> Because of their inability to speak German, ... officers have tended to put undue trust in Germans who could speak English. As this is by no means a good criterion of political reliability, they have often been led by the nose. (In fact, of course, the educated classes where English speakers are chiefly found contain most of the ardent nationalists.)[33]

Those Germans who were employed by the British, whether as interpreters, support staff or officials, occupied the classic position of the 'inside outsider'. Kept at arm's length from the British community, with no access to British social life or living spaces, they were often on the point of being discredited in the eyes of their own local communities, either by virtue of the position they held or because of the clearly ambivalent attitude which the occupiers had towards them: 'We must be particularly careful to avoid discrediting the German officials through whom we work in the eyes of their own people.'[34]

The French occupation zone meanwhile had been even more intensively staffed than the British zone: there were 18 French administrators for every 10,000 Germans, compared to ten administrators in the British zone. Whereas, however, the hallmark of the British zone was the retreat of the occupiers behind the plate glass walls of their own language and their cultural separation from the local community, the ethos in the French zone was to take the native language of the occupiers out to as wide a general public as possible. To begin with, the concern was to spread French cultural values: by 1946, France had already mounted a wide range of cultural tours in occupied Germany: 21 theatre groups and 29 orchestras, performing to an estimated 600,000 spectators (Torriani 2005: 107). To access French culture properly, however, it was seen to be vital to transform the whole educational system so that the language of France could be available to all. The desire of the French administration to produce a lasting impact on the education of young

Germans was attested by the sheer number of school textbooks which were printed in record time: by 1947, the French authorities had distributed well over six million textbooks for their school population of 900,000 children, compared with the British tally of 12.5 million for 3.5 million students (Willis 1968: 44). Teaching the French language to all Germans became a major goal of the occupying authorities. One of their first measures, indeed, implemented before the end of 1946, was to make French the compulsory first foreign language in all secondary schools in the zone. French was to be given a pre-eminent place in the school curriculum, with 54 teaching hours a month to the detriment of several other subjects, including Latin (reduced to 24 from the pre-war 54 hours), Greek (reduced from 36 to 16) and history (cut down from 21 to four). To support this linguistic effort, nearly 300 French native speakers were speedily deployed into German schools and universities and some 300,000 French dictionaries and nearly 800,000 French language textbooks were allocated. By mid-1946, there were already 166 French lecturers and professors teaching in German further and higher education (Biddiscombe 2007: 156). The impetus to teach the French language, however, extended beyond the formal educational sector. French classes were established in adult education, with 29,800 Germans attending these in July 1946. Radio stations in the zone broadcast language classes aimed at the wider public: six hours of French language a week were already scheduled in the autumn of 1945 (Torriani 2005: 111).

Whereas the British largely dealt in their own language with key German personnel who could then translate their wishes and execute their orders, the ambition in the French zone of occupation was for all Germans to be able to understand some of the French language and hence to have direct access to authentic French culture. In this representation, the language itself went hand in hand with a desire to create new governing institutions. Significantly, when in October 1946 plans were discussed to set up a French training school for civil servants in Germany, to be modelled on the newly established Ecole Nationale d'Administration, the proposal also included the parallel establishment of an Interpreting School at Mayence-Germersheim (Hudemann 1997) whose aim would be to develop 'interpreter-translators for the zone, and, at the same time, provide junior managers for administration as well as for industry and commerce'. A knowledge of foreign languages, and above all of French, was conceived as the principal means by which French influence would be spread in the occupied zone (Defrance 1994: 76).

Conclusions

Attitudes towards the native language of each occupying army played a
key role in framing relationships between the military and the civilians
on the ground. In the French zone, the French language itself immediately became a prime instrument of occupation policy. One of the
main goals of the French occupiers was to ensure that the majority of
civilians in their zone of occupation were learning, or at least had the
means to learn, as much as possible of the French language. To this end,
educational systems were radically modified, French language teachers
were drafted in, and cultural and publishing policies were mobilized in
order to support the spread of the French language. In the British zone,
the English language was represented as the language of the governors,
a mark of political power which excluded those who did not speak it
as effectively as the barbed wire which protected British military compounds. For the French, interpreting and translating could be seen as
an intrinsic part of the spread of French language and civilization, a
means of ensuring that French culture, and correct French, would per-
meate the whole occupation zone. For the British, a somewhat ad hoc
system of interpreters and translators transmitted British administrative wishes to a population which was accepted as being linguistically
apart. Linguistic distance and separation typified the British approach,
with the English language as a barrier to protect the occupying community. Linguistic intervention characterized French policies, with the
spread of the language as a key signifier of the success of the occupied
presence.

With the international political pressures of 1948, when the Foreign
Office was beginning to encourage warmer personal interaction between
military and civilians in Germany, it was clear that the linguistic distance, now formalized and entrenched in the British zone, would make
closer cultural contact between the two groups highly problematic.
Without the expansionist first language policy pursued in the French
zone, the only alternative at this stage seemed to be a less coercive
system of voluntary language exchange between German and British
personnel. This however was difficult given that few Britons showed any
interest in learning a foreign language: 'German classes do not appear to
be much attended ... personnel ... begin to learn the language and usually drop it after a month or two.'[35] Language separation, the attitude
which the authorities had adopted towards English, was to make any
change in occupation policy extremely difficult to implement: 'I do not
think that the right kind of social progress will ever be made except in

cases where a nucleus of the British are prepared to do battle with the German language.'[36]

Notes

1. NA, FO 1060/874, SHAEF CA 6/44/209, issued to Army commanders, 27 September 1944.
2. Quotations from Hillel (1983) and Mombert (2005) are the translations of the present author.
3. *Yank* magazine (British edition), 30 April 1944.
4. *Yank* magazine (British edition), 12 November 1944.
5. NA, FO 898/478, Pocket Guides Education Sub-Committee, 9 November 1943.
6. IWMSA, E. Jones, 20894, recorded 2000.
7. IWMSA, G. Hayward, 18706, recorded 1999.
8. NA, FO 371/46730, report to PWD SHAEF of D. Lerner. For more information on this displaced population, see Reinisch (ed.) (2008) and Gemie and Humbert (2009).
9. IWMSA, J. Stafford-Baker, 5398, recorded 1981.
10. NA, WO229/5/1, Spot announcements: no. 1.
11. NA, FO 1060/874, Legal Division, 15 November 1944.
12. NA, WO229/5/1,SHAEF Psychological Warfare Section, 'To What Extent Non-Fraternisation Hampers Our Objectives', 30 May 1945.
13. NA, FO 1030/289, Report of Memo from Lord President of Council at second APW meeting, 25 January 1945.
14. NA, FO 1030/289, Montgomery to PM, 6 June 1945.
15. NA, WO 229/5/1, Notes on new policy for non-fraternization, undated.
16. NA, FO 1049/610, L. H. Sutton, Control Officer for University of Göttingen, January 1946.
17. NA, WO 229/69/9, Draft Instruction (undated); G5 submission, 7 December 1944.
18. NA, FO 1020/82, Allied Commission for Austria (British element), 12 January 1945.
19. NA, FO 1030/289, Policy and instructions on relations with the Germans of Allied Forces and Control Commission staffs in the initial period of control, undated [January 1945?].
20. NA, FO 1050/1104, Education Branch, Report on tour in French Zone by Educational Adviser and Director, Doc. 2a.
21. NA, FO 1032/2099, Second Report from the Select Committee on Estimates, Appendix, printed 23 July 1946.
22. NA, FO 936/236, Letter from Military Government Officer (Bunde and Hamburg), 8 February 1945.
23. NA, FO 936/236, Berensson to Robinson, 23 December 1945.
24. See for example, NA WO 219/3689 11th Wimbledon course, 4 September 1944.
25. NA, FO 371/46971, Balfour report, 10 August 1945.
26. NA, FO 1030/320, Notes on a visit to Germany, 30 December 1945.
27. NA, FO 1032/1465, Research Branch paper, 8 September 1945.

28. NA, FO 1032/1465, 'Behaviour of Officers to the Germans', 26 February 1946.
29. Reference provided by Simona Tobia.
30. NA, FO 1032/1353, Control Commission for Germany Pool of Interpreters (War Establishment), September 1945. The author is indebted to Simona Tobia for these references on the Pool of Interpreters.
31. NA, FO 1032/2099, Second Report from the Select Committee on Estimates, Appendix, printed 23 July 1946.
32. NA, FO 371/46730, *SHAEF Handbook* governing policy and procedure for the military occupation of Germany, December 1944.
33. NA, FO 371/46971, Balfour Report, 10 August 1945.
34. NA, FO 1030/320, 'Relations with German Officials and Official Bodies', undated [1946?].
35. NA, FO 1014/26, Clegg Report, 31 May 1948.
36. NA, FO 1014/26, Senior Control Officer (Hamburg) on Clegg Report, 13 July 1948.

8
Fraternization

'I struggled to keep the women interpreters out of bed with the soldiers. It's inevitable, war does funny things to you, but where women were married to Serb army commanders, not a good idea.'[1]

In September 1944, as the Allies were entering Germany, soldiers were ordered to obey a policy of 'non-fraternization'. In the words of the Allied command: 'non-fraternisation is the avoidance of mingling with Germans upon terms of friendliness, familiarity or intimacy, whether individually or in groups, in official or unofficial dealings'.[2] There was to be no visiting of German homes, no drinking with Germans, no shaking hands, no giving or receiving of gifts. Punishable infringements of the ban were set out under two headings, minor offences – ogling women, permitting children to climb on vehicles – and serious cases – drinking with Germans, associating with women.[3] Two principal cultural narratives attach themselves to this early phase of German occupation: firstly, that there was a before and an after in Allied–German relations, that non-fraternization gave way to fraternization, at which point soldier/civilian relationships were normalized; and secondly, that non-fraternization broke down because of the wholesale disobedience of troops on the ground who sought out sexual partners from among the local women. As early as May 1945, one military observer wearily commented that 'the policy [of non-fraternization] ... is widely disregarded particularly in sexual relations between soldiers and German civilians'.[4] Journalists reported that they often saw a 'Don't fraternize' notice right next to an arrow pointing to a 'Prophylactic station'.[5]

The connection between the word 'fraternization' and sexual activity was rapidly established at both an official and a popular level. The Judge

Advocate General advised that American troops should not be automatically punished for suspected fraternization simply because they had to receive treatment for venereal disease (Browder 1998: 11). By July 1945, the *New Statesman* was explaining to its readers that '[f]raternisation has become a word denoting sexual intercourse', with the verb *fratting,* and the noun *frat,* as in 'my frat'.[6] This characterization of the mass disobedience of non-fraternization orders through sexual activity has passed into contemporary usage, giving 'fraternization' a markedly sexual character, rooted in these Second World War experiences. Thus the *Oxford English Dictionary* defines it as '[t]he cultivation ... of friendly relations by occupying troops with local inhabitants ... used especially of relations with German women after the war of 1939–45', with the further gloss, 'frat: a women met by fratting', and 'fratter: one who frats'.[7]

Nearly 60 years separate the Second World War, when the terminology of 'fraternization' and 'non-fraternization' was first brought into being as a frame of norms for soldier/civilian relationships, from the peace operations in Bosnia-Herzegovina, where commanding officers enjoined troops to respect the principle of winning 'hearts and minds' in their dealings with the local population. Language, policies and practices had changed in the meantime. The slang of 'fratters' and 'frats' had fallen out of use, while the sexual connotations of 'fraternization' had expanded to take over the word entirely: Vanessa Kent, for instance, writes of 'countries that have successfully implemented strict non-fraternization policies' (Kent 2007: 53) during a discussion of how militaries in peace operations ought to prevent sexual exploitation and abuse. Enormous changes had taken place in the technology and materiel available to the military, and in the composition of a non-conscripted professional army in which women fight alongside men; indeed, by the 1990s, post-feminist framings of the role of women in society had problematized some of the 'givens' of male/female relationships in the 1940s. The work of Psychological Operations had, meanwhile, become central to peace support missions that were legally and conceptually based on the consent of the host government and its society. Winning over the hearts and minds which would restrain their local groups from resistance to foreign forces was, by the time troops deployed to Bosnia-Herzegovina, a clear military objective that would be put to counter-insurgent use in twenty-first-century wars.

This chapter examines the two case studies of soldier/civilian exchanges in the Second World War and in Bosnia-Herzegovina, which make it possible to discern important differences and continuities in policy and practice. Foreign militaries in both contexts occupied space and named their positioning within it, domesticating the foreign by creating an overlay of familiarized geography that permanent inhabitants of the territory experienced as alien. The asymmetry of soldier/civilian relationships was dramatized, in both case studies, by narratives of vehicle accidents, which introduced danger into local space even after wartime risks of violence had passed. In both case studies, the landscape was also gendered in particular ways, grounded in the gender orders of the 1940s and the 1990s. Questions of sexual fraternization itself, which had been actualized as a policy concern precisely during the Second World War, and of sex and language had taken on new meanings by the time of the Yugoslav crisis with the deployment of mixed-gender militaries, pushing sex away from the front stage of operations. Whilst there are certainly differences between the two time periods, a strong sense of continuity still emerges between soldier/civilian encounters in the Second World War and in Bosnia-Herzegovina. Overall, the language of military/civilian exchanges continues to be one of distance, of silence and of linguistic appropriation.

Occupation of space

Whatever the purpose of foreign troops entering a country – liberation, occupation, humanitarian assistance, peace enforcement – they occupy its space in the sense that they impose their own geography on an unfamiliar territory. The most significant sites to soldiers may well have figured in local geographies only as unremarkable or empty places. Military forces require bases, supply routes, air and sea ports and bounded areas of responsibility which may disregard or even consciously cross-cut political entities and domestic military delineations. The domestic map of BiH after the Dayton Peace Agreement, for instance, was characterized by two awkwardly-shaped political units (the Federation and Republika Srpska) plus the internationally-administered enclave of Brčko in the north-east; IFOR and SFOR maps of the country overlaid the boundaries of the coalition force's three Multi-National Divisions, effectively the British-, French- and US-led sectors, which each took in parts of the RS and the Federation. However, it is at the everyday level of the town or village where the invention of a new military geography becomes most visible. Whether troops construct new bases or reuse existing structures, they adapt local space to their own purposes and accommodate hundreds or thousands of foreign soldiers whose knowledge of local languages is usually minimal or nil.

The forces that liberated Western Europe in 1944–5 and entered Bosnia-Herzegovina on peace support operations in 1992 or 1995–6 both tended to make use of existing local buildings. In France, for example, American troops liberating Cherbourg in 1944 speedily requisitioned a huge number of buildings. At the heart of the town, the prestigious and centrally-located Ratti's department store was taken over as a Red Cross Centre for black American troops, despite the fact that the mayor had protested personally to the American authorities: 'Ratti was the pride of Normandy, . . . and it was necessary that such a store be in operation for the people of Cherbourg' (Thomson 1996: 84). Inevitably, the very same spaces previously occupied by the Germans were now taken over by US troop contingents, one occupation in effect replacing another. In the Reims area where US troops would be based from August 1944 until the end of 1946, the Allied military not only occupied spaces recently vacated by the German army but also followed its example in requisitioning local engineering and manufacturing workshops. The managing director of the well-known Usine Bauche et Bazancourt at Châlons complained bitterly that he had had to put up with the Germans requisitioning his factory from February 1944 until August 1944 and now would have to put up with another occupation:

> Unlike what occurred during the German requisition, there was absolutely no warning in advance . . . the American military personnel who came . . . simply told us what was going to happen, and in English. The takeover was immediately confirmed by the army placing sentries at the factory gates; none of them spoke French.[8]

Besides houses, factories and barracks, the Americans also required social space for their troops. In this, as in the requisitioning of the factories, there was a strong similarity between the places that the Germans had taken over and the cinemas, theatres and other facilities which the US authorities targeted for their personnel. The manager of the Palace Theatre in Epernay, for instance, saw very little difference between the two occupations' effects on its services: 'for five years my two operators and me . . . haven't been able to have the pleasure of any days' holiday, because we have had to be there, firstly for the Boches, and then for the Allied troops'.[9] By early 1945, the detailed list of American army occupation in Reims included 17 factories, 41 garages, five cinemas, four dance halls, three barracks, two hospitals, 68 hotels, 12 restaurants, 174 private houses, 122 flats, 260 rooms in private houses, five schools, the Stade Municipal, the municipal music conservatory, public gardens, and six of the major arterial roads in the city.[10] In effect, an extremely intense American occupation had taken over and extended the spaces formerly occupied by the enemy army, paralysing the life of the city and its surrounding region.

In Bosnia-Herzegovina, the typical base for foreign troops was an abandoned factory, one of thousands that had been left empty or sabotaged during the concurrent collapse of the socialist Yugoslav economic system and the violent struggle to reappropriate state-owned resources that characterized the ensuing armed conflict. British Army bases in Bosnia-Herzegovina included such locations as the Banja Luka Metal Factory (the headquarters of Multi-National Division South-West, actually located in the village of Ramići within Banja Luka municipality), the Kiseljak Brick Factory, the Tomislavgrad Cable Factory, the Shoe Factory and Bus Depot in Mrkonjić Grad, and the Aluminka factory in Šipovo. Mark Ferguson, an officer in the Royal Electrical and Mechanical Engineers (REME) who commanded a vehicle repair workshop based in the Aluminka factory, recalled that the factory had been put out of commission in 1995 when Croat forces briefly took Šipovo and then withdrew in compliance with Dayton (a skilled linguist in Serbian, he used the factory's local name rather than a generic name or translation):

> [W]e had to deal with basically what was a shell of a building – and indeed the chap who took it over is a friend of mine – in 1995, and they [the Croats] had wrecked all the machinery on it. By the time we got there, three years later, all had been swept out and taken away, and so we were working as just a shop floor, as a workshop, and we'd spent some time on it.[11]

The practice of occupying empty factories met the military need for premises spacious enough to hold large equipment and vehicles and provide improvised accommodation, yet had both practical and structural drawbacks. Factories were not immediately suitable for habitation: a female British soldier who was deployed to the tanning factory in Bugojno in 1993–4 recalled that the environmental health team had found raw chromium for treating leather in the water table and that the extent of privacy for female sleeping quarters was initially 'a cordoned-off area of the factory floor'.[12] The Ministry of Defence paid to lease factory premises (one interpreter who had worked in Šipovo recalled monthly rent payments of €10,000–20,000 for four factories in a list of positive effects of the British presence there), though in the chaos following the collapse of the socialist state that had owned those factories the legitimate destination of the rent could be unclear. Ferguson's construction of post-socialism led him to challenge a businessman who was presenting himself as the current factory owner and pressuring the MOD to either double the rent or allow him to put the factory back into operation:

> And it was a real indication, at the start, of how putting occupying troops – because that's effectively what we were – in the businesses really stifles the economy. And we shouldn't. And if we'd known we were going to be in Bosnia for long enough, and we've learned the lessons for places like Afghanistan, we'd have built specifically-built camps.[13]

Whereas most foreigners and locals (Communists aside) in the Western Europe of 1945 anticipated the pre-war economic system would be reinstated, in 1990s Bosnia-Herzegovina there could be no such expectation. The transnational collapse of Eastern European socialism meant that the foreign occupiers, as Ferguson on one level perceived them, would be implicated in building up a new economic system, in cooperation and/or competition with local entrepreneurs.

In liberated France, it had taken time for civil society to be re-established in those areas in which large contingents of Allied forces remained. Here, soldiers and French civilians tended to have very different priorities. Significantly, the Americans in the port of Cherbourg operated on a different clock from the French clock outside the base, one hour behind: 'American time', and 'French time', as the local press described it.[14] To some extent, the ways in which the two groups related to each other had much to do with this notion of separate time zones. US troops saw themselves as a community in transition, passing through the town on their way to a future, fighting in Germany and then hopefully returning home. The French, unable to reclaim their own urban space, moved to a space which was at least potentially open to them – the essentially-lost past community – and directed their concerns to recovering what had been lost in order to re-establish a permanent community. The past was of key importance in setting the terms of this civilian/military encounter. As the Mayor of Cherbourg explained to the Americans: 'The Frenchman lives with his past, a past of which he is justly proud and which he endeavours to preserve from the hands of modernism.'[15]

If post-Second World War had too little civil society, post-Dayton Bosnia-Herzegovina had too much: the civil society of socialist-era voluntary organizations had been destroyed, but the country's three ethno-political power bases (Croat, Serb and Bosniak) facilitated three civil societies which existed in antagonistic or semi-suspicious semi-allied relationships with each other, while a frequently non- or anti-nationalist civil society was located in the country's parallel NGO and project economy. What Steven Sampson critically terms 'project life' contained its own flows of resources, people, knowledge and language, creating a world of 'capacity building', 'target groups' and 'problem trees': 'Project life is a world with a premium on abstract knowledge, by which power accrues to those best able to manipulate the key symbols and concepts' (Sampson 2002). Bosnians working in the project economy tended to be younger and more skilled in Western European languages and often aimed to leave a country they believed contained few opportunities for a rewarding life. Most employed Bosnians depended for a livelihood on one or other of these civil societies or their associated political institutions rather than on industries oriented towards economic production.

Naming

Formal and informal military practices of renaming space are ubiquitous, and they exert 'the power of naming' perceived by Mary Louise Pratt (1992: 33) in colonizers' navigational mapping. The implication that naming equals possession is all too easily elided into the perception that, with space already in one's possession, one need not strive to understand it any further. As Alain Brossat (1994: 8) has noted, one of the first actions of people in liberated France was to tear down those physical marks of German occupation, the street signs and notices on buildings, which had marked out their former presence. In occupied Germany in the Second World War, the British occupation administration renamed the buildings they were using as offices and bases – 'Lancaster House' or 'Stirling House', for example, replacing the original German nomenclature. Roads around the offices were similarly signposted in English, and potentially common areas nearby, like bus shelters, were designated 'for Allied personnel only'. For the occupiers as much as for the occupied, the naming of these spaces in their own language undoubtedly reinforced what observers described as a 'compound atmosphere', experienced as a marked separation between the Germans, shut out of the spaces, and the British who had re-named and controlled them.[16]

Though foreign troops' presence in Bosnia-Herzegovina was discursively with the invitation and consent of all three main local politico-military forces, their naming of the local landscape (using English, the working language of the coalition) was strikingly similar, producing mental and physical maps quite at odds with local geography. The anthropologist Kimberley Coles (2007: 63) recalled that a fellow OSCE election monitor, seeing English-language route names on a foreign map of Bosnia-Herzegovina, had initially thought the mapped territory was part of the United States.[17] Route names – such as the UNPROFOR-era Route Triangle for the main mountain road from Tomislavgrad to central Bosnia, or Route Bluebird where British, Canadian, Romanian and Greek troops de-launched a temporary bridge near Mrkonjić Grad in a public relations success for SFOR in 2002 (Whitteaker 2002) – gained concrete existence in the landscape when nailed to telephone poles once or twice every kilometre. Coles argued that these naming practices caused 'internationals' to live in a 'hyper-Bosnia' where they shared nothing but space with Bosnians themselves:

> This organizational system and its referent map took a Bosnian actuality and created a separate and parallel reality for internationals from that used by Bosnians: a hyper-Bosnia.
>
> Hyper-Bosnia, a parallel world of statelike practices and institutions laid out on top of Bosnia proper, is a hyperstate. (Coles 2007: 64)

Officially mapped names aside, foreign soldiers further renamed the space around them as slang, abbreviations or corruptions of hard-to-pronounce local toponyms. Bugojno, much to the exasperation of the base's military interpreter, was most often 'Bugonyo' to the soldiers of the 1st Battalion, Duke of Wellington's Regiment stationed there in 1994. Gornji Vakuf, an important British base in the 1990s, became 'GV', and Mrkonjić Grad similarly 'MG'. Bosnians beginning to work as field interpreters with British patrols initially found the abbreviations alienating, yet sometimes integrated them into their own narratives of movement:

> After some time...I think August or September '96, I moved with the unit I worked for to a place, Gornji Vakuf, and the abbreviation (laughs) so many times mentioned by the soldiers was GV. And if you ask the soldier 'Do you know where Gornji Vakuf is?' he wouldn't know, but if you ask him 'Do you know of GV?', he says 'Yeah, man, I know.' So, we moved to GV, and I stayed there for another six months[.] ('Mitch')

The situation changed, and it depends where you were working. In big camps, like Banja Luka, or – MG, Mrkonjić Grad, MG, or – some other bigger camps, there were of course more interpreters. But here my first post was in a small camp, in Baraći, that's a village towards the border with Croatia. (Dubravka Jukić)[18]

One foreign military name, however, has entered local naming practices to symbolize what turns out to be a paradigmatic space of foreign military/local civilian interaction. Arizona Market, 'reputedly the second biggest black market in Eastern Europe' (Jašarević 2007: 274), takes its name from SFOR's Route Arizona between the cities of Doboj and Tuzla and occupies the space of a disused IFOR checkpoint in the former zone of separation established during the implementation of Dayton. While the US Army's start-up funding in 1996 suggests that foreign forces initially saw the initiative as encouraging 'local entrepreneurship and cross-ethnic reconciliation and interaction', Arizona Market grew into a site of smuggled goods and sex trafficking as well as small-scale sales of home-grown/home-made produce (Andreas 2009: 42–3). The international community continued to praise the market as an (illusory) myth of free-market economics empowering Bosnians to overcome ethnic hatred and trade together even as it acquiesced in human rights violations against women trafficked in and through the site. Later investigations revealed that members of the international community, including Russian and US soldiers, were themselves complicit in trafficking by using prostitutes inside the market space (Haynes, Dina 2010). Arizona Market, with its apt and problematic connotations of the United States' own frontier illegality, represents a site of criminality as well as consumption which would not exist without demand by foreign troops yet flourishes because it meets the needs of consumers and producers in BiH and the wider South-East European region.

Mobility

The privileged mobility of foreign troops involves two forms of power: the physical power to move (embodied in armoured vehicles, caterpillar tracks, haulage equipment and priority access to airspace) and the notional power to leave the country when a tour of duty ends. During the liberation of Normandy in the Second World War, a constant theme of Allied/civilian encounters was the different physical perspectives of those involved. The troops, in their tanks and armoured vehicles, were on the road, travelling through the villages and towns of Normandy – 'The front is on the move everywhere'[19] – whilst the local inhabitants were largely static, watching them as they passed by. As Simone Rose described the scene in Creully: 'We stood there looking, as in a dream, at the procession of this formidable war machine' (Herval 1947: 22; author's translation). Most frequently, Allied accounts speak of viewing the local inhabitants from above, from the top of their tanks, with the French looking up at them from the street below. A contemporary photo in the *Sunday Chronicle* classically imaged two soldiers in a jeep, looking down at a tiny French girl who was holding a small bunch of flowers up to them: 'For her, freedom', ran the caption, 'for them, flowers'.[20]

Privileged physical and notional mobilities intersect in the vehicle accident, the result of the size and weight of military vehicles combined with a reckless disregard for consequences. Both case studies in this volume contain a striking amount of material regarding road accidents caused by foreign troops. In Marseille in 1944, for example, the regional newspaper pointed out how vulnerable French civilians were to accidents caused by Americans who risked comparatively little by driving without due care: 'Every day, many of our citizens are paying the price for the carelessness of drivers, above all those who, perched on top of heavy lorries, are well protected from the accidents they cause.'[21] The French authorities complained that the effect of this heavy lorry traffic had been disastrous for the town's tram system, with 294 collisions involving 150 trams in September 1944 alone.[22] Many Bosnian interpreters interviewed for the *Languages at War* project recalled poor driving by foreign troops. Jovana Zorić, a student from Belgrade who worked for British forces in the RS during the late 1990s, had been upset by many incidents of bad driving by young and inexperienced soldiers:

[F]or me it was more about…am I going to survive this patrol, because this idiot 17-year-old driver, he just learned yesterday to drive and he is driving like mad, and he doesn't have a clue, and we're going to all die, right now. Because we're going to turn upside down, and that's it. For me it was more about that. Like a constant, 'OK, what are they going to do next?'[23]

Once, a 'young second lieutenant or whatever, 18–19 years old, just straight from the school' had disregarded a warning sign and driven his Warrior tank across a minefield with a colleague of Jovana's sitting in the back; another time, soldiers had been racing vehicles off-road so recklessly that, with no seat belts in the back of the Land Rover, she had been injured by a loose satellite phone case. Many interpreters told stories of fatal or incapacitating accidents in military vehicles involving others, and often complained that victims received no compensation or insultingly low pay-offs; the plot of Veselin Gatalo's semi-autobiographical novel *SFOR: siesta, fiesta, orgasmo, riposo* (Gatalo 2004) concerns an interpreter invalided out of work after a Spanish driver crashes his armoured vehicle. Road accidents as symbols of foreign military privilege and arrogance may in fact be a constant in the experience of hosting foreign forces. The sociologist Béatrice Pouligny found that 'problems of driving on the roads and accidents caused by international staff' were the most common complaints among local people she interviewed in several locations of peace operations, including Haiti and Cambodia: 'People were shocked by some accidents, and still more so by the scant attention paid to them and the lack of respect too often displayed by international staff' (Pouligny 2006: 167–8).

The perception of Bosnian roads as sites of danger dominates many British military recollections. The size and power of military vehicles often frustrated friendly informal communication with local civilians, and British UNPROFOR troops had the unpopular order not to hand children sweets, as one battalion commander recalled:

> I remember once stopping at a checkpoint, and it was pouring with rain – at a British checkpoint – and there was an armoured vehicle on a road junction, and I said to the soldier, to cheer him up, I said, 'Well, this is better than Northern Ireland, isn't it?' And he looked at me and said, 'No, not really, sir,' he said, 'In Northern Ireland at least I knew when they were abusing me, I knew what they were saying, but here,' he said, 'I'm not allowed to give sweets to the children in case it makes them rush out into the street and get squashed by passing armoured vehicles, and I haven't got a clue what any of the locals are saying to me, so actually I'd rather be in Northern Ireland.'[24]

Since the majority of troops could not operate in the local language, the emotional aftermath of military road accidents was outsourced to local people who interpreted in claims offices or worked as compensation clerks themselves. Slađana Medić, an interpreter from Banja Luka, narrated her time as a compensation clerk as a turning-point in her professional development of interpersonal skills:

> There were some situations when you had to translate a negative decision, where there were deaths involved in traffic accidents, and you

were supposed to tell the family that the British soldier who was driving is not at fault at all for the accident, and then there would be reactions, you know, emotional, aggressive – aggressive as in verbally, never physically. And then you were there like a buffer between your boss and them.[25]

In these case studies, the hugely unequal distribution of physical power between armed and mobile soldiers and unarmed civilians was sometimes imagined as a classic male/female power relationship, the protector and the protected. A famous press photograph of the Liberation of Normandy showed a large British soldier, fully armed, standing in a village street in France, with a smaller French woman hurrying past him, under the caption: 'It's a great day – the man who brings freedom and hope stands smiling in the village... With light heart this little French housewife hurries to the market and smiles good morning to the British paratrooper who stands guard.'[26] In photographs of peace operations such as those displayed throughout the 1990s in the British Army's *Soldier* magazine, however, the foreign soldier might equally be female, embodying the discourse of peacekeeping as a caring relationship to which female soldiers might be better suited than men (see DeGroot 2001).

The gendered landscape

Much of the landscape through which Second World War soldiers marched, and in which they would be stationed, was highly gendered. Allied troops entering Germany had been warned that they would have to deal with a robust German resistance which would seek to destabilize their operation, hence the early emphasis on the need for soldiers to keep the local population at a distance at all times.[27] What they in fact found when they entered Germany, as Petra Goedde (1999) has argued, was a female-dominated landscape, a society now composed of women, the very young, and the very old (see also Chapter 7). Women indeed were visible agents of reconstruction, clearing away rubble from ruined and bombed-out cities. In addition, it was evident that the civilians were in extreme need – desperately hungry, often homeless, and very frightened. The landscape in which soldiers and civilians would encounter each other in Germany was thus one 'infused with gendered meaning, creating the perception both among those who held power and those who submitted to it, that the asymmetry between them was a natural phenomenon' (Goedde 2003: xxi).

Dominant memories of this universe in the Imperial War Museum Sound Archive are of an asymmetry characterized by distance and separation, of a landscape in which 'the other' is largely perceived from afar: 'we didn't really come across many civilians...saw them, but not really to speak to';[28] 'Little contact with them...we were just there'.[29] The 'being there', the Allied presence in Germany, was framed as a presence related to conquest and power: 'They were beaten so we just steamed in and took what we wanted. If we wanted a car, we just went in and commandeered it. They hadn't got anything.'[30] Men and women recalling this time describe themselves as an occupying force, occupying German space from which local civilians had been forcibly displaced: 'Basically we had no contact with the German population at all because they'd all been turned out of their houses. We were living in them.'[31]

Memories of this landscape are often associated with the inside and outside of houses: those in power and those excluded from it. A naval officer in Minden, for example, recounted how the previous German owner of the house he was living in had come to beg a favour:

> the daughter of the crippled doctor who'd been moved out of his home came and asked for the wheelchair in the cellar...under orders not to do such things...but gave way. Told we mustn't let them have anything. We were to clear them out.[32]

In these memories, food symbolized the yawning gulf between what the Allies had at their disposal and how most German civilians were living. One ex-soldier described the experience of being watched by starving civilians as he ate his meal: '[I] remember them seeing me eat...and their eyes almost popping out of their head.'[33] In this situation of plenty alongside penury, relationships between soldiers and civilians were remembered in a strongly colonial framework: 'They hadn't got anything'; 'For a packet of fags you'd get hundreds of marks.... Money beyond our wildest dreams...so easy to get.'[34]

Bosnia-Herzegovina was a landscape similarly in decay, where asymmetry between foreign troops (or foreign civilian officials) and local people all too often went unquestioned. The post-war Allied 'being there' had its counterpart in the language of international 'presence' itself, which Kimberley Coles views as a key concept in the foreign-led transformation of BiH: 'Presence – an emic category and a fact on the ground – was a project and an intervention in itself, not just a logistical means of carrying out other projects' (Coles 2007: 86). The military presence secured and supported a much broader civilian presence which after the Dayton Peace Agreements gave a physical basis to the 'trans-formative ideology' of the project to promote democracy (Coles 2007: 88–9). Both dimensions of the indefinitely long foreign administration entailed privilege and separation for their agents, while contributing to new stratifications in local society.

Away from the sites of the worst massacres, Bosnia-Herzegovina was not so devoid of men as post-war Germany and was certainly not an economy where men who did return from demobilization or imprison-ment could count on finding work. Male war veterans, often struggling with endemically high unemployment levels as well as physical and/or psychological injury, in fact became 'a new and specific social group produced by the war' (Bougarel 2007: 167). Women were better able than men to take advantage of employment opportunities with for-eign forces because many of the jobs on offer were considered feminine in a gendered division of labour: laundering, cleaning, catering, textile repair and, to a certain extent, language work (experience in language teaching, a somewhat feminized profession, was a common route into interpreting for a foreign military). Although Robert Rubinstein (2008: 120) argues that employment opportunities with peace operations in general create a gender gap that benefits local men, the character of the pre-war Yugoslav workforce meant that in Bosnia-Herzegovina the opposite was the case.

British forces across three bases at Šipovo numbered approximately 2000 in 1998 – in a municipality with 15,000 residents on the 1991 cen-sus and likely fewer after Dayton – when they began a pilot project to hire local men as artisans and labourers. Mark Ferguson had played a leading role in interviewing and recruiting candidates, and had stood up to an attempt by the local mayor (a wartime power-holder) to mono-polize patronage in offering employment. In his narrative, the foreign force's ideal role was not to restructure the traditional gender order but to inject extra cash into the economy and foster a friendly atti-tude between locals and troops, objectives which were both achieved by creating employment for men as well as women:

[W]hen you – on a Saturday morning, if you took a walk around town, which I often did, because it sort of made the point of say-ing 'We're here,' and you got to sort of sniff the air and just say 'Right, what's happening in town?', you would know lots of the men. Because it was quite embarrassing, when I first got there, if you walked around town you'd know the women, but their husbands would sort of stare at you in rather a sort of, 'M-m-m, my wife goes up to your camp, I'm not entirely sure what she does all day, you know, m-m-m, I'm not sure I like this, because she's in control, she's got the money.' And you could really feel a sort of tension there. Whereas when you went downtown at the end, and you met the men, you'd be introduced to their wives and their children, and the wives were all smiling and the child, because of course he's now at work, he's bringing home money, and therefore the family's happy.[35]

Interpreting, the highest-paid form of foreign employment available to local people, attracted many men as well as women (interview participants recall a female/male ratio of approximately 60/40, including female interpreters in desk jobs with ordinary office hours). Male interpreters reconciled their status and the feminization of language work by using their narratives to construct spaces of male agency, focusing on (a) endurance in rough or outdoor conditions, (b) the use of street smarts, fast talking and resourcefulness to survive dangerous situations in the field and (c) their ease as a fellow male in all-male infantry patrols. Men spoke of weaponry more comfortably than women:

In one operation, for instance, we collected 62 tons of weapons. It was a huge operation, in an area called Dubica, and 62 tons. I was impressed, you know. Because the field was full, packed, with weapons. And many mortars. Howitzers. Hundreds of rifles. Automatic rifles. Semi-automatic rifles. Grenades. All kind of grenades. Fully charged. Anti-personnel mines. Anti-tanks. Anti-armour mines. It was shocking, you know, to see that in one place. (Stojan Radišić)

[E]ach time I couldn't understand a word, I would say 'Could you explain?' or 'Could you please point at what that is?' and then I would ask these Serbian experts, asking them 'How do you say that, in your language?' OK, so now I know the word, and write it down.... there's always something new, especially for a woman who has never seen, I don't know, a pistol or something, let alone knowing all the parts, like trigger and sight and what else. ('Sarah')[36]

In these militarized landscapes in which asymmetrical relationships were framed by the physical distance between soldiers and civilians, crossing over from one side to another – moving out of the silos created – could be perceived by both parties as potentially predatory, bespeaking hostile and subversive acts. In liberated France, for example, French civilians in Normandy complained that Allied troops were breaking into

their homes to pillage and loot: 'In the village, enthusiasm is wan-
ing. Soldiers are pillaging and breaking everything, entering under the
pretext of searching for Germans.'[37] In Troyes, a self-styled group of
'indignant fathers' banded together in order to protect their daugh-
ters from what they regarded as 'the vulgarity and attacks perpetrated
against our women and girls by the American soldiers'.[38] The Allies, on
the other hand, felt that the local population was deliberately setting out
to exploit them economically, with illegal traders trying to gain access
to soldiers in the bases in order to sell overpriced goods. The gendarmes
at Mourmelon intercepted a lorry which was regularly making the run
from Paris to Reims, carrying 1088 bottles of Armagnac, destined for 24
local sellers. The bottles, originally priced at 400 francs, were being sold
to the Americans for 850.[39] Troops involved in peace support in Bosnia-
Herzegovina had similar complaints, often relating to local exploitation
of foreign aid resources and directed at local civilian mayors. 'And then,
I mean, I'd go for meetings with lord mayors, and I'd say "Do you need
anything?", and he says, "Oh, we need food, we haven't got enough
food for the winter,"' ran a typical narrative from a military colloquial
speaker who served in the RS in 1999. 'And he'd have mates round his
office, in his building, and there'd be bags of UN rice, you know, that
he's nicked, that he's trying to flog on.'[40]

Even when military and local civilians worked side by side, cultural
distances between them could still be wide and key 'signature concepts'[41] misunderstood. In liberated France, labour relations presented
a particularly vexed area of cultural exchange. When French dock-
workers in Marseille, employed by the Americans to unload ships in
the port, went on strike to protest about their conditions of work,
the US authorities found it difficult to engage with a union tradition so very different from their own, as the minutes of the ensuing
Franco-American discussions recorded:

> Major Martin...noted that America was also a country where trade
> unions are recognized and encouraged, but union delegates are never
> tolerated actually in the yards, which is probably different from the
> French system. He would not want to give the impression that the
> Americans were opposed to unions...It was clear that some misun-
> derstandings are caused by the difficulties the American and French
> workers have in understanding each other.[42]

In Bosnia-Herzegovina, Steven Sampson argues, foreign democratiz-
ers failed to understand local networks of obligation, trust, patronage,

corruption, and extended family: those 'alternative social arrangements for achieving one's own strategies and for preventing others from achieving theirs' (Sampson 2002). These relationships in fact constituted Bosnian civil society and enabled successful local NGOs to function.

Sexual relations

One way in which both sides arguably moved out of their separate silos and sought more empathetic meetings was in the area of sexual relations, or fraternization in its popularly understood sexual context. These were overwhelmingly the encounters which soldiers preparing to enter liberated Europe in 1944 were expected to have. When the American Forces Network in Britain prepared its troops for the Normandy landings with a six-week radio course, the final week, headed 'Here ... are the ones you've been waiting for', gave the soldiers French phrases which were clearly expected to promote future sexual relations: 'Do you want a cigarette?'; 'I am/am not married'; 'My wife doesn't understand me'.[43] The approach continued in the troop press after the landings, with an explicit presentation of the French language as a vehicle through which soldiers could meet girls: 'This is no college course, it's just intended to provide a couple of laughs and a couple of phrases which might come in handy, somewhere in la belle France. Pick out the ones that fit and try 'em on your French girl-friend (petite amie – pe-teet ahmee)'.[44]

In occupied Germany where fraternization 'on the ground' had challenged SHAEF's original policy of non-encounter, sex between the military and the local women was framed as 'natural': 'fellas obviously wanted to go down the towns and fraternize, go out with girls as men do ... there was no way they were going to stop it'; 'Most young men think about girls'; '[non-fraternization] almost impossible to enforce. People being what they are. Nature being what it is'.[45] Sex could be seen as part of the overall colonial transaction between highly unequal forces – 'Amazing how well chocolate and bars of soap were used to good effect'[46] – with German women constructed as objects which could be transported to different locations: 'A number of senior NCOs did take German women with them ... down to our next point of call ... I had them smartly sent back ... the German women had been transported in army transport.'[47] This construction was still in play, though could be challenged, in 1990s Bosnia-Herzegovina. The commander of 1st Battalion, The Coldstream Guards contrasted his battalion's attitude to that of his predecessors in Vitez: 'I think we had a slightly different moral standpoint on it all from some of the previous battalions, in that

I don't think we took advantage of them [female interpreters], or indeed took any of them home as trophies after the war.'[48] Home, for this Coldstream battalion, was Germany, where he reminded the battalion that '[w]e've left three hundred and fifty wives behind' and to where he promised to return violators of the marriage contract.[49]

Language itself was a marker of asymmetrical relationships in many accounts of sexual fraternization in Germany during and after the Second World War. Running through the memories like a refrain is the sense that it is the woman who crosses the linguistic space, who has to speak a little of the occupiers' language: 'The girl spoke pretty good English'; 'She spoke quite good English'.[50] On occasions the language competence of a woman could be set within a framework of patronizing humour: 'claimed she was a Pole, spoke excellent German. She used to turn up every night at the back fence...she only had two words of English, "All right!" '.[51] Communication in this situation appeared to have been largely a one-sided affair: 'as I didn't know the language I thought it was rather a waste of effort, and I would only really talk to anybody if they would speak to me in English'.[52]

Whilst in the Second World War military/civilian sexual relations were in some senses expected and normalized as 'natural', the question of sexual fraternization had taken on a new dimension by the 1990s when troops from more than 30 countries served in Bosnia-Herzegovina. Liberal feminist pressure in many of these states during the 1970s and 1980s had persuaded many governments to open military jobs to women, though women were often still excluded from specialisms or units that would require them to 'close with and kill' the enemy in combat (Woodward and Winter 2007: 53–6). Most national contingents of the peace support forces in Bosnia-Herzegovina could not be thought of as exclusively male groups of soldiers; indeed, an emerging discourse grounded in an equation of femininity/peacefulness and masculinity/aggression held that female soldiers were an asset to peace operations because peacekeeping was based on consent rather than coercion or intimidation and because women were less prone to uncontrolled aggression (DeGroot 2001: 33–5).[53] After incidents such as the Tailhook case in the USA or sexual exploitation of women by UN peacekeepers in Cambodia, western democracies' armed forces came under much greater scrutiny regarding soldiers' use of local prostitutes and indeed sexual harassment within militaries themselves.[54] Civilian political awareness of feminist concerns affected military culture such that the construction of troops as sexual actors seeking partners among the local population was not officially foregrounded and sometimes, in contingents with 'non-fraternization' policies, even denied – at least on the front stage. Commanders' backstage strategies for managing male soldiers' heterosexual demands might include the displacement of sexual services to R&R sites in neighbouring countries or the tacit approval of certain brothels as suitable and safe for troops to visit (Enloe 1990). A portion of that demand might also be satisfied through sexual relationships with female soldiers in mixed-gender militaries, nurses or humanitarian workers.

In this context of heightened sensitivity, the relationship between sex and language was very different in Bosnia-Herzegovina than it had been after the Second World War. French (though not German) vocabulary provided for English-speaking troops during the Second World War had included language for complimenting women on their physical attractiveness, which was likely to be used in initiating a sexual relationship. *Stars and Stripes*, the US troop newspaper, included phrases such as 'Vous avez des yeux charmants' (15 September 1944) and 'Vous êtes très belle' (13 February 1945)[55] (see Chapter 4). Such phrases did not appear in official vocabulary cards for BiH (which would, of course, be seen by female as well as male soldiers). Instead, strategies for seduction and obtaining sex in the local language would be imparted informally: soldiers on pre-deployment language classes might request them (perhaps embarrassing a native-speaking female instructor in the process), or they might be obtained from local interpreters (especially from males) during long patrols or drives. Jovana Zorić resented being used as an adviser or go-between in this way:

> [S]oldiers, officers, you know, British forces, British Army, they would ask questions, 'So how do you' ... I mean, soldiers, they would always ask 'How do you say "good tits"?' And you say, 'You don't say that.' That's like a cultural thing. That's not a compliment. In my country that's a serious insult. You don't want to, you're not going to pull a girl like that (laughs), saying things like that.[56]

On the front stage of military operations, sex was far less present in the experience of garrisoning BiH than it had been during the Second World War. On the back stage, soldiers continued to make arrangements for sex, with varying degrees of connivance or obstruction from their superiors. At one extreme was the Coldstreamer colonel who ordered his battalion to 'behave like a bunch of monks who have all gone to war'.[57] At the other extreme, another interviewee for the *Languages at War* project reported that a hairdresser working inside a British base had been removed when she turned out to be using the space for providing sexual services. Other studies have found members of the international community in Bosnia-Herzegovina to have benefited from, and to have personally engaged in, human trafficking of women from countries such as Ukraine, Romania and Moldova.[58] This practice imported, endangered and exploited another, unprivileged group of foreigners with no social connections in the locality. It therefore avoided upsetting local males who might object to even the most frontstage and legitimate form of sexual fraternization, romantic relationships that led to marriage and a local woman joining a foreign man's household in his home country. The observations by the Coldstream battalion commander, for whom 'home' in 1993 meant Münster, points to a long-term consequence of the Allied occupation of Germany. Even when the country had been returned to Germans' political control and even after the Cold War division of Germany had been reversed, British troops had remained in Germany long enough to construct spaces they understood as 'home', with British place-names, British cooking, British families and British schools. The marriages of Bosnian women and British male soldiers based in Germany introduced a new kind of foreignness to the military near-abroad which had emerged from the long-term failure of non-fraternization policies after 1945.

Conclusions

The foreign soldier physically and linguistically present in a local community takes on an outsider status by virtue of his or her mobility. The soldier, who in contemporary deployments will leave the territory on a known date and resume his or her personal life in a different locality and state, resembles the figure of Georg Simmel's 'stranger': 'the fundamentally mobile person comes into contact, at one time or another, with every individual, but is not organically connected, through established ties of kinship, locality, and occupation, with any single one' (Simmel 1950: 404).[59] Troops in Bosnia-Herzegovina constructed a parallel layer of geography in the space they shared with locals; troops at the Cherbourg docks constructed a parallel layer of time. Even when a deployment is not constructed as an occupation in legal and political terms, troops remain occupiers in a spatial sense. As occupiers, they are not 'at home' but in a place where they possess certain measures of power and authority and which they can leave at will (though normatively at the will of the organization rather than the individual). Therefore, the space is appropriated linguistically as a means of re-establishing a usable conceptual home. In so doing, the occupier and renamer reinforces the distance between silos and the dichotomy between inside and outside. This phenomenon appears to be a constant throughout the case studies in the *Languages at War* project and is likely to hold true for other military deployments.

In this comparison, the largest set of differences in military/civilian interpersonal relations concern the extent and visibility of sexual fraternization. The militaries of 1990s western democracies carried out their overseas activities cognizant of the gaze of a potentially critical domestic public opinion and within a conceptual framework that the limited operations in which they engaged should not alter or threaten social relations at home (unlike the paradigm of 'total war'). Bearing in mind Cynthia Enloe's observation that 'marriages up and down the international pyramid can jeopardize power relations between governments if the women refuse to play their parts' (Enloe 1990: 11), one imagines that the wife of a volunteer professional soldier would not long retain her confidence in the military institution were she to discover her husband and his comrades were being taught how to explain to local women that 'my wife doesn't understand me'. The sexual dimension of fraternization thus became even more informal, backstage and contrary to frontstage foreign aims of promoting gender equality.

The construction of a given sexual encounter as legitimate rather than forcible (at which point the initiator becomes an aggressor, subject to civil or military justice) rests on the notion of consent, which is conceived as a negotiation between two individuals of equal status yet which often masks inequalities between one party and another (Pateman 1980). Language for obtaining female sexual consent, as opposed to language for initiating an encounter through complimenting the female body, was noticeably absent from Second World War military vocabulary instruction (and, in the language encounters described during our interviews, was not sought out by foreign soldiers in Bosnia-Herzegovina). A meaningful understanding of consent, argues the ethicist Joan McGregor, must involve the production of consent through some form of speech without coercion, deception or incapacitation: 'Consent is performative; it is something that an agent does' (McGregor 1996: 193). To produce and understand the performance, both parties to a relationship must share a language. When the foreigner does not speak the language of the other, as is frequently the case in sexual fraternization, it is unclear whether the encounter can result in meaningful consent.

In any military operation other than a hostile invasion, consent regulates not only troops' off-duty sexual activities but the existence of the operation itself. The classic concept of peacekeeping stipulates that the foreign military force is present with the belligerents' consent, and international politics too contain the possibility that consent may be given grudgingly, contested or denied (Ratner 1995). Even in peace enforcement settings such as IFOR, where the consent of the belligerents is legalistically not required, militaries acknowledge the need to achieve and maintain the consent of local populations where possible, for the sake of security and to facilitate reconstruction and civil affairs work. When a military presence is contested, the power to label a deployment which political representatives have contested as a conceptual 'occupation' is a forceful moral claim that troops' physical occupation of the space is illegitimate, whether turned against SFOR bases in Republika Srpska, US bases in Japan or nuclear weapons sites in 1980s Britain. The privilege and asymmetric power of military forces and bases raises the same problems of language and consent that underlies the question of sexual fraternization. Is consent possible without language, and can meaningful consent exist without a *mutual exchange* of language where both partners are forced to cross the linguistic divide?

Notes

1. Interview, 26 February 2009.
2. NA, FO 1060/874, SHAEF 6/44/209, 27 September 1944.
3. NA, FO 1060/874, Memorandum of punishment for fraternization, 30 March 1945.
4. NA, WO 229/5/1, SHAEF Psychological Warfare, 30 May 1945.
5. *Maple Leaf*, 11 June 1945.
6. *New Statesman*, 14 July 1945, 20/3.
7. *Oxford English Dictionary*, 2nd edn, 1989, Vol. 6: 151, 152.
8. AD Marne, 16W 269, note to Ingénieur en chef, 7 November 1944; 3 November 1944 (author's translation).
9. AD Marne, 16W 4835, Epernay Palace to Prefect, 3 July 1945 (author's translation).
10. AD Marne, 3Z 874, Service d'Aide aux Forces Alliées de la Mairie de Reims to sub-prefect, 8 May 1945.
11. Interview, 3 November 2009.
12. Interview, 26 February 2009.
13. Ferguson had drawn on this experience on a later tour in Afghanistan (a country with far less of an industrial base), where he had been in charge of the support command: 'I sort of made the point of saying, "We weren't in Bosnia for 14 years, we were in Bosnia for one year repeated 14 times. Because

we never went beyond a year in terms of foresight".' Interview, 3 November 2009.
14. *La Presse Cherbourgeosie*, no. 74, 26 September 1944.
15. *La Presse Cherbourgeoise*, no. 106, 5 November, 1944 (author's translation).
16. NA, FO 1014/26, Clegg Report, 31 May 1948.
17. A similar map dominates the space beside the ground floor lifts at Hotel Saraj in Sarajevo, perhaps left behind or donated from one of several defence conferences which plaques at the reception desk boast the hotel has organized since the late 1990s.
18. Interviews, 5 and 9 May 2010.
19. IWMSA, M. Crawford, 94/34/1.
20. *Sunday Chronicle*, 11 June 1944.
21. *Midi-Soir*, 27 November 1944 (author's translation).
22. AD Bouches-du-Rhône, 150W, 178, 20 November 1944.
23. Interview, 18 November 2009.
24. Interview, 18 May 2009.
25. Interview, 4 May 2010.
26. *Sunday Pictorial*, 11 June 1944.
27. See for example NA, FO 1060/874. SHAEF CA 6/44/209, orders issued to Army Commanders, 27 September 1944.
28. IWMSA, 18785, recorded 1999.
29. IWMSA, 17995, recorded 1998.
30. IWMSA, 15733, recorded 1995.
31. IWMSA, 17995, recorded 1998.
32. IWMSA, 20894, recorded 2000.
33. IWMSA, 5398, recorded 1981.
34. IWMSA, 15733, recorded 1995; 20202, recorded 2000.
35. Interview, 18 November 2009.
36. Interviews, 10 and 11 May 2010.
37. Mme De Vigneral, IWM 78/35/1.
38. AD Marne, 16W 266, unsigned letter to mayor of Troyes, 8 August 1945 (author's translation).
39. AD Marne, 16 W 266, Commissaire de la République to Ministère de l'Intérieur, 13 August 1945.
40. Interview, 27 July 2009.
41. See Tymoczko 2007: 238.
42. AD Bouches-du-Rhône, 149W 182, Civil Affairs Conference, 18 December 1944 (author's translation).
43. *Yank*, 23 April 1944.
44. *Stars and Stripes*, 28 September 1944.
45. IWMSA 20202, recorded 2000; 20062, recorded 2000; 20894, recorded 2000.
46. IWMSA 13420, recorded 1993.
47. IWMSA 17330, recorded 1997.
48. Interview, 18 May 2009.
49. Interview, 18 May 2009.
50. IWMSA 22370, recorded 2002; 24611, recorded 2002.
51. IWMSA 20370, recorded 2000.
52. IWMSA 18706, recorded 1999.

53. When NATO militaries became involved in Afghanistan and Iraq after 2001, a further practical reason for using female soldiers emerged: in order to conform to the discourse of winning 'hearts and minds' by respecting local cultural norms, women were needed to search and address women.
54. See, for instance, Enloe 2000; Whitworth 2004.
55. 'You have charming eyes' / 'You're very pretty'.
56. Interview, 18 November 2009.
57. Interview, 18 May 2009.
58. IPTF officers were implicated in the sex trade at Arizona Market (Haynes 2010: 1796), and Human Rights Watch accused eight contractors from the US firm DynCorp of purchasing and selling Moldovan women for prostitution (Human Rights Watch 2002: 63–8). The HRW report found little direct evidence of SFOR soldiers themselves trafficking women but pointed out that US civilian contractors, not subject to military discipline, were more freely able to move in Bosnian territory and were not banned from visiting nightclubs and discotheques where prostitution took place. Ukrainian and French troops in Sarajevo were investigated for running a prostitution and smuggling ring in Sarajevo in spring 1993 (Pouligny 2006: 167), and Ukrainian UNPROFOR soldiers in Žepa and Sarajevo were also known to be smuggling fuel, cars, cigarettes and alcohol (Andreas 2007: 46–8).
59. The authors are indebted to Stephanie Schwandner-Sievers for this observation.

Part IV
Communicating Through Intermediaries

Undoubtedly, the military have a significant problem of capacity in languages and cultures. Planners suddenly realize that they need large numbers of people to meet the pressing needs of the conflict, but they struggle to identify and assemble enough people with a suitable range of skills. Their initial response is to look for linguists who are 'ready to go', already equipped by family background, education, training or personal experience to carry out the tasks that require language expertise. The second response is to find ways of training people in the skills required. However, language competence is only one part of what a linguist requires to function in a conflict situation. They may be required to deploy a wide range of professional expertise, to translate, interpret, investigate, interrogate, liaise or resolve problems.

Meeting language needs is a challenge, since expert personnel may be in short supply. Languages are embodied in people, and military commanders are required to weigh their operational language needs against the different national, social and professional profiles of the language intermediaries who could meet them. The intermediaries, for their part, often experience their allocated roles as conflicted and chaotic. For some civilian interpreters, their role might be a professional one. But many locally-employed staff are inexperienced and have to learn on the job, balancing their duties with their own networks of family, friends and obligations.

This Part examines the experience of translators and interpreters in a wide range of contexts and explores their identities, their loyalties and the difficulties they faced in carrying out their important work. Chapter 9 reflects on how a 'linguistic space' was created and developed in the post-war occupation of Germany and how an interpreting system was developed incrementally and 'on the ground'. It highlights the

Pool of Interpreters, established for the Control Commission Germany, whose members were used for the day-to-day needs of occupation. And it suggests that an effective 'linguistic space' in the judgement and punishment of war crimes was created in the Nuremberg trials and in the British war crimes trials, both of which had an impact on the professionalization of interpreting in the following decades.

Chapter 10 examines the local interpreters who were employed by the UN and NATO forces in Bosnia-Herzegovina. They were frequently students, teachers or professionals with some foreign language knowledge, who spent much of their time in low-level language support, accompanying troops on patrols and in liaison meetings. They had few opportunities for professional development or advancement and relied on their own interpersonal skills and informally-acquired strategies to win the confidence and trust of their interlocutors. Chapter 11 studies the role of language intermediaries in both conflicts on a spectrum from invisibility to activism. There are many positions between these poles. Hence, there may at times be a 'divided loyalty' between the ethnic group to which an interpreter belongs and their employers, who may be a foreign army. The resulting tensions suggest that users need to develop a more complex understanding of interpreters as neither just inanimate mouthpieces nor persons who cannot be trusted. Underlying all these issues is the difficult question of the professionalization of interpreting in war. The language intermediaries whose voices we hear in Chapter 11 sit uneasily in most of the professional models currently available.

9
Military Interpreters in War

> It was also noted that there had been a failure in the interpre-
> tation at more than one recent trial...at the abortive trial of
> Dr. JUNG the interpreters, who were Dutchmen, were able to
> speak neither English nor German.[1]

Throughout the course of the Second World War, linguists and foreign
language speakers were employed by a variety of different agencies,
such as the armed forces and their auxiliary services, the Foreign
Office, and other ministries. When the liberation of Europe was almost
accomplished and the conflict drew closer to its end, preparations for
the occupation of enemy territory had to include the governing and
administration of all aspects of life. Slowly, the importance of language
intermediary roles for the military during liberation/occupation and
later in regime change became clearer, not least given the requirements
of denazification. This chapter reflects on how a 'linguistic space' was
created and developed in the post-war occupation of Germany and on
how an interpreting system was developed by the military incrementally
and 'on the ground' to respond to the needs of military effectiveness.

It is clear that military and occupation authorities initially considered languages as only one of a range of skills needed for deployment
in post-1945 Germany and for denazification in particular. This became
particularly evident in 1944, when a specific Pool of Interpreters for the
Control Commission Germany (CCG) was established; recruitment to it
remained problematic because of the need to reconcile security requirements with linguistic facility. Interpreters from the Pool could be used
for various activities to respond to the day-to-day needs of occupation,
but this system proved insufficient to create an effective 'linguistic space'
in the judgement and punishment of war crimes. This chapter examines

and compares the development of interpreting in two similar, yet very different judicial settings: the Nuremberg trials and the war crimes trials held in the British zone of occupation of Germany (the so-called 'zonal military trials'). The 'linguistic space' was conceived of in very different ways in these two situations, yet both settings would have an impact on the professionalization of interpreting in the following decades.

Interpreting in occupied Germany

The occupation of Germany by the Allies after the end of the war in Europe, with its internal networks and dynamics of power, provides both the social space in which interactions took place and the framework in which a new profession was born, before the creation of any of the recognized codes of practices and ethical rules for interpreting which had become more widely accepted by the 1970s. At the end of the war in 1945, defeated Germany was in chaos. Allied authorities had to cope with its administration and reconstruction and also with a practical and ideological purge of the local regime.

The decision to divide the country into four zones of occupation (US, British, French and Russian) had been taken at the Yalta Conference in February 1945. Allied authorities started to run the country at first through a Military Government, and then, after summer 1945, through the Control Commission for Germany (CCG). Through the British Element of the Control Commission, or CCG (BE), the British tried to achieve the so-called 'four Ds' – demilitarization, denazification, democratization and deindustrialization. It was expected that occupation would involve the military in a range of situations in which translation and interpretation would be vital in the implementation of British occupation policy. In the same way, interpreting and translating were vital in the process of denazification, especially regarding the dispensation of justice and the punishment of war crimes. Languages, translation and interpretation were related to the occupation and deeply implicated in how the country was to be run. The most important step in the establishment of an official interpreting and translation policy for the occupation of Germany in the post-war period (see also Chapter 7) was without doubt the creation of the Pool of Interpreters for the CCG (BE), which oversaw the British zone of occupation.

The establishment of a Pool of Interpreters was initially conceived at the beginning of September 1944. On 22 September 1944, the War Establishments Committee, the Treasury and Norfolk House (the London seat of the Control Commission Germany) agreed on the creation and development of a Pool of Interpreters which had to meet the requirements of the CCG's headquarters, of the Berlin Local Government Control and the staffs operating in the British zone. Its development began in autumn 1944, with the aim of serving the British zone and the Berlin area, providing military and civilian interpreters in German, Russian and French, and pursuing the principle that 'the first essential in an Interpreter is his skill, and his rank is a much less important consideration'.[2] In general, interpreters and translators were to maintain their ranks in posting to the Pool. Rank would not have been a constraint and would have had little bearing on the level at which they were to be employed, but because resources were so limited it was necessary to obtain suitable interpreters in whatever rank they might happen to be. The first essentials for interpreters were their language skills. On the other hand, language skills were seen just as a means to serve other higher purposes and were not considered important or prestigious enough to be the sole grounds for an improvement in rank. The rank of Lieutenant-Colonel, for instance, was added just to broaden the field of search for suitable candidates, because experience in recruiting had shown that many of the best interpreters held that rank.

The Interpreters' Pool was led by a Chief Interpreter, who initially was to hold the rank of colonel and who after September 1945 held that of brigadier. He was responsible for the general management and administration of the Pool, and for policy arrangements with the Chief Interpreters of the commissions in the other zones.[3] The Control and Co-Ordination Branch was formed by officers who dealt with policy and with the use of the various categories and grades of interpreters in relation to the different types of service required, and it had to manage the allocation of interpreters to users in accordance with their requirements. Since resources were so limited, no user was allocated interpreters or translators on a permanent basis. Instead, it was decided that 'everything possible will be done to ensure that each large user has at least a few Interpreters on a semi-permanent basis, so that the personnel concerned may become used to the work of the user and its technical aspects',[4] as for example was the case in British war crimes trials. The Control Branch had an Administration Section which dealt with the management of human resources, including recruiting and testing new interpreters and translators, giving them instructions and keeping records of the work done based on users' reports. It also included a Clerical Wing in charge of typing foreign documents and correspondence.[5]

The Pool included three language divisions: the German, Russian and French Branches. These contained both military and civilian interpreters and translators and were headed by a Lieutenant-Colonel who was responsible for the actual work of all the personnel in the Branch, for detailing personnel to Divisions in accordance with the directions of the Chief Interpreter and for apportioning work and ensuring efficiency and economy. He thus had to keep personal liaison with the 'users' and with the interpreters with a view to ensuring that interpreters allotted were suitably employed.[6]

Throughout the spring and summer of 1945 the total number of personnel employed in the Pool varied, but it always remained in the range of a few hundreds, out of a total of tens of thousands of CCG employees (see Chapter 7). Very soon, however, in August 1945, the huge amount of translation work called for a change in the organization of the Pool, and it was decided to include a Translation and Training Branch. The Pool was by then entirely responsible for the translation work required by all divisions of the Commission: requests had been received for the provision of 4800 staff hours translating per week. As a result, the Pool of Interpreters was revised in September and October 1945: the number of staff was hugely increased to reach a total of 1520 but was still a very small percentage of the total CCG staff.[7]

The first problem military authorities had considered when they initially conceived the Pool of Interpreters before deployment had to do with security issues, and concerned the nationalities which could be viewed as acceptable. Shortly before recruitment started, in September 1944, the Foreign Office had ruled that interpreters and translators of different nationalities were suitable depending on the grade for which they were to be recruited. For example, only British- or Dominion-born subjects were considered suitable for officer or civilian-officer grades, and naturalized British subjects could only be accepted in lower ranks if MI5 had cleared them for the class of work for which they were wanted, whilst those of enemy origins could not be accepted at all. Russian interpreters of all ranks could be of any nationality other than enemy, provided MI5 accepted them, whereas German interpreters had to conform to the officer, warrant officer and 'other ranks' requirements.[8] However, in January 1945, shortly after recruitment had begun, things changed: the difficulties in finding suitable linguists made the Foreign Office drastically change its security policy for the recruitment of interpreters and translators so that naturalized British subjects of enemy origins could now be accepted.[9] Clearly, the shortage of skilled linguists was such that it called for a sharp change in policy during the actual deployment.

As soon as it had been created, the Interpreters' Pool had to face huge problems regarding the recruitment of suitable personnel. Enlistment and recruitment of interpreters had begun in the fall of 1944 right after the Pool's creation, and the CCG had agreed with Supreme Headquarters Allied Expeditionary Force (SHAEF) that civilian linguists would be recruited in the United Kingdom by means of attractive advertisement, announcement by broadcast and through contact with universities; Russian speakers were to be recruited by the Control Commissions for Germany and Austria, and military German speakers would be found by 21 Army Group.[10] The task was nonetheless a very hard one, and by the spring of 1945 it was clear that it was impossible to reach the expected goals to fulfil the interpreting needs of both SHAEF and the Control Commissions: the military kept statistics of all foreign language-speaking personnel in the Forces, but only a handful of those were available for use as interpreters under the existing conditions of employment and pay. Furthermore, it was estimated that no more than 2000 civilian German and Russian speakers could be found in the United Kingdom, a lot of whom would not accept a job in Germany because they were otherwise employed, viewed it as unacceptable to relocate to Germany or considered it unacceptable to work for a lower salary and for a lower social status than the one they were holding.[11] Other difficulties were caused by security concerns as well as Foreign Office and MI5 restrictions: of the personnel interviewed, the proportion finally approved by the Foreign Office and MI5 was about one in three at the end of January 1945.[12] Difficulties in recruiting civilian interpreters led to the conclusion that arriving at the required number was nearly impossible. Additional military interpreters were thus required, and a record of all returning prisoners of war was requested to discover those who were proficient in Russian, French or German. In May 1945, it was also decided to assess the language skills of all members of the CCG (graded Fluent, Moderate, Poor or Nil) and establish exactly to what degree 'business could be conducted without the assistance of Interpreters'.[13]

The grading procedure, applicable both to military and civilian personnel, was determined in a memorandum issued by Norfolk House on 8 February 1945. Three grades were established as a result of marking: Grade A (85 per cent), Grade B (56 per cent), and Grade C (50 per cent). The marks were obtained from a written test[14] and an oral test, consisting of about 30 minutes of conversation, designed to examine the candidates' academic knowledge of the language. In addition, candidates were also assessed as to their personality: S.1 (all persons who could be introduced to the highest society); S.2 (all persons who were in every way well educated and well mannered but fell short of the requirements of S.1); S.3 (all others).[15]

The task of training interpreters had clearly been underestimated upon creation of the Pool. In July 1945, the CCG in Germany wrote to Headquarters 21 Army Group that the most important task for the Pool was to assemble as many German, Russian and French linguists as it could, but 'since only a negligible percentage of those available has ever previously interpreted, next in importance comes the training of Interpreters'.[16] The letter emphasized the need for the provision of language refresher courses and intensive courses in interpreting, and in July it was also decided that training in the German language was to be given in Germany rather than in the United Kingdom or even in Brussels,[17] because the courses currently held were clearly not effective at all. Training in Germany, instead, was closer to where the work had to be performed, and it could be carried out on the job and with the help of the best linguists who were already working in the British zone. The establishment of an interpreters' school within 21 Army Group was under discussion in July, but the project was probably abandoned later, as no other reference to its existence can be found in the archives. It is therefore unsurprising that court interpreters were not fully prepared for their heavy task. In fact those of them who actually had some kind of training had been sent to a military interpreter's school in Brussels for a week-long course in which they learned mainly how to ride a motorbike, which was the best means of travelling quickly between interpreting assignments.[18] Walter Richards, who was only 18 years old when he attended the school, recalls having to learn how to ride a motorbike for two or three hours each day, but mentions no other aspect of the training. Clive Teddern, on the other hand, remembered that:

> [T]he course itself is fun with role playing and generally erring on the side of obscenity. I sit next to the man who achieved the impossible; failing the Interpreters course. I look over his shoulder as he translates 'Tief-Flieger Angriff' (low-level air attack) as 'underground air battle'.[19]

The greater part of interpreters' training, as will be seen later, had to be done 'on the job'.

At the time the Pool of Interpreters was established, the skills needed for interpreting were not very clear and requirements were mainly predicated on what available resources could offer. The Pool had been conceived in a way which aimed to provide language intermediaries for all the different needs of occupation and reconstruction of a denazi-fied Germany. The creation of a professional model was irrelevant at this stage, and what mattered most was the 'on-the-ground' need of effectiveness in communicating in war. Before the professionalization of interpreting, when no ethical codes of practice had yet been envisaged, the concept of interpreting was mainly conceived of as linguistic accu-racy. The Pool of Interpreters therefore created a 'linguistic space' within the domain of war, which was deeply resistant to ethical issues but on the other hand assumed unquestioning loyalty to both the employer and the institutional process. In fact, the interpreter's profile created by the Pool was (a) security-cleared; (b) socially acceptable; (c) multitasking; and (d) actually available on the ground.

This system, however, initially failed to recognize the specific require-ments in the different operational fields in occupation. The units especially created to deal with the judgement and punishment of war criminals are a prime example of this. This case poses in acute terms the issues of accuracy, ethics and neutrality which were to be at the core of the post-war interpreting profession. It was precisely in this field of court interpreting that a profile of skills for interpreters other than 'just' lin-guistic accuracy was developed incrementally in response to operational requirements and regime change.[20]

Professionalizing interpreting and denazification: Nuremberg

The question of the right to an interpreter in courts of justice has been the object of debates in the context of human rights over the last few decades. For example, the defendant's right to 'be informed of the charges in a language which he understands' and to 'have the free assistance of an interpreter if he cannot understand or speak the lan-guage used in the court' (Mikkelson 2000: 11) was specified for the first time in Europe in the Convention for the Protection of Human Rights and Fundamental Freedoms, adopted in 1950. Article 14 of the 1966 United Nations International Covenant on Civil and Political Rights also establishes that the defendant has the right to 'have the free assistance of an interpreter if he cannot understand or speak the language used in court' (Karton 2008; Mikkelson 2000: 10–11). The right to have an interpreter is thus linked to the notion of 'linguistic presence', meaning that defendants cannot be present at their trial if they do not under-stand the language of the proceedings. Court interpreting has therefore been acknowledged as a highly specialized profession, rather than just simply a role that any bilingual person might play, a profession which requires specific and dedicated training. Yet even today there are many veteran court interpreters who began their profession just because they spoke the language required for a court case, and later learned the techniques 'on the job', by a process of trial and error. Regulations in this field, especially concerning the quality of interpretation in the judiciary, only developed in the late 1970s. These basically required interpreters to demonstrate proficiency by passing a certification exam (Sweden, 1976; the USA's Federal Court Interpreters Act, 1978; Australia, 1978; Canada, early 1980s).

Modern-day interpreting must also cope with high ethical standards and codes of practice which are particularly important in the legal environment because the potential for and risks of miscarriages of justice are so high. The three most important canons of modern codes of interpreter ethics are fidelity, confidentiality and impartiality. Fidelity, sometimes also described as accuracy, refers to conveying the meaning of the speaker's message in an accurate and complete way. Confidentiality is particularly important in court interpreting because of the high stakes involved, and interpreters are not expected to take advantage of any information obtained during their work. Impartiality, or neutrality, is said to be important in all interpreting settings, but it is essential in court interpreting, where the parties involved are in conflict with each other and the interpreter must not favour any side. Interpreters are today seen as neutral participants in the court process.

Back in 1945, however, these acts establishing the rights to 'linguistic presence' and to the services of an interpreter, not to mention the codes of practice and the sets of ethical rules mentioned above which contributed to creating a 'linguistic space' in courtrooms, were still to be conceived. Interpreting during investigations and in court was only one in a wide spectrum of activities that all those with linguistic skills were expected to perform in the highly unstable environment of British-occupied Germany.

As the trials of the major war criminals at the International Military Tribunal (IMT) in Nuremberg between 1945 and 1946 were perhaps the most famous interpreted trials in history, this event is universally regarded as a watershed for interpreting in general, and for court interpreting in particular. Many see it as the only starting point for the history of official court interpreting as it is known today. Yet what was created at Nuremberg, however, was the conference interpreting paradigm, which has dominated interpreting for many decades since, and which was given professional existence in the apprenticeship model developed by the Association internationale des interprètes de con-férence (AIIC), the professional association for conference interpreters. The Nuremberg trials were a very particular and one-off event, with an extremely high profile, which received enormous publicity from every point of view and had massive political repercussions.

The specific linguistic needs of the Nuremberg Trials, due mainly to the number of languages involved and to the number of people who needed to interact, was evident to all those who worked on its organiza-tion. It was established early on that defendants had the right to a fair trial to be carried out quickly, meaning that consecutive interpretation was just not feasible. The interpreting system employed at Nuremberg was the Filene-Finlay Hushaphone, which had been patented in 1926 and was used before the war, especially at the League of Nations con-ferences in Geneva, either with 'simultaneous successive interpretation' (which involves at least one consecutive interpretation, while the oth-ers are simultaneous with each other) or 'simultaneous reading of pre-translated texts' (Gaiba 1998: 30–2). Because of the IMT's special linguistic needs, the Filene-Finlay system was used in a new way in Nuremberg and made simultaneous interpretation possible for the first time. One Mr Suro, Chief Translator of the American State Department, had to face the problem of recruiting interpreters who could work with this new system. Suro decided to organize recruitment in two phases: the first stage was only about language knowledge, whereas the specific ability to listen and translate at the same time, required by the new simultaneous technique, was tested in a second phase. The recruitment process included mock-trial situations, where potential interpreters were placed in booths and asked to interpret. To be successful, candidates had to have an exceptional knowledge of two languages, a broad cultural background, composure and the ability to remain calm in very stressful situations. Recruiters later said that the best interpreters were bilingual, rather than multilingual, and between 35 and 45 years old; those who had been educated in their own country and later had professional expe-riences in another country were considered the best. Academics were not necessarily part of this group, because even though they had excellent qualifications and background culture they could not always cope with the subjects raised in the trials or with simultaneous interpreting itself (Skinner and Carson 1990: 15–17). Training for those selected included mock-trial sessions and could last a couple of months or just a few days, depending on the ability of the person and on the demand.

George H. Vassiltchikov was a Russian civilian émigré who between 1942 and 1945 had been in France working with the Resistance.[21] He was recruited in Paris as an interpreter for the Nuremberg trials in 1945, when the IMT had already been established and when rumours were circulating that there were terrible complaints about the Russian interpreters. Vassiltchikov went to 'the French Ministry of Justice in the Place Vendôme'[22] to meet a recruiting officer, and although 'the Russian mafia immediately organized itself, I was among the group of Russians who went there to offer their services. Those who were recruited spoke languages very well and had a background which seemed to be OK. We were all flown to Nuremberg.'[23] Vassiltchikov had a stammer and therefore was initially recruited as a translator, 'but once there they found out that again those who had been recruited as interpreters were not very good'[24] so he was asked to try to interpret: 'I was submitted to a test and I passed, I do not stammer when I interpret. And I became their number one Russian interpreter.'[25] The test consisted of a text being read for him by a member of the prosecution team, and he had to interpret while being recorded. The interpreting was then played back and checked against the original text. Of his experience of being recruited and trained to work at the IMT, Vassiltchikov remembered that he had had to work for hours and hours as he had not done that kind of interpreting before: 'I was literally thrown into the swimming pool without knowing how to swim.'[26]

Recruiting interpreters for the IMT was difficult because of the high skill levels required, but it could not match the difficulties faced by those who were trying to manage the Pool of Interpreters of the CCG. In fact, although the required skills were far more general, the Pool could not offer the prestige, the comparatively higher salaries ('we received a fair amount in dollars for our Nuremberg work. It was the first time in my life I was not either poor or very poor'[27]) and overall the very good life and good future employment opportunities that Nuremberg interpreters like Vassiltchikov enjoyed.

The section in charge of language services in Nuremberg was called the Translation Division, headed by Léon Dostert and his executive officers Alfred Steer, Peter Uiberall and Joachim von Zastrow. It consisted of a Court Interpreting Branch, with a pool of three teams of twelve simultaneous interpreters, and an auxiliary team of twelve consecutive interpreters; the Translating Branch, with eight sections of about twenty-five translators; the Court Reporting Branch, consisting of twelve people for each language; and the Transcript Reviewing Branch, of about 100 people. According to Vassiltchikov, the Germans had a team of very good interpreters, who were mainly German émigrés from North America; the French were a mix, but in general some interpreters were outstanding and some others were average, but 'there were no bad ones'.[28] Working hours were not considered too tough for the times, as interpreters worked two hours in the morning, from 10.30 to 12.30 am, and two after the lunch break from 2 to 4 pm. As a rule, interpreters changed teams, but Vassiltchikov did most of the interpreting during the presentation of the 'Offences against Civilians and Crimes against Humanity of Eastern and Southern Europe' by Chief Counsellor Justice Lev Nikolaevich Smirnov, of the Russian Delegation. Vassiltchikov felt very anxious regarding his ability to interpret in that particular context, which was highly charged not only because of the crimes committed but also because it was a very public and high-profile part of the trial itself. He decided to ask Smirnov to read the documents to be used in court, which were in English, as he felt it would be easier for him to quote from the original rather than translating back and forth from Russian. Initially Smirnov had many concerns regarding the risks of information leaking to the defence, but then he and General Rudenko, the Chief USSR Prosecutor, decided that this request was reasonable and in their own interests, so Vassiltchikov spent several days working closely with Smirnov in his office.[29]

A very special system was thus created, tailored to the peculiar needs of the Nuremberg Trials. Surprisingly, however, this excellent organization, which was well aware of the importance of language issues and of the fact that this particular business could not be done without suitable language intermediaries, was not to be reproduced outside Nuremberg. The situation in the British zone, for example, was very different. At the end of the Second World War, at least 19,500 alleged war criminals were in the custody of British authorities (Bloxham 2003: 105). War crimes tribunals were set up in the British zone under the law known as 'Royal Warrant', and tried a number of very well known cases after 1945, such as the 'Belsen' and 'Ravensbrück' trials. In this situation, British as well as German, Austrian, Czech and other Jewish people would have to be employed as interpreters and translators, clearly placed in an institutional setting where they were not neutral but nonetheless had a key function in communicating the conflict during the process of judgment and punishment of their stated enemy. Adequately trained linguists who could satisfactorily interpret allowing the smooth running of trials were very rare, as were those who could at least speak some German.

Interpreting developed incrementally

The British war crimes courts set up in Germany under the Royal Warrant were scheduled to try 500 cases by 30 April 1946, but in fact were able to hold only 200 trials by that date. The numbers of cases pending were high. In fact, in March 1949 Christopher Mayhew, Under Secretary of State for Foreign Affairs, reported that 937 people had been tried for war crimes by British military courts, Control Commission tribunals had tried 148 people for crimes against humanity, and 2180 persons had appeared before German courts with the same charges (Sharman 2007: 224). These figures were only a slight percentage of the alleged war criminals in custody, but they give an idea of the considerable number of cases involved. As a consequence, interpreting needs were massive, both for the trials themselves and for the investigations preceding them. The great majority of defendants and a good number of witnesses and defending counsels in fact only spoke German; their 'linguistic presence' (De Jong 1992: 11–13; Gonzáles *et al.* 1991: 57–67; Mikkelson 2000: 12) in a British tribunal where the official language of the court was English had therefore to be provided by court interpreters. How did the British authorities cope with these enormous interpreting and translating needs, in a situation where every resource was lacking, especially that of skilled and trained personnel? The answer to this question is still relevant today, since it raises issues which have not yet been entirely resolved in the wider interpreting profession.

As has been seen, the occupation authorities initially failed to recognize the special needs of denazification and the Pool of Interpreters of the CCG was not in a position to supply suitable personnel. In court interpreting, both skills and ethical standards were essential, because if they were not guaranteed a miscarriage of justice could result. The situations involved were highly emotional for all linguistic mediators. Jewish ex-refugees working in Germany in 1945 had had to leave their countries and families because of Nazism, and many of their relatives had died in concentration camps. British interpreters would have to facilitate trials in which the defendants were accused of heinous crimes against Allied and in particular British servicemen. Working in these difficult trials, neutrality and detachment were likely to be very difficult. The problem in the British zone was solved by developing on the ground a system for court interpreting which could help to effectively employ the resources which were actually available rather than those ideally desirable.

The situation which presented itself in January 1946 was far from ideal:

It was also noted that there had been a failure in the interpretation at more than one recent trial – [at] ALMELO the standard was lamentable, at WUPPERTAL the Court sent away the interpreter provided after a few minutes, and at the abortive trial of Dr. JUNG the interpreters, who were Dutchmen, were able to speak neither English nor German.[30]

In a conversation between Group Captain Somerhough[31] and Colonel Harden,[32] it was also pointed out that bilingual trials were very much dependent on the skill and experience of interpreters and that 'more was needed to interpret in a court of law than the mere ability to translate from one language to another – there must be a complete mastery of the languages and idiom, ability to convey the fine shades of meaning from one to the other, and above all the ability to do this instantly'.[33] Somerhough and Harden were clearly aware of the fact that interpreting in a court of justice required more than the ability to translate, but even so they only referred to language skills, failing, interestingly enough, to recognize that interpreting, and court interpreting in particular, might also require other fundamental skills.

To deal with the problems of court interpreting for war crimes trials, it was agreed to nominate a Master Interpreter with the following duties:

> To go round the Corps areas, instruct the Interpreters on trial pro-
> cedure from an Interpreter's point of view, watch them at work, and
> report on their ability to Corps HQ. By this means, in due course each
> Corps will be sure of its ability to produce a first class German speak-
> ing interpreter for any trial which it may convene. And, moreover,
> in certain unsolved cases, and where public interest is aroused, the
> Master Interpreter could himself take some part in the interpretation,
> doing either the accused or a 'star' witness.[34]

The master interpreter also had to advise on the selection, training and ability of interpreters and report to the authorities on any points con-cerning interpreting. Captain Peter Forest was chosen for this role; he had been Senior Interpreter in the Belsen trial, where 'his performance of the task was the admiration of both the lawyers and the press, and he was the subject of a special commendation by the President'.[35]

Forest's task was initially to interview interpreters from the Inter-preters' Pool and select those who could be suitable for war crimes trials. It was thus a two-stage selection process, because these interpreters had already been selected to be included in the Pool. At the beginning it was quite hard for Forest to find suitable interpreters, but when supervis-ing the trials he managed to find a few outstanding ones. The skills he sought were quite basic if compared with today's standards: those who were rejected either had insufficient knowledge of languages or were not 'quick enough', or became too excited to give exact translations. Later on he started to consider other issues such as behaviour in court and respect shown to members of the court.

In April 1946, however, another letter of complaint from a President of a military court was received, reporting that interpreters provided 'were so far below the required standard that it was at times difficult to carry on with the trial'.[36] The system created by Somerhough was not working, and the reason was very clear to him: whereas the original plan was that the Master Interpreter would identify and notify the names of suitable interpreters and that these would be made available by the Pool, the selected interpreters later became so important for the Pool that they were never available for war crimes trials, showing that denazification, and war crimes trials in particular, became increasingly less important in the reconstruction of Germany, as resources including good interpreters were allocated to other more urgent tasks.[37] As a result, it became more and more difficult for Forest to find interpreters who could be recommended as first-class court interpreters: 'I arrived now at a stage where I am happy to find anybody who shows some promising qualities and who – after some training, coaching and experience – might prove useful for our trials.'[38]

Forest consequently decided to create his own new system: he had to work with resources which were actually available and also quickly accessible. He decided to recruit those who showed some signs of promise and send them to work in court as 'on instruction': 'My idea is to take the first above mentioned six NCOs[39] "on instruction" to the next trial at Wuppertal (JAG [Judge Advocate General] Mr. Stirling). I shall try to train them there, to work with them, to raise their standard of interpretation and find out how their knowledge and efficiency could be improved.'[40] His system thus consisted in training interpreters 'on the job' but under his close supervision: 'I go myself to the trials and work together with the NCOs, helping them, encouraging them and giving them confidence in the strange Court atmosphere. That is the only way to train them and to build up a pool of real Court Interpreters.'[41] In this sense, Forest had a clear view that the 'linguistic space' in court was a special one.

Furthermore, in the reports that the Master Interpreter regularly wrote after each trial he attended and sent to Somerhough, he evaluated each interpreter's performance in order to be aware of those who were improving and reject those who proved unsuitable. About a month later, he expanded his system by selecting the best interpreters and putting them in charge as supervisors in subsequent trials. Thus there was a hierarchy of interpreters in each trial. This was important in order to supervise the work of the less experienced and to help them, which could not be done by Forest alone. Among those considered suitable to be supervisors was Clive Teddern: 'Sgt. Teddern – This NCO is getting better and better. He is quite capable to take charge of a smaller team.'[42] This method allowed acceptable, if not good, interpreting at trials throughout their existence; in 1948, Forest was still pointing out that they could not always find good NCOs but 'one first class interpreter together with a mediocre one, is almost the best we can achieve during the present shortage. And, of course, with some experience they would improve, I hope.'[43]

As to the risk of misinterpretation, the Master Interpreter was not very concerned by the performances of non-commissioned officers and of Jewish refugees who in various ways had joined the British war effort, like Anderson, Richards and Teddern. In fact, all those involved in the establishment of British policy regarding war crimes trials had been so keen to avoid accusations of 'victors' justice' that the legal system paid close attention to the possibility of the mistreatment of defendants (see Bloxham 2001, 2003; Sharman 2007). A good number of those who came to be tested by Forest and proved to be the best were in fact non-commissioned officers. What preoccupied Forest instead was the risk involved in the use of German nationals as interpreters at trials. The difficulties in recruiting suitable interpreters had called for an extension of the search for interpreters to include German civilians: Forest mentioned this possibility for the first time in June 1946, emphasizing his reluctance to employ German civilians because of the delicacy of the task, which in his opinion could not be performed by those who just a few months before had been enemies. Nonetheless, he had to test a couple of them and they proved to be suitable, but he still stressed that in his opinion former enemy civilians had to be employed in war crimes trials only in cases of extreme emergency.[44] Although in 1948 Forest found that German civilians who had been employed in the Hamburg courts were very good, he felt they needed to be very carefully selected and tested before being allowed to work, and 'even then they must never be allowed to work alone; always together with a British Officer or NCO. The risks of misinterpretation are too big.'[45] Interestingly, impartiality was only mentioned in the case of German civilians, and not mentioned at all in the case of British interpreters or Jewish non-commissioned officers interpreting either in cases involving crimes against British soldiers or against fellow countrymen and other Jewish people. The reason for this 'one-way impartiality' lies in the broader policy which had generated the whole war crimes trials system, where the question of impartiality had been addressed at a much higher level as part of the overall legal infrastructure.

Forest's system relied on using available skilled resources in other units, with his biggest challenge being to actually locate people who could be considered suitable as interpreters beyond the Interpreters' Pool itself: 'I cannot be simply satisfied if I am told that there are no Interpreters available. They are available. We must only find them. And we shall find them. War Crimes Trials are going on.'[46]

Conclusions

Languages were seldom considered as a valuable form of cultural capital by military and occupation authorities during and after the Second World War. Instead, they were seen as one of a range of skills needed to perform occupation duties satisfactorily and efficiently. Likewise, interpreting was conceived of as a task which required mainly (if not only) linguistic accuracy rather than a more complex set of skills including, for example, ethical neutrality. Even so, a particular interpreter paradigm emerges from this case study. It can be exemplified on the one hand by those working in the high-profile Nuremberg trials, carefully selected and trained, and who enjoyed comparatively high salaries and social status, and on the other hand by those working in the British zone of occupation, where the situation on the ground was more complex and a new working system had to be developed in order to guarantee smooth proceedings.

When the Pool of Interpreters was created in 1944, recruiting suitably qualified interpreters who could satisfy the security requisites established by MI5 and the FO was highly problematic. The interpreter's profile developed at this stage was focused mainly on issues of loyalty to the military and identity: it included three main characteristics: being security-cleared, being socially acceptable and being able to multitask, to adapt to very different tasks in the same day. Authorities started to be more relaxed about security issues once the war was over and when it was clear that the need for language intermediaries was very considerable.

In the more specific context of denazification and the trial of war crimes in particular, a different system was needed. The CCG could not afford to attract as highly skilled people as the IMT, where something more than language skills was expected, and where a more rigorous selection and testing was carried out; however, the need for effectiveness, getting the trial expedited, led to the incremental development of a profile of skills and a system of interpreting decades before a professional code of practice and a set of ethical rules were established. The study of court interpreting in the British zone of occupation in Germany highlights the importance of a language organizer figure, here identified as the Master Interpreter, who was responsible for the selection of interpreters, for on-the-job training and for supervision.

Court interpreters in British war crimes trials after the Second World War were working in a highly dynamic and unstable environment, where operational rules and a professional code of practice were still to be conceived. Their ethical role was thus situated and enacted rather than responding to pre-established norms: they were more concerned with effectiveness, with 'getting the job done', rather than with complying with ethical rules, and so were their employers. It is clear from the evidence that the conference interpreting model inherited from Nuremberg, which has dominated the world of interpreting, was largely irrelevant in real 'on-the-ground' conflict situations such as the liberation and occupation of Europe after the Second World War.

In a trial, the outcome of a good or bad interpretation is not only immediately evident but can also have the very serious consequences of a miscarriage of justice. It is probably for this reason that Forest – the Master Interpreter – had quite high expectations of interpreters in terms of the standards of those times and environments. But he also had to confront other groups who were not as strongly convinced of the importance of a good standard of interpreting, and as he could not always find suitable linguists he had to work with those who were available: often unqualified interpreters who did not have time to prepare adequately for the trials in which they were to work. Forest thus established what we can call a selection/supervision system, based on the careful choice of available linguists and on their training on the ground, under the supervision of the Master Interpreter or of another more experienced and more skilled interpreter who then acted as a mentor. After the performance, another report assessed results and improvements, rejecting those that in practice proved unsuitable. The supervision system also made it possible to reduce the risks of deliberate misinterpretation, which might have occurred in such a highly charged environment, especially with the employment of former enemy nationals.

This selection/supervision system may be of relevance to those having to provide language support in more modern conflicts, in situations where finding suitably qualified linguists is problematic and where the

wide use of local civilians as interpreters and fixers can often pose security issues in an environment where it may be difficult to tell friend
from foe. Interpreting in the Second World War was developed 'on the
ground': the policy established at the beginning was far from the actual
operational reality and, in order to cope with the huge interpreting
requirements, those on the ground continually had to report to those
higher in the hierarchy and work with them to review and develop policy according to the actual situation. Effectiveness, requirements and
practice therefore influenced the development of an interpreting policy, adapted on the ground in order to bridge the huge gap between
what was needed linguistically and the resources available to meet the
language needs.

Notes

1. NA, WO 309/7, 11 January 1946.
2. NA, FO 936/116, 15 September 1944.
3. NA, FO 936/116, 6 February 1945.
4. NA, FO 1032/1350, 6 February 1945.
5. NA, FO 936/116, 6 February 1945.
6. NA, FO 936/116, 6 February 1945.
7. NA, FO 936/116, 5 October 1945.
8. NA, FO 936/116, 15 September 1944.
9. NA, FO 1032/493, 3 January 1945.
10. SHAEF commanded the Allied forces in North West Europe from late 1943,
    and was headed by General Dwight D. Eisenhower. 21 Army Group was a
    British formation composed of British and Canadian forces which operated
    in the North-West European theatre under the command of SHAEF. After the
    end of the war in Europe, it became the British Army of the Rhine (BAOR).
11. NA, FO 936/116, 6 April 1945.
12. NA, FO 1032/493, 30 January 1945.
13. NA, FO 1032/493, 3 May 1945.
14. Unfortunately, no documents are available to give us more information
    about this test.
15. NA, FO 1032/493, 8 February 1945.
16. NA, FO 936/116, 23 July 1945.
17. Initially, many of those who were hired to become interpreters in the Pool
    in the last months of the war were sent to a week-long interpreters' course
    in Brussels, which was not very useful at all.
18. It must be pointed out, however, that the only references about this facility
    were found in testimonies from the IWM. No reference to it was found in
    official documents from the NA.
19. IWM, Written Documents, Clive Teddern.
20. The phrase 'court interpreting' is used today to refer to legal interpreting,
    which can take place in several contexts, including interrogations during
    investigations, police departments, customs offices, immigration authorities

and other settings. Here, however, the phrase is used to indicate legal interpreting that takes place in courtrooms and tribunals.

21. IWMSA 10938, George H. Vassiltchikov.
22. IWMSA 10938.
23. IWMSA 10938.
24. IWMSA 10938.
25. IWMSA 10938.
26. IWMSA 10938.
27. IWMSA 10938.
28. IWMSA 10938.
29. IWMSA 10938.
30. NA, WO 309/7, 11 January 1946.
31. Officer in charge of War Crimes Group – Legal Section, North West Europe.
32. Head of JAG Branch (War Crimes Section), Headquarters British Army of the Rhine.
33. NA, WO 309/7, 11 January 1946.
34. NA, WO 309/7, 11 January 1946.
35. NA, WO 309/7, 11 January 1946.
36. NA, WO 309/7, 16 April 1946.
37. NA, WO 309/7, May 1946.
38. NA, WO 309/7, 4 June 1946.
39. Non-commissioned officer. Officers of foreign origin who had joined the British war effort, like Clive Teddern, were in this category. They could have various ranks such as sergeant or warrant officer.
40. NA, WO 309/7, 4 June 1946.
41. NA, WO 309/7, 14 August 1946.
42. NA, WO 309/7, 28 October 1947.
43. NA, WO 309/7, 7 January 1948.
44. NA, WO 309/7, 21 June 1946.
45. NA, WO 309/7, 7 January 1948.
46. NA, WO 309/7, 5 September 1946.

10
Civilian Interpreting in Military Conflicts

> 'None of us at the time was a professional interpreter. Very few people actually had a degree in English Language. No. Never. We kind of learned along the way.'[1]

Between the end of the Second World War and the beginning of the conflict in Yugoslavia, civilian interpreting had become formalized as a profession. The technique of simultaneous interpretation through booths that had arisen during the Allied war crimes tribunals in Germany (Chapter 9) became a dominant image of the interpreting profession after its adoption by the United Nations. An international association for conference interpreters, AIIC (Association internationale des interprètes de conférence), was founded in 1953 and laid down standards for working conditions and hours as well as committing interpreters to a code of professional ethics. The language needs of Cold War militaries, meanwhile, had developed in a more functional way. Linguists' most overt military roles were in the Military Liaison Missions in Germany, in the arms control inspections that accompanied détente and as defence attachés in important embassies. Under greater secrecy, military intelligence services depended on linguists to make sense of intercepted communications and trained linguist/interrogators in anticipation of a conventional war with the forces of the opposing bloc. Although military linguists derived a strong sense of professionalism from their subjectivity as members of the armed forces, their role had evolved in the perennial trade-off between training times, costs and requirements rather than being conceived and re-conceived in step with the professionalized linguist in the civilian world. The professional model of language intermediaries' careers and activities remained largely irrelevant to military language support even in the 1990s, 50 years after the formalization of professional civilian interpreting.

The militaries that contributed to the UN Protection Force (UNPROFOR) were still largely on a Cold War footing when the conflict in Bosnia-Herzegovina broke out and contained very few personnel who already spoke the language they had known as 'Serbo-Croat' (Chapters 2, 7). Their experiences from the smaller UNPROFOR deployment to Croatia and from reconnaissance missions to locations earmarked for national contingents' bases made it apparent that a high level of language support would be required to interact with the armies involved in the conflict and with local civilians. The solution was to hire local interpreters for every UNPROFOR office, every military observer team and the bases of the many battalions which formed part of the UN force. These employees were frequently students of foreign languages or professional disciplines requiring foreign language knowledge; some were teachers and others had been professionals in different fields until the Bosnian economy had collapsed. A remarkable number of interpreters, particularly around Sarajevo, were engineering students and/or the children of engineers. In small towns it was not unknown for units to hire resourceful teenagers, leaving UNPROFOR's age limit of 18 unenforced. Successful candidates received payment in hard currency, a job while troops were stationed in their location, and access to necessities in short supply during the war such as shelter, protection and food.

Many local people hired to provide military language support spent most or all of their time as field interpreters, accompanying troops to patrols and liaison meetings, rather than operating in more formal conference-style settings; a significant number also provided language assistance in office environments as media analysts or civilian clerks. Despite the changes in the character of the linguistic profession between 1945 and 1992, very often neither the local interpreters nor their supervisors situated their roles in that professional continuum. Indeed, most local interpreters lacked opportunities for professional development or advancement, while soldiers who had undergone crash courses in the local language before deploying to Bosnia-Herzegovina themselves struggled to find a career path in an organization that privileged other criteria far above language skills. This chapter highlights three particular sites of language support – the interpreters' cells at British UNPROFOR bases in central Bosnia, the network of bases centred on the British IFOR (Implementation Force)/SFOR (Stabilization Force) divisional headquarters in Banja Luka and the Linguistic Services Branch at HQ SFOR in Sarajevo. Two major issues are raised: (a) How did norms of professionalization and professionalism actually influence the work of these civilian and military linguists on the ground?[2] (b) To what extent did the post-1945 discourse of the linguist professional frame the experience of those who worked as interpreters in Bosnia-Herzegovina?

'Cracking on': the UNPROFOR years

The first local interpreter recruited by British troops as they arrived in Vitez in December 1992 – accompanied by one military linguist, Captain Nick Stansfield of the Royal Army Educational Corps (RAEC) – was hired after a chat over coffee with a salary of 200 Deutschmarks a month (Stewart 1993: 83). Over the next few weeks, Stansfield assisted in recruiting six to eight more interpreters from Vitez and nearby towns when his skills were not needed elsewhere in theatre. The quartermaster and other officers tasked with assembling this first interpreters' cell applied the British military mindset of 'cracking on', or persevering even in unfavourable conditions. Any military linguist stationed in Vitez was expected to manage the local interpreters' cell, even if – like Miloš Stanković, one of only three Anglo-Serbian members of the British Army – their own skills were in combat and command not language instruction. The dual process of recruiting interpreters and giving soldiers realistic expectations of how to communicate through them was refined by one of Stansfield's successors and RAEC comrades as the military supervisor of interpreters in Vitez. Fred Whitaker had worked with Dobrila Kalaba (a local interpreter and former English teacher) on an embryonic testing regime for interpreters:

> And so we devised a sort of rudimentary test for interpreters. I have to say it wasn't anything very scientific. But at least we required them to have an interview in English, to give them a situation, to require them to do a translation. So we weren't just taking the word of people. And then, this question of developing the interpreter, as much as anything, was briefing the interpreters on the situations in which they were likely to find themselves, and building them up, trying to do what limited amount we could not to put people in positions beyond their ability and to build them up to it. And of course they did get lots and lots of language practice within the unit, and of course they were with people who were speaking English the whole time. And so that was a help. Sadly, that young woman was killed, which was a great shock to everybody. She was shot, and...by a sniper, which was very sad. But that was, I think, as far as we were able to go.[3]

Feedback from the RAEC interpreters after their returns from theatre had a direct effect on developing British military language training

(Chapter 5). Both men shaped and taught on 'Serbo-Croatian' courses at the Defence School for Languages, while DSL also provided a 'use of interpreters' package for battalions' pre-deployment training once it became apparent that the Army's first 'military colloquial speakers' (who had passed through three-month crash courses for Russian-speakers and troops who had declared other language qualifications) had not been fully used in the field. Officers had simply been led to expect an 'interpreter', and with no more preparation than that might have expected linguists of the standard they had encountered during military liaison and arms control missions in the final years of the Cold War rather than soldiers who had been prepared with a strictly functional vocabulary limited to military tasks.

DSL's courses for military colloquial speakers contained, one attendee recalled, participants between the ranks of lance-corporal and major whose personnel records showed an aptitude for languages, in most cases a degree but sometimes A levels. Russian-speakers were preferred, since they would already be familiar with Slavonic grammar and (if there was a large enough group) could be taught on an accelerated conversion course; in practice, the demand for colloquial speakers exceeded the supply of Russian-speakers and brought in volunteers who had acquired French or German in mainstream education. Two Army corps, the RAEC (the home corps of military language instructors) and the Royal Corps of Signals (which had trained Russian linguists for signals intelligence purposes), seemed to supply a large number of trainees. Military interpreters took on rewarding and essential tasks but were detached from their own units and could not fully participate in the practices of re-affirming battalion and regimental identity which formed an important part of British military culture. This remained a source of regret and potentially left individual attachments at a long-term disadvantage in dealing with their experiences from the field.

Expanding the British military commitment in Bosnia-Herzegovina by deploying a second battalion to central Bosnia (the so-called BRITBAT 2) cascaded the interpreters' cell system beyond its original location of Vitez. At the same time, the complicated local ceasefires being agreed at the end of the Bosniak/Croat conflict – which had caught the Lašva Valley towns of Vitez and Travnik on a new front line – required ever more intensive use of interpreters in military liaison meetings. 1st Battalion, Duke of Wellington's Regiment (1 DWR), the first BRITBAT 2 battalion, ended up employing 41 interpreters in and around Bugojno. In this physically, socially and economically devastated area, demand for employment with the peacekeeping force was high. 'You only have to tell one person locally that there's someone giving work', the first military supervisor of interpreters in Bugojno remembered, 'and you're fighting them off at the door.'[4] Sinan Halilović, who had been hired as an 18-year-old when part of 1 DWR moved into Goražde (and who had interpreted for foreign militaries and police organizations ever since), was socialized into the requirements of the job and the alien culture of the British base by more experienced interpreters who had travelled with the British soldiers from Bugojno. His impression of their interpreting background was close to that formed by Whitaker and Kalaba in Vitez:

> Some of them were studying English. The others didn't.... I can't remember now. I know for two. These two who were working at the CO [commanding officer] level, they were English students, I know that for sure. The others were not. The others were kids like me. Like common kids, youngsters who were able to pick up some English. Who were able to learn English in high school and pick it up to the level sufficient to get a job. They were not trained, really. I wasn't trained. I was – I had to do it myself. I had no-one who would sit me down and say, 'Listen, this is how you do things.' I'm not trained to be an interpreter, I'm just, you know... this probably wouldn't be my career if there was no war. Probably not. Definitely not.[5]

Interpreters' military supervisors were also responsible for equipping them. 1 DWR required every patrol to have an interpreter on the grounds that, without communicating with the locals, the infantry could not perform its primary role of dominating the ground and gathering intelligence. This policy contrasted with the Dutch approach to patrols during the UNPROFOR period, where an interpreter would usually not be taken even on the 'social patrols' which aimed to 'take the pulse' of the civilian population through informal conversations – although by 1999 the Dutch troops in SFOR were 'often' taking an interpreter on social patrols (Bureau 1999; Frankfort 2002). Given the constant risk of sniper fire while outdoors, obtaining protective equipment for civilian interpreters was a matter of survival. Louise Robbins, the interpreter/supervisor in Bugojno, found she had to negotiate with the battalion quartermaster for flak jackets and helmets and protested that '[y]ou can't send soldiers out with flak jackets on and protection and the interpreters without, 'cause a bullet will go straight through them, you know, it's not fair.'[6] However, precautions were not foolproof if interpreters removed the jackets' protective plates – for sale or simply for comfort on hot days – or if they chose through solidarity with fellow townspeople not to wear the equipment. Practices of individualizing the uniform in non-functional and therefore non-military ways (such as leaving jackets open or hair loose) could frustrate supervisors, since it undermined the protective rationale behind all members of a patrol looking more or less the same (see C. Baker 2010).

Wartime interpreters in other parts of Bosnia-Herzegovina were employed by different national contingents, the UNPROFOR headquarters or the UN Military Observers (UNMO) organization. In contrast to the post-Dayton period, all fell nominally under UNPROFOR's bureaucracy, although the remoteness of many locations made UN procedures difficult to enforce or even implement. The UN ID card, supposed to facilitate local interpreters' crossing of checkpoints, required a photograph, which candidates displaced from their homes might not be able to obtain. For all the lengths interpreters and supervisors went to obtain cards, the card in practice had limited legitimacy in the eyes of local armed forces. Crossing a checkpoint operated by soldiers from the 'wrong' ethnicity – that is, from any force currently at war with another force associated with the ethnicity to which the guards ascribed the interpreter – remained a fearful moment for interpreters. It was not unknown for interpreters to be detained when a UN convoy passed through a checkpoint, and many more were threatened with detention: the outcome depended on the negotiation skills of the convoy's soldiers. Lejla Delibašić, who had worked as an interpreter for international forces since 1993, recalled that one woman had been detained for two weeks after an UNPROFOR officer agreed with checkpoint guards that she should leave the convoy. After other UN officials achieved her release, she quit the job and left Bosnia-Herzegovina. She herself had once been intimidated at a checkpoint:

I had a similar situation at the checkpoint, but the liaison officer for whom I was working, he said, 'No, it's none of your business,' he didn't actually say 'It's none of your business what her ethnic background is,' he said, 'She works as an interpreter for UNPROFOR, she has a UN ID card, you can allow us safe passage or not. You cannot, you know, take people off our vehicles and cars.' Then we had to stay at this checkpoint for about 40 minutes, until all the phone calls were made, and we were ordered to go back. We were not allowed to pass through, and then we had to file a request for a clearance for me to go back to Sarajevo with a strong recommendation that in the future we always announce our movements. But, I mean, I was not detained, you know. Yes, I had to go back to Kiseljak or wherever. So ... and it's not a good thing when you depend on the personality of your next superior. You want to have a system, you know, you want to have a standardized system in which you are working.[7]

Interpreters themselves were anxious to be situated within a more clearly defined structure and to be less dependent on informal commitments such as these. The inconsistent management of interpreters during the UNPROFOR period did little to advance the professionalization of interpreting in Bosnia-Herzegovina, especially when individuals were socialized into the job without the supervision of trained linguists.

Interpreting as logistics: the British divisional headquarters

The end of UNPROFOR's mission in December 1995 with the signing of the Dayton Peace Agreement brought massive organizational change to the multinational military mission in Bosnia-Herzegovina, though units already on the ground just removed their UN insignia, painted vehicles in camouflage colours instead of UN white and (often gratefully) adopted more robust rules of engagement. As time went on, units and individuals who returned for second or third tours acquired a greater reserve of local language capacity: for example, the liaison officer of 2nd Battalion, The Light Infantry in 1995–6 had already served a tour in Goražde in 1994–5 and fed his experiences into the battalion's pre-deployment training for platoon commanders (Barry 2008: 45, 54). This was still never great enough for units to do without local interpreters. Local interpreters employed by national contingents kept their jobs and many more were hired as the force expanded into new locations: British forces, for instance, ended up with most of the western Republika Srpska (RS) in their area of responsibility, the new Multi-National Division (South-West) (MND (SW)), and had to set up a divisional headquarters in the Banja Luka Metal Factory (BLMF). UN civilian agencies such as the United Nations High Commission for Refugees (UNHCR) remained in place, but the UNPROFOR headquarters and the UNMO organization were quickly dismantled, forcing their local language staff to seek other jobs (some moved easily from the UNPROFOR HQ to the HQ of the new force, which for the first year was supplied by the deployed HQ of NATO's Allied Rapid Reaction Corps). UNPROFOR had never interfered in low-level language support arrangements such as how interpreter cells were managed or how local interpreters were trained – indeed, it had not even expressed an opinion on how armies should balance their language needs between hiring local staff and training their own personnel.

Its absence nonetheless left language support in the post-Dayton mission even more decentred. Even the different units in Sarajevo and various branch offices that made up HQ IFOR/SFOR operated widely divergent hiring, training and staffing practices for language staff until a professionalization process was investigated in 1998 and began to be implemented in 2000.

The *Languages at War* oral history interviews contain two particular clusters for the period after Dayton: international and local civilians associated with the HQ SFOR language service and local staff employed by British forces in and around Banja Luka. Whereas interpreters at HQ SFOR were formally tested in 2000–2 and if successful became employed in a centralized language service with professional standards of staff development and translation revision, no such advancement was on offer to the employees of British forces or any other national contingent. In human resources terms, the British Army's interpreters throughout MND (SW) were the responsibility of logistics personnel at the Banja Luka Metal Factory who arranged contracts and dealt with complaints that could not be resolved between interpreters and their supervisors. Day-to-day management and tasking was the responsibility of a supervisor who might be, but increasingly (given the larger number of bases) was not, a military colloquial speaker with some knowledge of the local language and experience of the strains of interpreting.

Besides the cadre of field interpreters, BLMF as the divisional headquarters also required two other forms of language work: (a) a small team of office-based translators who concentrated on legal documents and contracts and (b) commercial, claims and finance offices whose local staff routinely worked between English and the local language. Training for the financial roles was much more advanced than training for interpreters. Jelena Vlahović, a former hospital interpreter who became a finance officer, attended three courses in the UK and Germany for Army finance clerks as her job expanded during the civilianization of certain support roles:

> I went to Glasgow, and I had Army finances training. I had three sets of training, like when I first started I was taking a job from a corporal, so the rank was corporal. And I was sent to Glasgow for two weeks' training. That was the Army Personnel Centre, where all the personnel requests and issues were processed at one place ... And I was trained there. Actually, I think I was the only civilian at that time there. It was all corporals and young soldiers who were getting trained for the trade. On the next training, that was a sergeant-graded

training, again in Glasgow. It was only I think five days or something like that, and it was at the time when the euro was introduced. So from Deutschmark to euro, because we had ... every finance office had a satellite phone, so every day after I closed my safe I had to submit a safe closure report to Glasgow. And it was done through the satellite link. ... And the third training is actually – ha, I think it's still a sub-officer [NCO] rank, because I always had a captain as my superior. ... [T]he finance office was at the same time a central admittance point for all arriving slash departing soldiers. ... [F]or the central admittance point, that was the third training I had ... So that's Army finances, training. And it was easy. Because I was already, every time I went for that training I had already been trained by my superior at home to do that. So I would go there after a few weeks doing that job already, so being trained, starting doing it, under the supervision of my boss, and after the training when I got my formal certificate, then it was done by me, without supervision.[8]

Sladana Medić, initially a field interpreter, similarly recalled being sent to procurement and negotiation courses in the UK once she started working for the division's civil secretariat. The resources and formality of this finance training compared to the ad hoc advice which was available to interpreters suggests that ensuring the highest standard of accuracy in financial reconciliation was perceived as far more mission-critical than achieving similar standards in translation. Yet interpreters themselves often remarked that they would have preferred more training in interpreting. 'Mitch' (his British Army nickname), who had worked as a field interpreter since the initial British recruitment drive in the RS, considered that the success of a mission could be in jeopardy if a lack of testing and training had produced an unprepared interpreter:

I know it's a difficult time, when you have to find a lot of people in a short period, when you are desperate for people, but even if you have employed somebody who doesn't know English, and you haven't checked properly at all, because nobody has given you any oral examination or had a real conversation with you, if you know what I mean – that, for my understanding, is even worse than just the fact that that person doesn't know English, because later on ... in the encounter situation, when there is some conflict involved, or when it might expand into something bigger or something that is dangerous ... I think that sometimes the interpreter can have the key role in resolving the misunderstanding or the problem, and in this case you would actually have a person who is unable to do anything. So you would have two opposite sides, and nobody in between to – maybe even to get them together or get them closer.[9]

The supervisory relationship between interpreters and their officers-in-charge was disrupted every six months as troops rotated in and out. A new rotation might bring a sudden change of workplace culture (if, for instance, a unit's commander preferred soldiers not to socialize with local staff or attempted to extend a curfew to interpreters' accommodation). It was at the beginning of a new rotation when local interpreters were most likely to transcend the role of facilitator and become impromptu cultural and political advisers to the military, for example when counselling liaison officers on the best way to achieve positive results when they met the local mayor. In the case of those British and US units recruited from particular regions of their countries, rotations would also force interpreters into rapid acclimatization to an unfamiliar and non-standard accent and dialect of English. Encountering a regiment on one's first day at work whose soldiers spoke Scots, Geordie English, a Welsh/English mix or even (in the case of Gurkhas) Nepalese instead of the 'BBC English' taught in Yugoslav schools could understandably shake the confidence of a new interpreter: indeed, another piece of training that Banja Luka interpreters wished they had had in advance was briefing about the UK's linguistic diversity. Supervisors might stay in post for longer under the outsourced interpreter recruitment system used by US forces, which relied on private military contractors to test and recruit two separate groups of interpreters (local people hired at the base itself and security-cleared US citizens hired in the USA). However, in this case too the officer directly in charge of interpreters would rotate in and out with his or her unit, forcing interpreters and the new soldiers to build up trust relationships once again.

A professionalized service: LSB at HQ SFOR

Unlike any other branch of the multinational force in Bosnia-Herzegovina, HQ SFOR after 2000 represented an exception to the semi-professionalized concept of the locally-employed interpreter, and it offered the most developed career structure to individuals who were able to adapt to and take on its new professional norms. The introduction of a centralized professional language service, the Linguistic Services Branch (LSB), was recommended in 1998 by the senior linguist at Supreme Headquarters Allied Powers Europe (SHAPE), NATO's own HQ, whom the deputy chief of staff in Sarajevo had invited to review language support at HQ SFOR. Having visited ten HQ SFOR locations and found that interpreters had not been professionally trained or assessed as linguists, he proposed centralizing the system and recruiting two native-English-speaking experienced language professionals to replace the dozens of military supervisors. Soldiers requiring interpreting or translation would thenceforth need to request the work through the LSB's front desk officer, introducing a welcome intermediary between the linguists and the pressure of competing demands from different parts of HQ. The LSB's chiefs would revise translations in order to provide on-the-job training and quality control, job descriptions would be written so that managers could assess what qualifications were required for each job, and existing staff would be evaluated to make sure they met the new standards. The review identified 54 posts for local nationals, 23 in a central pool in Sarajevo and 31 at those SFOR offices which would remain open after a drawdown of troops. In September 2000, 48 locally employed linguists were tested for the positions. Eight or ten had their rolling three-month contracts terminated after poor test results, while the rest were given longer contracts and assigned to jobs on the basis of their qualifications and professional experience. A further manpower and organization review in February 2001 recommended 44 linguist positions overall, with sixteen located in the central office (including the chief, Louise Askew, and her deputy chief) and the remainder elsewhere.[10]

Language support in the LSB after 2000 came closest to the paradigm of professional interpreting. Goran Šiljak, a young man who had been working as an untrained interpreter for a multinational intelligence battalion, thrived on the new professional subjectivity he was able to obtain after the centralization. He came to realize the quality difference in feedback from professionals rather than untrained supervisors and eventually put himself forward for training in the most demanding technique, simultaneous interpreting using a conference booth:

[F]ollowing the test, out of 54, I think more than 20 were let go, because they did not pass the test, which was extremely difficult, and later on when I discovered other tests that are out there to be taken, like TEFL or [the] British Council test, I think that this one rates higher when it comes to difficulty level than most of those. Anyways, those who passed the test remained, and Mrs Askew decided to pull all of us, or most of us, into the central pool. So I came to the Linguistic Service Branch very cocky, self-assured, and utterly convinced that I was an excellent interpreter. And it took me about fifteen minutes after I had met my new colleagues to realize that that was nowhere near the truth (laughs), because I didn't even know the theory. I couldn't even explain what it was that I was doing when I went into a meeting. And then I kept my head low for a while, trying to learn first of all what it really meant to be an interpreter-translator, because there is obviously a difference, which I didn't know before that.[11]

Similarly, Zorica Ilić, a former teacher who had been interpreting for the UN and NATO ever since 1993, first began to think of interpreting as a profession when the LSB reforms caught up with her office in Banja Luka:

I did a lot of reading, especially off the internet, about interpreting and translating, of course, but it was not official, it had not been done by my bosses, by anyone from the organization, it was on my own. And so it [at the LSB] was the first professional linguistic approach that we had. And I do not know to what extent it changed our habits during meetings, during interpreting, or when translating the texts. But we started thinking in that way now, officially (laughs).

...we stayed there [in Banja Luka]. Until reorganization, and Louise, I believe you know her, she established and transferred everything. And then it was the first time when we heard about (laughs) professional development, career (laughs). To think that we might, that we actually have careers, it was a career, it wasn't just surviving (laughs).[12]

Even after 2000, however, professional norms had little impact on the ways in which the roles of locally-employed interpreters were conceived outside LSB. Some individuals with language degrees who had worked as field interpreters during or shortly after the war progressed into professional interpreting with other organizations and settled abroad; some others built on their work for the military force to establish themselves as freelancers, supporting themselves with a portfolio of short-term contracts with agencies, international conferences and NGOs. Boba Vukojević, who had obtained a postgraduate languages degree from a foreign university just before the war, had worked as an interpreter for journalists and UNPROFOR during the siege of Sarajevo then become a media consultant. During her interview, she expressed concern that an influx of untrained interpreters had not only driven down rates for professionals but exposed the interpreters to complaints and blame:

> I suppose, I can't tell you with a hundred per cent certainty, but I suppose when you are not good in the language, you can make a lot of mistakes. In such a difficult environment, such as the war, and very delicate and sensitive situations, it could provoke additional problems if you are not translating and interpreting in a good way what two sides want to say. I've heard some stories that people in conflict complained about translators. Because they couldn't understand each other well. So they complained about them. But also, I know some stories when they wanted to put guilt on the translator, if the interpreter translated something in a good way, and ... they didn't want a certain situation to have been done in a good way, so they accused translator and interpreter for misinterpreting, or for mistranslating, et cetera et cetera. So I think that it's a really delicately-positioned profession.[13]

Local linguists working at all levels of the profession in Bosnia-Herzegovina – whether field interpreters like Mitch, professionalized translator-interpreters like Šiljak and Ilić, or experienced freelancers like Vukojević – would clearly have preferred their functions, strength and limitations to have been better understood.

Conclusions

The individuals who facilitated conversations during meetings, patrols or interrogations, who advised their military employers or fellow soldiers about the history, culture and society of the area and who acted as fixers and liaisons in roles which sometimes went well beyond a narrow definition of 'language support' were universally referred to in military and journalistic English as 'interpreters'. Very few of them, however, would have been trained or classified as interpreters (or translators) according to the paradigm and standards of the profession itself. Experienced professional translators from former Yugoslavia had been recruited very quickly; language teachers were the next best option for an employer seeking local 'interpreters', although there was no guarantee they would be competent in translation or interpretation skills (Dragovic-Drouet 2007: 34). As the provision of language support for peace operations in Bosnia-Herzegovina moved from desperation to professionalization, some local staff were able to accumulate cultural and social capital within the 'field' of the linguistic profession, such as the woman who began as a field interpreter in the early 1990s and by 2009 had become chief of the LSB at HQ SFOR. Professional advancement as a linguist was in fact more difficult for military linguists from the troop-contributing nations, where career structures for linguists tended to relate only to intelligence work rather than the emerging idea of 'operational language support', which was only in its infancy – if that – during the Bosnia-Herzegovina intervention.

The experience of peace operations in Bosnia-Herzegovina, combined with NATO's mid-1990s preparations to incorporate Central and Eastern European states in enlargement pre-discussions, nonetheless began to lead some military planners to give languages more consideration – although their policies and practices would be revised again after the forces' first engagements in Iraq and Afghanistan in the early 2000s. NATO's Ad Hoc Group on Cooperation in Peacekeeping recommended in 1997 that NATO members provide their soldiers with more training in the common language of the mission (effectively, in English) and also in the local language:

> There is a need for a common language capability among units deployed on missions. This is essential to both the execution of the mission and the day-to-day administration of deployed forces.... With regard to local language capability, access to competent interpreters and translators is required as an integral part of the mission, since it may not be possible, or desirable, to rely entirely on locally-recruited staff for these roles. (Ad Hoc Group on Cooperation in Peacekeeping 1997: 23)

However, no force was able to commit the resources in personnel, money and time it would have taken to meet all its language support needs internally, producing a constant demand for locals to work as linguists.

Local interpreters who had remained in the job until the late 2000s often looked back on the turn of the 1990s/2000s as a high point of the role: the years when international organizations' demand for interpreters had been greatest, the hard currency salaries had had the most purchasing power to compensate for the hardships of the work, and the contact with native English speakers (something interpreters valued highly) had been most frequent. The gradual drawdown of the multinational force in the 2000s (by the time SFOR handed over to the European Union-led EUFOR in 2004, only 7000 troops remained) reduced the

198 Languages at War

number of available posts and sometimes led to mass redundancies, such as those experienced in Banja Luka when the Metal Factory closed in 2007. The new contingents that replaced longer-standing deployments (which had often pulled out because of those countries' military commitments elsewhere) tended to pay lower rather than higher wages. Looking to the future, interpreters anticipated even less demand for work like theirs: English-language knowledge in the general population of Bosnia-Herzegovina was not the scarce resource it had been in the early 1990s, and in particular the military English programmes being carried out to prepare the Bosnian armed forces to join NATO meant that local soldiers would increasingly be able to participate in liaison meetings without needing an interpreter at all. Some former interpreters had returned to the profession they had previously been studying to join, had become full-time homemakers, or moved abroad for family reunion or education. Others had supported themselves through even less secure project work for NGOs or even by taking jobs such as logistics supervisor with private military contractors in Iraq and Afghanistan.

The extreme pay differentials between employees of international organizations and their neighbours remained a characteristic of life in Bosnia-Herzegovina long after the Dayton agreement. According to Robert Barry, the US diplomat who led the Organization for Security and Co-Operation in Europe (OSCE) mission to Bosnia-Herzegovina, more should have been done to prevent a brain drain of local professionals into employment with the 'internationals' which ultimately damaged the Bosnian public sphere. Barry wrote in a lessons-learned document for *Helsinki Monitor* during the crisis in Kosovo:

> We should not let the international agencies and NGOs coming to Kosovo do what they did in Bosnia – bid against each other for qualified local staff. Doing so results in people who should be the judges and editors becoming the drivers and interpreters at wages higher than cabinet ministers receive. (Barry, Robert 1999: 102)

Locals who wanted to build long-term careers in the linguistic profession might have disputed this equation of their role with drivers. Others did, however, regard their jobs as sidelines or interruptions, or stoically viewed the work as a short-term adaptation to (post-)wartime circumstances rather than a lifelong career choice. One woman dismissed by SFOR during the establishment of the LSB replied 'I've had four great years ... maybe it's time for me to get serious' when her manager broke the news to her.[14]

Even though a recognized interpreting profession had existed for 50 years by the time the former Yugoslav conflict was internationalized, interpreting and translating for the peace operations in Bosnia-Herzegovina was organized hastily and without reference to its professional norms. Capable 'language organizers' such as the military educators who managed interpreter cells in Vitez or the professional linguists who took charge of HQ SFOR LSB after 2000 were in short supply even though they made appreciable impacts wherever they could be found. At a time of increased civilianization of administrative, financial and blue-collar support roles, most militaries aimed to meet their language needs by using more rather than fewer civilian staff, drawing away from the use of military linguists; some, such as the US Army, turned to private contractors to supply security-cleared citizens for tasks considered unsuitable for local eyes. How else could military language support for these operations have been shaped? Near the end of one interview in Banja Luka, Jelena Vlahović suggested that SFOR's public information campaigns (which communicated messages about reconciliation and landmine awareness through a range of media) could also have been used to familiarize the public with the concept of the neutral linguist and to deliver the message not to blame the interpreter. Had local interlocutors known interpreting was a profession with a norm of impartiality, she hinted, it would have been far easier for interpreters to work and made interpreters' personal lives in neighbourhoods suspicious of SFOR more comfortable. Comparing the roles of interpreters with medics, another profession with a highly developed ethical code, leaves even the most professionalized linguist at a disadvantage. Whereas medics possess and wear widely-recognized symbols of their profession and neutrality, and even the general public is likely to be aware that they normatively adhere to certain ethical standards, interpreters do not benefit from the same recognition. 'Conflict interpreter', unlike 'conflict medic', has not emerged as a codified identity with norms of loyalty on which the performer of the role and others with a stake in the role can agree: do conflict interpreters owe their loyalty to their employer? to the fidelity of translation? to reconciliation and peace? In low-level language support such as many of the situations encountered by the multinational force in Bosnia-Herzegovina, linguists relied on nothing more than their own interpersonal skills and informally-acquired strategies in order to provide their interlocutors with the confidence, impartiality and trust which civilian professional interpreters outside the theatres of war would have regarded as absolutely basic to their profession.

Notes

1. Jovana Zorić, an interpreter who worked for UK forces 1998–2001, interviewed 18 November 2009.
2. The NATO-led force that replaced UNPROFOR after the Dayton Peace Agreement in December 1995 was named IFOR until December 1996 and SFOR until EU troops replaced it in December 2004.
3. Interview, 24 July 2009.
4. Interview, 26 February 2009.
5. Interview, 29 October 2009.
6. Interview, 26 February 2009.
7. Interview, 27 October 2009.
8. Interview, 14 May 2010.
9. Interview, 5 May 2010.
10. Interview, 31 March 2009.
11. Interview, 26 October 2009.
12. Interview, 27 October 2009.
13. Interview, 28 October 2009.
14. Interview, 25 February 2009.

11
Being an Interpreter in Conflict

'Never anything else but English...and the desire to assimilate: we were British soldiers now, we didn't want to speak German. Unless we saw a German, then we might speak German to him.'[1]

'In 1995, in Bosnia, Serbs in Bosnia were under air strikes, and then in four years, again, Serbs were attacked by NATO. And I was in NATO uniform during that time. I was also, in my mind, against Milošević and the regime in Serbia, but I was in a really bad situation.'[2]

Conceptions of the ideal role of language intermediaries occupy a spectrum from invisibility to activism. Historically, translators have been expected to render themselves unseen in the work of producing a fluent target-language text (Venuti 2008: 1–2); standards for interpreters established since the professionalization of interpreting after 1945, based on the expectation of working in ordered institutional settings such as conferences and tribunals, demand a strict neutrality in which speakers, listeners and interpreters themselves accept the interpreter as a mouthpiece that faithfully facilitates comprehension of the source. At the other end of the spectrum, language intermediaries may approach their work with the goal of political engagement or supporting a particular cause (Stahuljak 2010; Tymoczko 2000). Between these two poles lie many degrees to which translators and interpreters become voluntarily or unwillingly implicated in disseminating, resisting, selecting and representing public narratives – processes which become far more acute and fraught when linguists are working on or in conflict situations rather than in spaces with agreed norms for interaction and the resolution of disputes (M. Baker 2006).

While interpreting as a profession demands neutrality, the users and employers of language intermediaries in conflicts demand loyalty. The loyalty and neutrality imperatives need not clash when every party to a language encounter, including third-party interlocutors or receivers of texts, understands what the work of translation and interpreting involves. However, as previously seen (Chapters 9, 10), interpreters' military supervisors and users are often not equipped to appreciate the precise nature of the work interpreters do; interpreters themselves have frequently started work without being socialized into the wider linguistic profession; and third parties hostile or obstructive towards a foreign military force may treat interpreters supplied by the force as representing the force's own objectives and values. The experiences of interpreters in conflict – whether they are locally-recruited, members of the military, or security-cleared foreign civilians – are therefore situated in an arena structured by the limitations of expected or imagined loyalty. This structuring effect even extends beyond the conflict zone to affect the positioning of interpreters in asylum cases (Inghilleri 2007) or of foreign translators physically removed from the conflict when the society of the source language they work from is undergoing crisis and fragmentation (Jones 2004). Eduardo Kahane, a member of the Association internationale des interprètes de conference (AIIC), thus uses the problem of loyalty in conflict interpreting to question whether the professionalized notion of neutrality is appropriate in these situations:

> The notion of the unsullied interpreter who extracts the essentials of a message and transforms them into another language without sharp edges and roughness in the interests of communication and on the fringes of the contexts and intentions that exist well beyond the act of communication is a recent idea – what are 60 years? – that sits awkwardly with the profession's history and with the world we live in. (Kahane 2007)

The contemporary paradigm of conflict interpreting raises the expectation of divided loyalties. They are present in the ethical dilemmas facing translators in the War on Terror who must balance loyalty to their state and military with international law and moral norms (Inghilleri 2008); they emerge from the biographical narratives of many locally-recruited interpreters who participated in the Bosnia-Herzegovina case study, such as the Serb man quoted at the beginning of this paper who had to reconcile loyalty to his NATO employers with sympathy towards relatives and other members of his ethnic group who had suffered as a result of

NATO air strikes, *as well as* with his own political views that placed him in opposition to the Milošević regime. The study of interpreting during the Second World War, however, shows that interpreting in conflict may also be a matter of shared rather than divided loyalties. Whereas the course of events in 1990s Bosnia tended to position interpreters within clashing fields of loyalty, the nature of the Second World War meant that interpreters' organizational and personal loyalties became closely aligned. This chapter examines the experiences of Second World War military interpreters, particularly of those Jewish refugees from Germany who dealt with denazification and of those Britons who had been inspired to learn German before the war. It suggests that these shared loyalties just as much as the divided loyalties of contemporary conflict interpreting raise uncomfortable questions about the possibility of neutrality during and after war.

Bosnia-Herzegovina

Acting as an interpreter during and after the conflict in Bosnia-Herzegovina implicated every person who took on the role in an ongoing process of contesting or acquiescing in others' attempts to situate one within collective identities: 'locals', 'internationals', 'the Serbs', 'the Croats', 'the Muslims', 'the Brits', 'the UN', 'townspeople', 'refugees'. The ethno-political logic of the war and indeed of the peace settlement conditioned these collectivizing responses but also had roots in longer-term legacies of trust and mistrust, including the vestiges of militaries' experiences in previous conflicts (producing the idea that soldiers could only trust fully vetted members of their own armed force). To work as an interpreter and embody the position of language intermediary was therefore to attempt to find agency and individuality in normatively invisible acts of translation and interpretation. Unlike the Second World War, where the Allies had been able to provide a few thousand linguists in widely spoken languages, in Bosnia-Herzegovina even the forces that invested most in military language training (such as the UK and Denmark) were able to meet only a fraction of their language needs themselves. The vast majority of people who interpreted for foreign forces in Bosnia-Herzegovina were thus locals from that country or other parts of former Yugoslavia, selected for their spoken English, confidence and self-reliance.

This section explores the ambiguities of conflict interpreting by introducing an extended extract from an interview with 'Mitch', one of the longest-serving interpreters for British forces in the Republika Srpska (the Serb entity that governed 49 per cent of Bosnia-Herzegovina's territory under the Dayton Peace Agreement). Mitch (who chose to be referred to by his Army nickname) described himself as 'a Christian Orthodox, Serb by nationality' and had come to Banja Luka from Croatia at the beginning of the Yugoslav conflict. He went to Serbia in 1994 rather than take part in the fighting and, on returning to Banja Luka in December 1995, was one of the first interpreters recruited as British forces took up new areas of responsibility and the operation passed from UN to NATO command, tasked to implement Dayton and ensure local forces withdrew from the so-called Zone of Separation either side of the new Inter-Entity Boundary Line. An incident during one patrol, which Mitch narrated at length, exemplifies the difficult ethical decisions interpreters regularly faced:

> [W]e were on a patrol in one rural area near a town called Bugojno, when...coming out of the forest there were two locals who had machine guns or had rifles, and when we saw them, of course...one of the main assignments for the military is to take all the weapons from the locals, to reduce the number of weapons present. And especially the fighting weapons, the long-barrelled weapons. If somebody had a pistol, he was obviously supposed to have a permit for it. So we came across to the two men, who were apparently from the village nearby, and both of them had AK-47s, you know, which is an assault rifle. So we said, 'OK, what are you doing with it, where are you going?' They said, 'Oh, we went to the woods, we went hunting.' 'OK, we appreciate that, but we have to take the rifles off you.' They said, 'No you won't.' Now again it was up to the interpreter to try to, let's say, to talk out the whole situation, to calm down the whole situation first, to try to talk them into giving the rifles to the soldiers and to try to relay to the soldiers as much information as possible for them not to react hastily, or not to react in a bad manner, or not to escalate the whole situation. So in that particular case, we had...come across two pretty stubborn men, you know? So they didn't want to hand over the weapons.
>
> The result, or the biggest problem, occurred when – although I've tried my best to try to talk them into giving the weapons to us, because [I was] always trying to present myself as somebody who is closer to the local than to the soldiers, in order to try to establish a friendly relationship to the person that I was talking to, I would tell them, 'These soldiers have their orders, you know what it was like during the war, if you didn't obey the order you would have

some problems, they were told that if they find somebody with a weapon they have to take it off them, it's better for you to give them the rifles than to cause any troubles, if you don't give them the rifles they will call the police then you will have to go to the jail,' na-na-na-na. I mean, I've done my best. Then again, you know (laughs), you come across the usual question. 'Where are you from?' I said, 'Well, I'm... I'm from Banja Luka.' 'Oh, so you are a Serb.' I was talking to the two Muslim guys. I said, 'Yes, but guys, believe me, it doesn't mean anything.' 'Oh, so you were fighting against us?' I said, 'No I wasn't, I was away from the war, I came at the end of the war, at the end of '95, and I've got nothing to do with it, believe me.' Then I've started again lying, you know, 'I was brought up in UK, I come from a mixed marriage, my father is a Muslim, my mother is a Serb, but I have a Christian name [i.e. a non-Muslim name],' so la-la-la. And they said, 'No, we're not giving up our weapons.' That's what I've said to... And then, I always try to give my advice. I'm not saying that I'm the brightest guy in the world or that I'm the most experienced guy in the world, but out of all the experience that I have, I try to relay this to the soldiers, because in most cases they were just young soldiers who (laughs) can hardly clean their mouth after a meal. I mean, with all due respect, I know they are the people who are sent to the war and everything. But in these cases, you need somebody with a steady and calm hand. Because the easiest way is to pull out the rifle or the pistol and to shoot, because... but after that there is no turning back. So I said to them [the soldiers], 'Guys, please, take it easy, I'm going to try to talk them into coming down and everything.' So 'OK, OK, go on, but we're not letting them go with the rifles.' I said, 'OK, fine.'

And... after some time, and after an hour of persuasion, and trying to talk them into it, they were really stubborn and didn't want to give up. And they said, 'OK, so, you are a Serb, we don't like Serbs,' and everything, and he said, 'OK, well, ask your patrol commander, what will he do if we shoot his interpreter now?' I was like, 'Wow, hold on guys, please, calm down.' I mean, I wasn't feeling comfortable, I have to admit.... So the situation escalated and everything, and... they said, 'OK,' they've pointed the barrel at my head and said, 'OK, ask them now, what would they do if we shoot their interpreter?' because, again, I'm the one who takes all the blame and I'm being accused that I'm the one who has told the soldiers to get the rifles from them. Because if I wanted I would have told the soldiers to let them go. I'm always the one who takes the blame. And in general it is always the interpreter who is responsible for everything, unfortunately. In most cases without any true reason, but it is the easiest way to accuse the interpreter. And...luckily for me, another person, local civilian, has shown up from the village, he knew those people, and he was, whether a person of influence, or a person who was, let's say, in some way I would say educated and more...normal-thinking, to tell them 'Just give the rifles, we have as many as you like, somewhere stashed in some barn or something, just give them those two rifles, let them go, they're going to call the police and we [will] have troubles and everything.' So, you never know in a situation like this what can be next. Maybe, I don't know. Some soldier can be just nervous because he is in a situation like this for the first time and he just, if he draws the rifle or the weapon, you know...the shooting might happen, and you are always the first one on the line. Basically, someone in between. When I...so that was one thing.[3]

Mitch's story of the threat to his life on a patrol recaps several themes that recurred during his interview: the practical expectation that establishing rapport with an interlocutor was an interpreter's responsibility; the significance of his real name as 'Christian' (thus non-Muslim); the gap in maturity between young Bosnians and foreigners of the same age (their early twenties) as a result of Bosnians having lived through extreme instability; the effects of being addressed primarily as a member of a certain ethnic group; the interpreter being simultaneously the most vulnerable and the most crucial party in any encounter. A number of different subject positions were potentially open to interpreters for achieving the goal of rapport. In these fraught interactions, Mitch chose to construct himself as 'closer to the local than to the soldiers'. Others might invoke a discourse of professionalism that cleaved closer to the troops as employers, rely on the logic that wearing an army's uniform (non-badged uniforms were often issued to field interpreters) afforded one the protection of that state, or strive to convey an ethic of independence and neutrality to all parties involved.

Further complicating these subject positions was the reality that, since the war had been waged by elites constructing and exploiting inter-ethnic difference, language encounters in Bosnia-Herzegovina were mediated by a triangular pattern of ethnic relations as well as by the dimension of 'local' and 'foreign' (see, for example, Mujkić 2007). The same first name which marked Mitch as an ethnic antagonist in this incident near Bugojno (since a man with a 'Christian' name could normatively not be a Muslim) had served as a resource, in a confrontation with a group of Croat troops near Bočac, in an attempt to reduce the interlocutor's suspicion by removing ethnic antagonism from the equation (since his name was in common use among both Serbs and Croats). The heroic, agency-giving attributes of courage and fast talking that Mitch ascribes to his younger self in this anecdote were nonetheless constrained by the aftermath of violence in which 'identity' consisted of whatever the interlocutor projected on to a person's ethnicity, a frame he unsuccessfully attempted to escape by presenting himself as the child of a mixed marriage. The Anglo-Serbian British Army officer Miloš Stanković, whose memoir of his service as a military interpreter in Bosnia-Herzegovina operates within 'the idealized notion of the brave, heroic, strong warrior' (Duncanson 2009: 67), retells grudgingly playing on his Serb identity more and more frequently to develop a report with Bosnian Serb officers, and narrates it as taking an intense psychological toll on his self which eventually required therapy (Stankovic 2000).

Attempting to recover humanity and agency was all the more important to people displaced from or still living in villages, towns and cities on the front line, such as the Sarajevans in Ivana Maček's fieldwork of the siege: 'To lose control over one's life to some unknown person's whim was an utterly humiliating experience. To reassert some sense of control, at least to choose whether they would live in fear or not, enabled people to regain some pride' (Maček 2009: 47). Being forced to accept the status of a refugee or aid recipient, which might even force one to compromise ideals of a secular Bosnia and depend on religious organizations for humanitarian assistance, felt – in the words of Jelena Vlahović, an interpreter who had moved with her ethnically mixed family across three different towns in central Bosnia – like 'the greatest insult to any human'.[4] Working as an interpreter was one means of recovering agency and selfhood in besieged cities or even in economically depressed post-war towns where unemployment was endemic. Beyond the agency of producing translation itself, the job's hard-currency wages and improved access to purchasable goods allowed interpreters to provide for their families and reduced or removed their dependence on aid. Here too, however, they had to manage the contradictions of their position as intermediary.

In wartime Sarajevo, for instance, Boba Vukojević employed various levels of impression management within the ethic of shared suffering that dominated discourse in the city while interpreting for journalists and French troops. Practically, she strove to forestall malicious gossip by sharing the benefit of her work with her neighbours ('I always brought something for them, and ... never took money or anything'),

and symbolically she limited the amount of privilege journalists transferred to her by refusing to wear protective equipment during interviews
with fellow Sarajevans ('they knew that I was from Sarajevo, from the
same city, and for me it was really – I would be ashamed to wear a
bullet-proof jacket in front of them').[5] Even less extreme situations could
produce conflicting demands between one's private and work life. Bojan
Dragović had been a student at an academic-track secondary school
(*gimnazija*) when he began working for IFOR, and his mother supported
him in missing classes for his ten-day shifts: 'sometimes she did lie, yes,
about that, but of course it was necessary. It was necessary for me to
work, to help the family a little.'[6]

The interpreter's aim of successfully conveying meaning, an active
subjectivity, could often conflict with the ideal of interpreter impartiality, which demanded much more restraint from intermediaries.
Military interpreters, including graduates of crash courses at the Defence
School of Languages, were trained to minimize their presence in conversations, as Nick Stansfield, the British Army's first interpreter in
Bosnia-Herzegovina, explained: 'At Molesworth [airbase], the Americans
used to call the interpreters "lips". "Hey, lips," you know, and the lips
would come over and do the interpreting and they were supposed to be
invisible.'[7] They attempted to pass on this practice when acting as military supervisors to local interpreter teams. Soldiers expected this service
even of interpreters who were not fortunate enough to have been supervised by trained linguists. If left unchecked, troops were even prone to
viewing interpreters as tools or inanimate resources through a logistics
lens that the subjects of their gaze found dehumanizing and hurtful.
Jovana Zorić, who worked for British forces in the RS in the late 1990s,
complained of being likened to a toolbox:

> [T]hat was our favourite briefing for soldiers when they were going on
> a patrol. Don't forget your kit. I don't know, helmets, body armour.
> Don't forget your satellite box, the orange box of the satellite phone.
> Don't forget your interpreter. And we were like, as if I am a tool, sorry,
> excuse me? (laughs) I'm human, you know, kind of thing.[8]

Interpreters forced to devise an ethical code autonomously, without
access to professionalized support or training, often returned to an
image of the interpreter as mediator, which might be upset rather than
reinforced by a mouthpiece approach to translation. Sinan Halilović,
who interpreted between British officers and both the Serb and Muslim
forces at Goražde, had sometimes chosen not to translate personal

insults: 'I didn't only have to be an interpreter, I had to be a mediator, and soften some hard words said at those meetings.'[9] He saw this
not as a breach of duty but as the very opposite, a convenient fiction that enabled communication to continue and achieved his team's
higher-level aims:

> [D]on't get me wrong, people could understand. Although they
> couldn't understand the words, they could understand the facial
> expressions, really. You can't hide the hate on a face. You cannot hide
> that there is a sentence of twenty words and you're just saying 'How
> are you.' Of course, I couldn't fool anyone. The British could see that
> there was something going on, really. But I would be just dropping
> these things, in order for the communication to continue. That was
> the main thing.[10]

Many local interpreters who worked during and shortly after the
Bosnian conflict were university age or younger – though age and maturity were different concepts. (In the Bočac dam story, Mitch constructed
himself as psychologically older than a fresh British lieutenant of the
same age: 'I was 19 years old, and... I'm not saying that I've seen many
atrocities during the war, but at least I've seen them on the televi-
sion. But many soldiers who came to Bosnia didn't even know where
Bosnia is.'[11]) Most had no background or support that amounted to
professional training. Long-term residents of towns behind the lines,
such as Banja Luka, might have their first personal encounter with
the aftermath of violence during an early interpreting job: 'I didn't
see the war at all until that point' was a typical comment, made by
Slađana Medić remembering her arrival in a burnt-out Mrkonjić Grad
with British troops in January 1996.[12] These visits could often also be a
first, hard-to-deny witnessing of what had been done in their own name
by armies claiming to represent and defend them ethnically. Serbs in
particular were often forced to confront hostile foreign discourses about
the group identity with which they were under strong pressure in their
own communities to identify. Serbs who still lived in the RS, such as
Stojan Radišić (who had worked for British and Dutch soldiers), often
spoke of their attempts to add nuance to foreign soldiers' initial understandings of the conflict while also distancing themselves from their
own group's wartime nationalist leaders:

> [M]ost of the military in the peacekeeping forces, they came here
> with the opinion, good guys, bad guys. Serbs are bad guys. The rest

of the nationalities or ethnic groups are good guys. And it was black and white. So . . . we, Serbs, Serb interpreters, somehow tried to change that picture. Many times, my reaction was, 'Oh come on, come on, wait, wait! You know nothing about it. Wait.' And then we had a conversation about it. On a friendly basis. It was possible to talk without any anger, without any problems, without any . . . you know, it was possible to talk. Not with Dutch all the time. Because they had a very negative experience during the war in former Yugoslavia.[13]

With the exception of the Dutch, whose failure at Srebrenica was inescapable, most foreign soldiers were not forced to be as reflective about the actions of others wearing the uniform of their own nation-state. Foreign military linguists who did not have an ex-Yugoslav family heritage to negotiate had to confront instead their own lack of language capacity, since the time and cost pressures of military training produced linguists with only a baseline knowledge and limited vocabulary. Louise Robbins, a British military interpreter who served in Split and Bugojno in 1993–4, was conscious that her own skills equipped her for routine conversations but not to carry a high-stakes conversation on her own:

[I]f it's in a social situation you can make mistakes and everyone can laugh and it's fine, but there were high-level situations . . . where it's not good to make mistakes or it's not good just not to be good enough, and you need to take back-up with you, and say [to a local interpreter], 'Darija, come and help, I can't understand this.'[14]

Whether local residents or foreign visitors, whether military or civilian, and whether ethnically connected to the region or not, the interpreter remained, in Mitch's words, 'always the first one on the line'.

The Second World War

Being a linguist in the Second World War, and particularly during the liberation and occupation of Europe, also positioned individuals in very problematic situations. Those who were called upon to perform interpreting and translation duties, or more generally acts of linguistic mediation in encounters with speakers of a different language, were a mixed group, with a variety of different backgrounds. Their experiences as mediators between different cultures all highlight analogous paths of recruitment and training (or lack of it) to become interpreters and a similar 'situatedness' while acting as linguists. Among these interpreters/translators were British soldiers or civilians who had learned

German for a variety of reasons, foreigners who spoke at least some English, and a group of German or Austrian Jewish refugees who had left their countries of origin, arrived in Britain just before or at the beginning of the war, and then joined the British forces. The cultural belonging of interpreters and translators has been recognized as a problematic element in conflict situations (Palmer 2007: 13–14), where the relationship between commitment and interpreting is a key element in interpreters' and translators' roles. Where did loyalty stand in the process of translation and interpretation at a time when ethical rules focused on neutrality and impartiality were yet to be developed? The very nature of this conflict, which not only involved many different countries but also whole ethno-religious groups and the Jewish people in particular, was the basis of a 'shared loyalty' which characterized all those who joined the Allied effort against the Nazis. Possible legacies of longer-term trust and mistrust did not play a major role during the liberation of Europe, nor in the early occupation of Germany and Austria. By 1944, loyalties had been clearly defined within the logic of the conflict and proven through years of service with the allied forces. Those linguists who were called upon to act as interpreters, translators or more generally linguist/mediators therefore shared their loyalty to a common cause. Despite their differences, they united to fight a common enemy, the Nazis. This section will explore the experiences of interpreters on the ground at different stages, from the path to becoming an interpreter, to the flexibility of the role both in the liberation and in the occupation of Europe, and the role that languages played in the definition of identity and shared loyalty.

Interpreters and translators were mainly recruited because of their knowledge of the required language which they had acquired for various reasons during their pre-war lives. They were largely put to work with no – or very limited – interpreting training, which would later cause different levels of anxiety depending on the task they were called upon to perform. Lieutenant Charles Gowenlock Hopton Bell describes in his memoir his experiences as an interpreter dealing with Italian prisoners of war in Britain during the Second World War, initially as a civilian attached to the Ministry of Works and Planning and then as a subaltern in the Army. While working for his family business importing fruit from Italy (where he had started as an office boy at the beginning of the First World War), he had learned Italian. Here is his account of how he became an interpreter:

Business in imported fruit diminished very much month by month, ... At length, even this slender income became so inadequate in my case, that I faced the facts, . . . so I instructed my wife in the necessary formalities of it's [*sic*] day to day working, and visited the Labour Exchange, where I filled in an application form with such qualifications I possessed.

Two posts were offered me almost at once, although both necessitated leaving home.

One of these was with the BBC monitering [*sic*] Italian (now enemy) broadcasts, working in watches round the clock.

The other, which I decided to accept, was with the Minister of Works and Planning as Italian Interpreter at one or other of the many prisoner-of-war camps being constructed largely with the labour of Italians themselves.[15]

After quite a long wait, Bell received the long-awaited communication from the War Office, inviting him to attend a selection board. He spent a day 'doing intellectual tests and solving problems which became progressively harder',[16] and shortly afterwards he received word from the War Office: 'I was hard and fast in the Army, for better or worse.' His destination was a camp in the Midlands. He was a Second Lieutenant and was part of the Pioneer Corps.

R. L. Crimp, on the other hand, was an interpreter in Austria between May and August 1945. In his diary, he betrays a lot of anxiety about his lack of specific training and about the perception that his ability to speak and understand German might have been overestimated:

10th May:

Spend afternoon reading German. It looks as though my perennial 'language qualifications' will soon be put to some practical testing. What's going to complicate matters is that these Austrian [*sic*] are supposed to speak a very peculiar brand of the lingo.[17]

Basil Farrer, meanwhile, had spent the war largely in Britain before receiving an offer to serve as an interpreter at Headquarters 21 Army Group in North West Europe. In 1944, before being posted overseas, he was sent to an interpreters' course in London. Like the great majority of the testimonies of Second World War interpreters, Farrer's account of the interpreters' course is dominated by motorbike training, highlighting a seemingly greater need for mobility and independence than for the ability to do the actual job of linguistic mediation:

Then one day the officer in charge said to me: do you ride a motorbike, Sergeant? I said no.

I reported, and I met the corporal who was there to teach me how to ride a motorbike; at 47 years of age!... Eventually I was going around this field, and the first day I learned how to start and stop.... They wanted you to be independent from transport. For me it was a big thing to drive these motorbikes.[18]

Walter John Richards was the youngest person on the interpreters' course held in Brussels, which had the reputation of being very easy to pass. Richards, however, has memories of a more thorough training in actual interpreting techniques, such as interpreting in court.

We had to learn how to ride a motorbike and went out every day for two or three hours, but we also sat in the class. Everyday we did exercises of interpreting and translation; some of it was interrogation work, some of it was as Court Interpreter. When you're a Court Interpreter you have to stand there to listen to a person talk and you have to stop them, because the brain only absorbs so much, and at the same time you have to have a quick thinking in order to be able to translate into English or vice versa, what the person has said.[19]

Although training was quite limited in time, and not offered to everyone, it clearly addressed what were conceived of as the essential requirements of a specialized interpreter who had to work in occupied Germany: from the ability to move quickly using a motorbike to the crucial skill to interpret consecutively. The role of language intermediaries was flexible in all situations and theatres, and often went well beyond interpreting or translating. For example, Bell, who was billeted as an interpreter in a POW camp for Italians in Britain, was sometimes charged to be Orderly Officer. He had to count the thousand or so prisoners, inspect the meals of the British guard company, hear complaints, pay them, and more generally supervise the camp and see that everything was carried out according to regulations.

After finding out that in Austria 'everything was unintelligible'[20] for a British chap who had some basic knowledge of German, Crimp had to start his 'nattering duties'[21] negotiating with a local brewery for the consignment of some drinks. He spent his days in occupied Austria mainly accompanying an Intelligence Officer outside, or in his office where people were brought whenever a linguistic mediation was needed.

Still plenty of work in the office. Even when, like Achilles, I've retired to my tent, I'm always being bowled for across from the house to deal with some local or other who's appeared on the scene or been hauled in for questioning. The other interpreter – the 'official' chap – is only here on rare occasions. Practically all day long he's out in town, which he knows as well as any Klagenfurterer.[22]

Farrer had to carry out his flexible interpreting duties in the immediate aftermath of violence, and he describes his role more as one of psychological mediation to provide a 'friendly face' and win the hearts and minds of the locals in war-torn France:

Our duties were very strange duties. It was July '44. There was fighting in the whole area. When the British troops would capture an area, we would go in immediately after, the officer and I, and when the civilians did eventually flop back, we were letting them know that we would do anything to settle any claims for looting. This was a psychological thing to soften the blow, 'cause we were doing a hell of a lot of damage. Not war damage, looting.[23]

Tony became an interpreter while in Germany because he had studied languages at school. He was assigned to the Technical Maintenance Office, but his description shows again how flexible the ostensible role of interpreting was:

I was assigned to the TMO, the technical maintenance office ... to get the telephone exchanges working, and so I had to learn a lot of technical terms, although I was in signals I had to learn a lot more ... and then I had to take over with Petley two things, we had a number of prisoners of war .... We had to go and inspect them, to make sure they were all right, read them various orders and so on and so forth, and they did various jobs for us, you see, running around.[24]

Initially, Tony was not very confident of his ability to perform his role and of his knowledge of the language, and so he made an effort to prepare as much as possible by studying every night: 'I had very good grammatical [...] but not a lot of vocabulary. So I had to work every night to try and increase my vocabulary'.[25]

During the war of liberation, troops often encountered members of the local resistance who were very keen to cooperate with the Allies. These were local interpreters who could be used as fixers (Salama-Carr

2007: 2), for their knowledge of the territory as well as for their languages. In more contemporary conflicts such as Bosnia-Herzegovina, Iraq and Afghanistan, linguists recruited locally continued to have to cope with a stressful and problematic positioning between their fellow countrymen and the foreign militaries for whom they are working. This problem of 'divided loyalties' was not a matter of great concern in the war for the liberation of Europe. Members of the local resistance were in fact 'local interpreters', but their primary concern was to take part in the war of liberation itself and so they shared their loyalty to the same cause as the allied troops who hired them.

Henry Siraut was a member of the Belgian Resistance when a White Brigade Lieutenant, Vivian Esch, met him near Ghent in Belgium in 1944. Siraut was very young, only 18 years old, and he spoke very good English, so he was invited to attach himself to Esch's troop, C Squadron, 11th Hussars, as interpreter:

> I joined your Squadron beginning of September 1944 in Belgium. I was dressed in civilian clothes with the Belgian secret army badge. I was only 18 years old. The driver from a Scant cars sent you a message. I told the driver I was Belgian and could speak English, German and Dutch that I wanted to fight under your regiment's banner. Than [*sic*] you came in your Armed car.[26]

In this case loyalty was clearly shared, yet it is also worth stressing that Siraut did not attach himself to the British squadron because he wanted to be an interpreter, but mainly because he wanted to join the fight. He exploited his fluency in so many useful languages as a tool to make himself needed. Later, during the occupation, linguists, interpreters and translators conceived their role as a very privileged one. Not only were they 'the occupiers', but as linguists they had the power to understand both the language of the occupier and that of the occupied. Lieutenant H. B. Moyse had his first test as an interpreter with 1749 Naval Party in Minden, Germany, where his primary duty was to accompany the requisitioning officer, but he also had to interpret for the doctor, for the Military Police and even to trace witnesses for courts-martial. Clearly, military interpreters in this situation were much less concerned with being the 'friendly face' for the occupied population and were instead the 'face of the authorities'.

Being a linguist, particularly an interpreter, as the face of the occupation authorities was clearly conceived of as a highly desirable post, at least for somebody like Arnold Horwell. Horwell did not have any trouble in speaking both German (his mother tongue) and English, as his letters to his wife indicate: 'Well, this is it, at last! Harvey is the fellow who tested me and then sent me to Beule. Apparently the post at Main HQ has meanwhile been given to somebody else, and I just go through the pool like all others.... Darling I am so excited; I don't think I can find sleep tonight!' Two days later he added: 'My only dearest love, I am still in a dream, dearest,... I am going to attend the interpreters course after all...it is scheduled for 10 days.'[27]

Being an interpreter towards the end of the war and then in occupied Germany meant working in a flexible, and often a very highly charged situation. These interpreters' duties could include more complex jobs which required skills other than just language fluency, such as requisitioning, interviewing and interrogating. There were however many advantages: 'I find myself more and more getting used to the differences here and so feel more and more that these people are not "foreigners".... One of the advantages of being an "interpreter", I always have an excuse for talking to Germans.'[28] It is interesting that Horwell puts the word 'interpreter' in inverted commas and mentions being able to talk to Germans as an advantage. These linguists felt that languages and their language skills were important because they gave them status and power. Not only were they part of the victorious and occupying forces, who for example were able to live in 'luxuriously built and exquisitely furnished'[29] requisitioned accommodation, but they had one enormous advantage compared to everybody else: they could understand and speak both the language of the occupiers and of the occupied. Interestingly, there is no difference between British and non-British soldiers in the way they conceived of language skills as something which gave them status.

Tony met 'an enormous number of Germans there'[30] during the occupation and his memories are of a very pleasant time:

> I had my 21st birthday there, and I was the only English man there (7th June 1946)...anyway my birthday party one of the factories...she had this beautiful large house...and I was interested in singing and she taught singing, she'd been the pupil of Elena Gerhardt and so I studied singing with her but I had my 21st birthday party in there and there was a very good concert pianist...so that was very enjoyable.[31]

For British soldiers, language was mainly seen as a mediating tool and identity was seldom an issue precisely because language was never represented as a means of performing a different identity. However, there is a tension worth mentioning. Those British soldiers or civilians who contributed to the war effort as interpreters had learned their foreign languages in an entirely different situation (generally a deep interest for the foreign culture, which might have taken them to study in pre-war Germany; roots such as business relations with the country, as in Bell's case; family roots, as with children of mixed marriages). During the conflict, the situation in which they were called upon to act as interpreters or language intermediaries was entirely different from the one in which they had learned the language. When they first acted as interpreters, they had to assess their loyalty and conceive of that same foreign culture that had interested and fascinated them as 'enemy', although not entirely 'other'. This did not appear to be a difficult process in the Second World War, and the reason is to be found in the particularity of the nature of the war and of the enemy itself. During occupation, however, when the chance for occupier/occupied contact was greater, this fascination with the foreign culture was renewed through language. Those who became interpreters viewed their ability to speak German as a privilege.

A further group of German-language interpreters in British uniform were drawn from the 75,000 German and Austrian Jews who had come to Britain as refugees from Nazi oppression between 1933 and 1939 (Fry 2009: xi). Approximately one in seven, a total of 10,000, enlisted in the British forces and contributed to the Allied victory over Nazism. They swore allegiance to King George VI and became known as the 'King's most loyal enemy aliens' (Fry 2007). At the end of the war, the vast majority of these 'loyal aliens' were transferred to the BAOR, the Control Commission Germany and Austria (CCG and CCA), and were sent back to their countries of origin to join the denazification effort. They spoke both English and German, their loyalty had been proven during the war years, and they were eager to take part in the process of dispensing justice at the end of the conflict, just as they had been eager to take part in the fight against Nazism in the war. The choice to employ them seemed an obvious one, especially – but not only – because of their knowledge of the language. They were chosen because they could perform multiple identities: a German/Austrian identity, a Jewish identity, and a British identity shaped presumably by the British system of recruitment and training of this group of refugees. However, to what extent was coming to Britain as a refugee and being recruited and trained by British forces synonymous with the complex process of becoming British, of owning a British identity? These soldiers' identities were cultural constructs

(Anderson 1991), shaped and performed (Schechner 2002: 151) through the use of languages.

German or Austrian Jewish refugees in occupied Germany (and also when fighting with the British forces) used different ways of expressing and displaying their identities. For instance, they adopted linguistic devices such as accents to establish themselves and to negotiate their social roles, performing a British identity and hiding their German (or Austrian) former self. The fact that Jewish refugees changed their names during the war years to avoid the treatment reserved to traitors in case of capture by the Germans, and the fact that they all had to swear allegiance to the King before they could actually enlist in the fighting forces are just the most evident examples of how national and cultural identities were shaped in this context, while the naturalization process to achieve British citizenship showed the extent to which identities were performed and at the same time the extent to which this performance itself shaped identity. Language played a central part in this process. Whereas, according to Colin 'there was no psychological difficulty about accepting a change of name',[32] speaking English reflected 'the desire to assimilate. We were British soldiers now, we didn't want to speak German. Unless we saw a German, then we might speak German to him.' Willy Field went even further:

> When fighting according to the British authorities and in the eyes of everybody else I had lost my German identity, to become a British soldier.
> Being a British citizen meant a hell of a lot to me.[33]

Although some of these narrators still had very strong foreign accents when they spoke English during interviews in 2009–10, they did not seem to recall particular concerns regarding the way they were perceived by their fellow British soldiers. Colin, for example, thought that they were seen as 'British specialists. They didn't know and I didn't want them to know that I was technically still German of course.... The people we were attached to accepted the fact that we were attached to them, they didn't ask a lot of questions...security procedures were so strong and pervasive in those days that you automatically didn't ask people many questions...strictly everything anyone said or asked was on a need-to-know principle.'[34] A huge difference between ex-refugees and their fellow British soldiers concerning identity and language therefore emerges: British soldiers performed a different identity through language, but their identity was not shaped by this process.

German/Austrian former refugees, on the other hand, performed British identities in several ways: name changes, becoming part of the British war effort, fighting the Nazis, and speaking English without telling anybody of their true national origins. This performance quickly became part of their everyday life and started to shape their identity. When they were called upon to speak German again, for example to interrogate a prisoner of war or to act as interpreters, their origins had to remain hidden, with no questions asked. 'One didn't have to explain, I spoke German like a German of course... it was while interrogating Germans, German soldiers, that I might be asked how come you speak such good German, and at that point I might have to remind them that I was here asking questions, and they would please give the answers.'[35]

Conclusions

It seems ironic that while the role of interlingual mediation is widely described as a site of conflict in itself (see Salama-Carr 2007: 1–9), the role of those who have to provide the very act of interpreting and translation in conflict (fighting, liberation/occupation and peace operations) is viewed as one of negotiation and mediation, in which the element of neutrality or impartiality is one of the most important requirements in accepted professional ethical rules and codes of practices. In fact conflict situations are sites of open political, cultural and ideological confrontation, in which the interpreter is usually involved from a position of deep commitment, and in which the notion of neutral mediation is difficult to sustain.

Examples drawn from both case studies in the *Languages at War* project have identified an area of tension in the lived experiences of interpreters (or linguists who are called upon to act as interlingual mediators) in conflict: interpreters can occupy different positions along a spectrum between the two extremes of invisibility and activism. Their position is determined through resolving or failing to resolve the tension between their expected neutrality or impartiality, which requires loyalty to the act of translation/interpreting in itself, and their loyalty to a specific cause, which can be political, cultural and/or ideological. This might be described as a tension between theory, the ethical requirements of neutrality/impartiality inscribed in the codes developed for the profession after the Second World War, and reality, more specifically the reality of war, the need to work 'on the ground' with resources which are actually available.

Testimonies from the two case studies suggest a range of tensions around the idea of interpreter loyalty. A 'divided loyalty' emerges from the biographical narratives of many of those who worked as interpreters in Bosnia-Herzegovina, such as Mitch, who explained how he had to make sense of his loyalty to his own ethnic group, and of his loyalty to his employers, a foreign military force. At the end of the Second World War, on the other hand, the very nature of the conflict positioned interpreters and linguistic mediators within a game of shared, rather than divided and clashing, loyalties. Nevertheless, the assumption of shared loyalty had personal consequences for those, particularly native-speaking Germans, who were valued by their military host community primarily because of their ability to speak the language of the enemy. National assimilation through foreignness, in effect assuming the identity of the Allied brother through the language of his enemy, was one of the many paradoxes which faced those who interpreted in the Second World War.

Loyalty, whether divided or shared, does not necessarily need to be the opposite of neutrality. In war, the tensions highlighted in this chapter are most likely soluble only by accepting the particularity of war 'on the ground'. Whilst a policy of selection, training and staff development to familiarize linguists with the wider linguistic profession may be highly desirable, what emerges from these experiences of interpreters in conflict is the urgent need to humanize rather than professionalize the process of interpreting in war, to help military users and supervisors to stop seeing interpreters as 'assets', inanimate mouthpieces likely to betray, and to develop instead a more thorough sense of them as the individuals we have seen in this chapter, people placed by virtue of their role in a variety of tense situations, to whom all sides in a conflict will owe a duty of care and respect.

A commitment to neutrality has, of course, been the foundation stone of the professional subjectivity in interpreting that has developed between the aftermath of the Second World War and the present day. The voices of interpreters in this project show that being an interpreter in war and conflict deconstructs this paradigm of neutrality. Indeed, the paradigm itself may serve to reify the interpreter as a tool or machine rather than a person whose physical and moral discomfort must be considered. Whether conflict places interpreters in a situation of shared loyalty as in the Second World War, or a situation of divided loyalty as often in Bosnia-Herzegovina, language intermediaries are themselves positioned and implicated in these loyalties. Intermediaries in either type of situation have agency in war, and the intermediary above all should be aware of and understand this agency. With the possession of agency comes a weight of responsibility, and this responsibility is ultimately personal rather than professional.

Notes

1. Interview, 10 December 2010.
2. Interview (Stojan Radišić, Bosnian interpreter), 11 May 2010.
3. Interview, 5 May 2010.
4. Interview, 14 May 2010.
5. Interview, 28 October 2009.
6. Interview, 12 May 2010.
7. Interview, 17 September 2009.
8. Interview, 18 November 2009.
9. Interview, 29 October 2009.
10. Interview, 29 October 2009.
11. Interview, 5 May 2010.
12. Interview, 4 May 2010.
13. Interview, 11 May 2010.
14. Interview, 26 February 2009.
15. IWM Documents, 92/13/1.
16. IWM Documents, 92/13/1.
17. IWM Documents, 96/50/1 & PP/MCR/245.
18. IWMSA, 9552.
19. IWMSA, 17355.
20. IWM Documents, 96/50/1 & PP/MCR/245.
21. IWM Documents, 96/50/1 & PP/MCR/245.
22. IWM Documents, 96/50/1 & PP/MCR/245.
23. IWMSA, 9552.
24. Interview, 4 June 2009.
25. Interview, 4 June 2009.
26. IWM Documents, 67/384/1.
27. IWM Documents, 91/21/1.
28. IWM Documents, 876–88/55/1.
29. IWM Documents, 91/21/1.
30. Interview, 4 June 2009.
31. Interview, 4 June 2009.
32. Interview, 10 December 2009.
33. Interview, 2 December 2009.
34. Interview, 10 December 2009.
35. Interview, 10 December 2009.

Conclusions

The *Languages at War* project was initially designed to explore the interaction between policy and practice where language issues arose in two conflict situations: the Allied presence in continental Europe from 1944 and the NATO operations in Bosnia-Herzegovina from 1995. The first major finding challenged the initial design of the project: language issues far exceeded the scope of explicit policies, making it more productive to begin by examining the broad range of language practices in the two conflict situations. It is clear that languages are woven through all aspects of the two conflicts. The interaction of languages occurred in many key areas of military operations in these conflicts, and permeated the entire experience of conducting war and managing peace. In this sense, the research has opened up new areas of enquiry, which are more extensive than was expected, and which were previously almost unexplored. As the structure of this book suggests, there are four main areas in which languages have proved to be particularly important:

1. *Intelligence.* Knowledge of other languages and cultures proved crucial to understanding the different parties to the conflict, whether through monitoring media and communications, through investigation and interrogation, or through contact with other intelligence sources. A key element in this is the framework of understanding within which language resources are mobilized and directed.
2. *Preparation and support.* To operate effectively, the armed forces need to be prepared for their encounter with relevant languages and cultures, and provided with professional support services. In some cases, the preparations in this area proved to be less extensive than were required on the ground, and language support was at times very ad hoc. Moreover, decisions made by the military on how to approach

languages may cast a long shadow over the countries in which they are deployed.

3. *Meetings between the military and civilians.* The battle for hearts and minds emerged as a key requirement in both conflicts. Capability in language and culture proved useful in supporting peace-building and reconstruction in partnership with civilian populations. However, there were complexities and tensions in the 'fraternization' of military with local civilians, which highlighted the fundamental asymmetry of relationships on the ground.

4. *Communicating through intermediaries.* The availability of military linguists was limited both by the shortage of trained personnel and by the difficulty of providing recognition and incentives for military personnel to take up specialized language roles. In both conflicts, civilian interpreters and translators played a vital role in communications. They were often locally-employed civilians, whose relationships and loyalties were a cause of frequent concern. But they often provided important links with the community, local expertise and even a degree of continuity between successive deployments.

Although these areas of activity are closely interconnected, each has its own logic and culture, and its own relationship to policy. The conclusions that emerge from them can usefully be presented separately.

Intelligence

Intelligence gathering and analysis are closely connected to a country's level of preparedness to face potential risks and threats, and hence to be able to survive in an unpredictable and changing world. Its capability in this area is intimately linked to its ability to understand foreign languages and cultures. Failures of intelligence are often blamed when states are taken by surprise by events or when they are unable to react rapidly enough to the implications of what is actually happening around them. Whilst commentators may argue about the exact causes of one of these specific intelligence failures, there is nevertheless a broad consensus about the type of problems that typically engender errors in intelligence.

Some intelligence failures are clearly systemic, intrinsic to the intelligence systems that have been established. There may, for example, be lacunae in the processes by which intelligence is gathered. There may be shortcomings among the diverse agencies engaged in intelligence in the ways in which they share vital information, and hence build up a coherent picture of the risks presented by certain situations. The failure to anticipate attacks from the outside – Pearl Harbor in 1941, the 9/11 Twin Towers assault – are often given as examples of these types of failure. Other causes of intelligence failures, however, are ascribed not to ignorance or poor intelligence organization but rather to the frameworks of analysis, interpretation and reception, which are applied to the information once it has been gathered. This has emerged as a significant issue in what has been called the 'post-normal science' scenario where 'typically facts are uncertain, values in dispute, stakes high, and decisions urgent' (Funtowicz and Ravetz 1993). In these scenarios, reliance on traditional tools of scientific methodology, such as testable assumptions and hard empirical evidence, may prove inadequate and even damaging. Heazle (2010) helpfully distinguishes between tactical and strategic assessment. Tactical assessment makes specific assertions about the existential and the spatial (what exists where), strictly related to the present. Strategic assessment, on the other hand, is more clearly interpretive, placing information gathered within the context of 'an existing logic and accepted set of assumptions' (Heazle 2010: 294). At this point, what clearly comes into play are the frameworks of analysis, those attitudes and assumptions which are held by analysts and observers. These often develop into consensus perceptions, where a healthy attitude of questioning disbelief is submerged in shared a priori assumptions: 'confronted with evidence which did not fit their assumptions, the reaction...was to question the motives of those who produced it' (Watt 1989: 529). Language issues emerge with urgency in the formation of the beliefs and disbeliefs which are key to the strategic assessment of intelligence. Critically, they concern the 'foreignness' of the material with which intelligence typically deals. Foreignness needs to be transmuted into something sufficiently accessible and domesticated for planners to make strategic assessments. But, on the other hand, unreflecting domestication can eliminate the unfamiliar context and patterns of thought that give character and specificity to the intelligence gathered. This has proved to be an issue whatever the source of intelligence: directly available open material, covert operations, signals intelligence, personal reports, investigations or interrogation. The role of foreignness is most often a missing dimension in traditional understandings of intelligence. Foreignness affects perceptions of 'the other' and hence the frameworks that are adopted in order to select and analyse the intelligence that has been gathered. A recognition of foreignness enables intelligence to be viewed as a more complex product, which has passed through a medium of exchange, a translation, which is neither transparent nor neutral. It also enables a clearer understanding of the personnel who must be recruited to mediate this foreignness. Their knowledge and competence may prove difficult for all involved.

A large proportion of intelligence information emanates from foreign sources, arriving in its raw form, written or spoken, in a language that is not normally that of the planners and must therefore be translated for them. This process of mediation, of rendering the foreign intelligible and therefore assessable, is an integral part of the way in which beliefs about 'the other' in intelligence terms are constructed. A notion that what is at issue here is the apparently simple one of accuracy, of producing a translation in English faithful to the original, fails to engage with the fact that translation is neither transparent nor neutral as an exercise. Features quite external to the translated words themselves may provide framings that will condition responses to the material. The current knowledge of the intelligence community about terrorist threats, for example, relies for much of its open material on well-funded translation programmes which select, translate and distribute an enormous amount of documentation on the Arab and Muslim worlds. As Mona Baker has argued in relation to one of these translation programmes, the Middle East Media Research Institute (MEMRI), the languages (and therefore countries) from which MEMRI chooses to translate its texts, the selection of this material and the ways in which its translations are headed, grouped and cross-referenced to other translations all provide a framework through which particular representations of the documents are created, a process which is entirely separate from any intrinsic textual criteria of accuracy and faithfulness (M. Baker 2010b).

During the Second World War, the experience of Bletchley Park challenged the traditional separation of translation and analysis in dealing with foreign intelligence texts. The orthodoxy was that each piece of intelligence was separate and sacrosanct, and that the process of translation should avoid drawing relationships between documents, and thereby risking contamination. However, practice demonstrated that accurate intelligence could not be derived without a sophisticated linguistic infrastructure, and that each piece of raw intelligence had to be related to its overall cultural background in order to be understood and properly analysed. Conversely, divorcing the analysis of a foreign language text from its producing culture, and from other texts related to it, could lead to misinterpretations, with potentially dangerous consequences.

The continued invisibility of foreign languages within contemporary discussions of intelligence gathering and evaluation may relate in part to these broader issues of how the process of translation is regarded. A translated text is a constructed product, resulting from a series of judgements and decisions, at different stages, in which prior knowledge is a key factor. It may result in a foreign text being 'domesticated', screening out key aspects of its essential foreignness. This in turn can encourage recipients of such translations to maintain a type of cultural parochialism in which translated intelligence is compared only with similar texts and situations in English, rather than inviting speculation on what may be unknown and as yet, in intelligence terms, unthinkable.

Beyond the realm of the sort of material that is openly available for consultation, most intelligence systems depend to some extent at least on recruiting their own language intermediaries whether for covert operations, or to translate the signals or human intelligence that is obtained. Paradoxically therefore, the quality of intelligence assessment becomes at least partially dependent on intermediaries who will have derived their precious language skills either from birth within the community from which intelligence is sought, or from close association with the potentially hostile enemy country as a result of residence and/or long-term study of its culture and society. From the point of view of the intelligence institutions, the balance between on the one hand, security and trust, and on the other, the recruitment of the requisite foreign language and cultural competences, is an issue with which all intelligence operations clearly have to deal. The position of these vitally important 'alien others' within the system, and the attitudes of their employers towards them, have thus far been largely invisible in studies of intelligence. How do such language intermediaries understand their own role in the intelligence networks? And what effect does this holding of multiple cultural identities have upon them and upon their working lives?

The experience of British intelligence in the Second World War provides some answers to these questions. Perhaps the most striking feature is the breadth of intelligence roles for which competence in a foreign language was required, including operators intercepting wireless conversations and translators at the Bletchley Park nerve centre, among others. Language requirements were defined by the technical environment within which language skills were to be used. Language competence was rarely seen as a sufficient qualification in itself but was part of a broader profile of technical and intellectual expertise. The intelligence requirements of the Bosnia-Herzegovina conflict were considerably narrower, but knowledge of the language and culture proved valuable for a field officer like Milôs Stanković (Stankovic 2000) or an investigator like Eric Wilson, whose role was to debrief refugees. The capability in psychological operations and media management was heavily dependent on civilian employees, but their military supervisors were more effective when they understood the material they were handling.

The position of linguists within the intelligence services raises questions of the foreignness of personnel. How can national authorities assure themselves of the loyalty of people who have close associations with the enemy culture? That association may be largely derived from education, but it will often be accompanied by personal experience of the culture and a degree of commitment to a place and its people. Since the supply of British-educated foreign language speakers is limited, language skills must also be sought from people with a family background in the culture and even from available non-nationals such as refugees or migrants. In all these cases, the intelligence services develop views on the acceptable compensatory limits within which difference can be safely and securely accommodated. The interaction between foreignness and security ensures that the issue of trust pervades all intelligence work and indeed extends to most other areas of military operations where languages are involved. In the Second World War the benchmark of trustworthiness was often that intelligence personnel, and especially interrogators, should show a hatred of the enemy. This fitted well with the attitudes of 'loyal aliens' who had themselves been the victims of Nazi repression, such as German Jewish refugees. However, a degree of suspicion still pervaded attitudes towards people who demonstrably had a deep knowledge of the foreign language and culture.

Linguists in intelligence appear to accommodate their own experience of cultural plurality in a variety of ways. For those in direct contact with the foreign culture, the likelihood of personal stress may be high. People intercepting wireless messages or listening in to conversations through bugging devices may feel ambivalent about their own position in eavesdropping on people with whom they sympathize culturally, the sort of people they may have met in previous encounters outside the conflict. People interpreting for interrogators may feel ambivalence arising from the intimate engagement with people face to face. And interrogators who bring their own knowledge of foreign language and culture to the role may feel this more sharply still.

For linguists who experience this type of cultural ambivalence or who are subject to mistrust within the intelligence environment, the principal strategy for dealing with it appears to be to focus on the professional aspects of their work rather than its human implications. They often develop a sense of solidarity with other language specialists and perhaps construct their own group identity within the intelligence structure in which they are placed. In the Second World War listening posts, those with foreign language skills seemed to bond together, operating in effect as a secret, and largely invisible, band of linguists inside the secret service. At Bletchley Park, linguists were subsumed into a broader grouping of academic researchers or female sections of ancillary language assistants. Loyalty to a broader ideal, whether the pursuit of knowledge or professional standards of working, were key elements in the identities they constructed.

The availability of suitable personnel is a recurrent problem, whether the need is for German speakers in 1945 or Serbo-Croat speakers in 1995. The eruption of conflict in Bosnia-Herzegovina highlighted the difficulties in finding people familiar with the language and culture of a small country that had not hitherto figured in the military planning of NATO states that were called on to intervene. The conflict revealed the limitations of intelligence capability, which was constrained by the marginal place of the region in the education systems of NATO countries like Britain. Much intelligence work was conducted within an ad hoc framework of understanding, stitched together from a collection of memories of the Second World War, cultural stereotypes of the Balkans as a fiery, unstable and ungovernable region, and tourist information presenting the warm and hospitable nature of coastal resort areas. This ad hoc framework was reinforced by the small amount of published material available, in the form of two language learning textbooks and a few literary translations. Where expertise existed, in a handful of universities, it was very much in the shadow of Russian studies and was regarded as a somewhat exotic elective subject. Even within Serbo-Croat studies, Bosnia itself rarely figured in its linguistic and cultural complexity. In many ways this situation can be represented as a crisis of understanding, since an urgent need to grasp the reality of the region remained largely unmet, at least in the earlier stages of the conflict.

To a large extent, Bosnia-Herzegovina is paradigmatic of the military and strategic landscape that emerged at the end of the Cold War. When conflicts flare up in little-known areas, international forces are called on to intervene but lack the intelligence capability to respond effectively. In the absence of native expertise, forces are obliged to act on the basis of ad hoc understandings, inherited from a diffuse assortment of historical fragments. These limitations were painfully clear to many of the people who were put in the position of remedying them, through language teaching, cultural briefing or operational training. Those who were interviewed for the *Languages at War* project had often worked extremely hard to set in place programmes for intelligence officers and military personnel more generally, to prepare them for their roles in operations. With time, these programmes offered effective preparation, but they continued to function against a background of relative lack of interest in wider society and within the education system in particular.

Preparation and support

The lengthy and detailed preparations for the liberation and occupation of continental Europe stand in stark contrast to the scramble that accompanied the first stages of the UN/NATO intervention in Bosnia-Herzegovina. Where the Allied forces were able to choose their timescale in the months leading up to the landings of 1944, the NATO forces were mobilized at short notice in the winter of 1992. The preparation for landings in occupied Europe began almost as soon as the USA entered the war in December 1941, though the build-up to the Normandy landings only gathered pace after 1942. The vast machinery of preparation focused primarily on training personnel for the ships, aeroplanes, munitions and other materiel, which were the means of winning the war. But the Allies nonetheless developed time and space in order to train in the so-called 'soft' skills that would be crucial to winning the peace. By contrast, the Bosnian intervention could not have been foreseen before the descent of Yugoslavia into open war in the summer of 1991, and at that stage it was not at all clear that British or NATO forces would become involved. The UN peacekeeping force (UNPROFOR) was established almost a year later, leaving little time for the British troops to make suitable preparations.

Where the Allies were able to prepare systematically for the battles to come and their longer term presence, NATO battalions had little specific preparation and no certainty about their future role. The Allied plan was to liberate the continent and to introduce a new post-war order on the rubble of Nazi Germany and its empire of occupied European countries. This was a project of historic magnitude, and was carefully planned over two years or more. The NATO forces had no such vision. The break-up of Yugoslavia was a regional sideshow in the context of the fall of the Berlin Wall and the collapse of the former Soviet and socialist states. The outside world was drawn in reluctantly and with a great deal of confusion over the precise nature of the job the armed forces were expected to carry out.

On the other hand, NATO was able to call on small battalions of highly-trained professional soldiers, whereas the Allies in 1944 had to manage huge conscript armies. The scale of the two operations was quite different, with thousands of troops committed to Bosnia whereas several million were involved in fighting and occupation at the end of the Second World War. Where the Allies were tasked with occupying, administering and rebuilding whole countries, the NATO forces were deployed with a more focused military remit, working alongside a host of civilian agencies. There were certainly advantages in being able to concentrate on a finite range of purposes, though in practice the military were increasingly used for rebuilding work and civilian/military cooperation (CIMIC).

What remains common to both the cases is an underlying conception of the value of preparation in language and culture. This can be simply stated as the acquisition of capability that can contribute to a successful outcome to operations. However, in acquiring the capability, the military applies a cost–benefit analysis, as was stated clearly in a NATO minute of June 2004:

> Whereas language is the most complex of human behaviors, and the attainment of high levels of language proficiency require lengthy periods of intensive instruction, it is important that language requirements such as the NATO Force Goal EG 0356 for language proficiency meet dual requirements of being high enough to meet operational needs while not being so high that training time and costs are prohibitive. (BILC 2004)

Military planners are required to appraise whether the cost of training is commensurate with the purpose it is to fulfil. In both conflicts, the ultimate mission and motivation centred on winning the hearts and minds of the target population and eventually being able to hand over to an appropriate civilian authority. Undoubtedly, it was recognized by planners that relationship building was a major priority and that language and culture would play a role. It is easy to understand why they were willing to invest substantially in a long-term conflict, such as the Cold War, but less willing to devote large sums to preparing for a conflict, such as Bosnia-Herzegovina, in which they considered they might not be involved for long. This has a direct implication for training in language and culture, quite apart from the uncertainties around the nature of the conflict. The length of time required to achieve high levels of language competence is very significant, and not very elastic.

Cultural briefing, by contrast, is comparatively inexpensive. Where language training is measured in weeks and months, cultural training may be measured in hours and days. It is not surprising that recent NATO doctrine has argued that 'Whilst all personnel can benefit from enhanced cultural capability, language capability will remain a specialization' (Ministry of Defence, Development Concepts and Doctrine Centre 2009: 1/5–1/6). A similar calculation was made by the Allies, who distinguished sharply between the preparations offered to the large masses of troops and those provided for Civil Affairs personnel, who were expected to be the main point of liaison with representatives of the former enemy.

Specialist language training was very different in the two conflicts. Training for civil affairs in the mid-1940s made some provision for language learning, though in practice it was largely squeezed out by the plethora of other topics these personnel required. Many military learners failed to see the point of the exercise. Often, the most significant part of their language preparation was the range of written materials in foreign languages that they would be required to use.

In the 1990s, by contrast, the notion of civil affairs officers was no longer in use, as a large proportion of military personnel in Bosnia-Herzegovina were engaged in relations with local civilians or paramilitary militias as part of their peace support operations. Preparatory language teaching was offered to a relatively small number of personnel who would be expected to use the language in theatre, and was typically organized as an intensive course of several weeks rather than as a minor portion of a more general course. The type of language teaching was initially rather haphazard, owing to the limited availability of staff qualified to teach Serbo-Croat. But, as provision developed, it was increasingly organized on a functional or communicative basis. Learning focused on tasks that might need to be carried out on the ground and included role-play and simulated scenarios. This largely replaced the grammar-translation approach, and proved more effective and more motivating to learners. However, it may not have achieved the integration of language and culture achieved by civil affairs officers in the 1940s as a side effect of their broader curriculum.

The great majority of troops deployed in both conflicts were non-specialists, whose language preparation was remarkably similar. The ubiquitous Pocket Guides, issued to all Allied service personnel, presented languages as part of a broader engagement with a foreign country. Rather than offering language learning, they focused on giving troops a meta-language, which would help them to develop their ability to make themselves understood (in English as well as in the foreign language), using any available elements of body language, tone of voice, sign language and strategies of discourse (don't ask open questions, look for yes or no answers). The handbooks of 1995 offered a dozen pages of useful phrases, along with summary ethnography, supplemented by language cards that troops could refer to during operations. The instructions on meta-language included how to use the cards.

The emphasis on cultural rather than linguistic training raises a concern that trainees may not move far beyond a superficial acquaintance with the prevailing stereotypes. For the Allies, these stereotypes were primarily functional, providing troops with the attitudes required in order to fulfil a particular task, whether through peremptory commands to hostile aliens or courteous requests to the grateful liberated. For the NATO forces, the stereotypes were aimed at providing ways of recognizing and dealing with warring factions. The US *Bosnia Country Handbook* (Department of Defense 1995), for example, devotes three paragraphs to this, under the title 'Ethnography', enumerating the ethnic groups, the language varieties and the religious groups. To some extent there was a difference of familiarity, in that the languages and cultures of France, Germany and Italy were well known to many in the British officer class, who could be presumed to be relatively comfortable with them. Bosnia-Herzegovina, by contrast, was a small country of which little was known, even by officers. The difference for the mass of troops may not have been so great between the two cases, since the rank and file of the era before foreign holidays may well have felt the near continent to be just as foreign as their later counterparts felt a small Balkan state to be.

A particular lesson of Bosnia-Herzegovina is that an international military force does not operate in a hermetically-sealed linguistic environment. There is clear interaction between an institutional language policy and the socio-political linguistic circumstances outside the force. This was scarcely seen as an issue in 1945. The Allied forces undoubtedly increased the use of English across the continent. And they certainly accelerated the importation of English or American words or phrases into French, German, Italian and other European languages. But they barely affected the status and identity of those languages. In Bosnia-Herzegovina, by contrast, decisions regarding language taken inside the force had ramifications for language issues in the wider society. The language policy of the UN/NATO forces evolved on the basis of a pragmatic response to the language demands of the former warring sides. These demands were part of the broader peace-building context and it seems likely that the force's language policy fed into the divisive post-conflict identity politics. By accepting the idea that Serbian, Croatian and Bosnian should be treated as three distinct languages, particularly in written translations of documents, the force contributed to the efforts of political and intellectual elites to keep the constituent nations apart and to use language as a tool of discrimination on an ethnic basis. Conversely, in a narrower context, the three-language policy may have facilitated the peace-building process by allowing for negotiations on the military aspects of the Dayton Agreement between the NATO force and the former warring sides to proceed smoothly. It may also have encouraged more tolerant approaches to language in more recent defence reforms.

More broadly, the question remains whether the lessons of language preparation and support identified through experience of the two conflicts were learned at the time and passed on to later cohorts. In both conflicts, the transition to other conflicts provided an obstacle to the process of learning lessons. The wars that followed the Second World War were of a different nature, with the Cold War setting an overall strategic context within which a multiplicity of small regional conflicts was pursued. The crisis of former Yugoslavia marked the end of this period and the beginning of a new world order, whose implications took several years to understand. A further factor working against learning lessons was the regular rotation of troops and consequent loss of institutional memory.

Meetings between military and civilians

Relationships with civilian populations are well known to be increasingly important for military interventions of all kinds, but especially for peace support operations. Effective counter-insurgency, for example, demands an understanding of those cultural environments in which troops are to be deployed. Kilcullen argues persuasively that: 'The bottom line is that no handbook relieves a professional counter-insurgent from the personal obligation to study, internalize and interpret the physical, human and ideological setting in which the conflict takes place... to borrow a literary term, there is no substitute for a "close reading" of the environment' (Kilcullen 2007).

In practice, military responses to this situation have largely been dominated by approaches drawn from anthropology, a disciplinary domain most famously embodied in the five-person social science teams (Army Human Terrain System) sent in to advise US military commanders in the field in Iraq and in the data sets of local information pioneered by the cultural anthropologist Montgomery McFate (McFate 2004, 2005). Academic anthropologists in the United States have been highly reluctant to support the close association of their discipline with military exercises, and the American Anthropological Association has condemned such activity (Weinberger 2008). However, anthropological models in preparing soldiers to meet local civilians have undoubtedly remained a central feature of pre-deployment training packages.

In perhaps the most developed of these programmes, for example, that of the US Air Force, the aim has been the generic rather than the specific, 'culture-general' competences rather than 'culture-specific' ones: 'The ability to quickly and accurately comprehend, then appropriately and effectively act, in a culturally complex environment to achieve the desired effect – without necessarily having prior exposure to a particular group, region or its language.' Overall, such an approach tries to ensure that students understand and engage positively with cultural diversity: 'Cultures are different, not one better' (Sands 2009). British training programmes similarly adopt a generic perspective, their experimental cultural analysis template for instance asking soldiers to consider what historical and ideological impetuses have created the groups they will be meeting: 'How does the group describe its history and where it comes from? What are the key formative events in the group's history?... Do the group members share religious beliefs... What are the important rituals that the group uses?' (Tomlinson 2009).

In general, what is at issue here is the creation of an intellectual atmosphere in which personnel can begin to think about the background of people they are about to meet. Whilst there is certainly a suggestion that looking at the practices of others may serve to relativize our own, the gaze of understanding is resolutely directed outwards. In a sense, the emphasis is less on an expected face-to-face encounter, soldier/civilian, and more on the generic situations in which military personnel might find themselves when on duty in foreign countries, so that 'intercultural communication' is placed alongside 'conflict resolution' and 'participant-observation'. Overall, the soldier stands at the centre of the training, with his sensitivities and emotional needs as key problems to be addressed: the Dutch teaching model, for example, describes the importance of minimizing the soldier's 'culture shock' and helping those on duty to become 'comfortable with difference' (Bosch 2009). Communication with local foreigners is arguably less important than enabling the military to come to terms with the fact of foreignness, in effect helping soldiers to domesticate this foreignness in order to become more operationally effective, what the American programme sees as making 'the foreign more familiar and more comfortable to operate in' (Sands 2009).

Sensitivity to cultural contexts does not replace language, however. Words, spoken or written, serve to condition the whole soldier/civilian encounter. However well-informed and friendly the 'Friendly Faces' of troops may be, the voices that issue from their mouths, or indeed their relative muteness, will have implications for their own behaviour and for that of others around them. Languages are a key element in setting the terms for putative soldier/civilian meetings in culturally complex environments of war. The most important element here is not the ease and linguistic fluency of these exchanges but rather the effect that military language policies, adopted either consciously or unconsciously, have upon the perceptions of those civilians in whose country the army has arrived and upon the efficacy of the operations themselves. Meetings between military personnel and foreign civilians in any conflict situation bring with them a set of assumptions about the languages of both parties which are as relevant to inter-cultural exchange as the histories, ideologies or beliefs of the two sides.

In 1945, the attitudes of two occupying armies towards the use of their own language played a key role in framing relationships between the military and the civilians on the ground. In the French zone, the French language itself immediately became a prime instrument of occupation policy. The goal of the French occupiers was to ensure that the majority of civilians in their zone of occupation were learning, or at least had the means to learn, as much as possible of the French language. To this end, educational systems were radically modified, French language teachers were drafted in, and cultural and publishing policies were mobilized in order to support the spread of the French language. In the British zone, by contrast, the English language was represented as the language of the governors, a mark of political power that excluded those who did not speak it. The two different approaches drew on the colonial model that each country had developed over the previous century or more.

This contrast was clearly exhibited in the different attitudes to language support services. The French saw interpreting and translating as a vehicle for spreading French language and culture. They used these services as a means of ensuring that correct French would be used at all times and in all places. The British, on the other hand, saw the English language as a barrier to protect the occupying community. They developed a somewhat ad hoc system of interpreters and translators, whose job was largely to transmit British administrative wishes to the population beyond. The impact of these policies was felt after the onset of the Cold War, when much warmer personal interaction between the occupying military and civilians in Germany was politically desirable. The reluctance of many British nationals to 'do battle' with the German language became a serious obstacle to cultural contact on the ground.

Languages are embodied, and communication is dependent on the circumstances and settings in which the physical entities involved, army personnel and local civilians, actually meet. The ways in which the military occupies the spaces it takes over in the foreign country, and its naming of those spaces, draw a landscape of war and conflict which positions speakers on all sides. The soldiers' comfort zone, which cultural preparations may have sought to establish as a buttress against unhelpful culture shock, is also one which, it appears, domesticates the foreign, providing troops with a vital temporary 'home away from home' for the duration of their deployment. Intercultural communication in war and peace-building is therefore neither neutral nor necessarily benign.

The foreign soldier physically and linguistically present in a local community takes on an outsider status by virtue of his or her mobility. Whether in 1945 or 1995, the soldier will leave the territory and resume his or her personal life in a different locality and state. In recent times, troops will often know the very date of their departure. During deployment, they have a degree of physical mobility denied to the local population, typically putting them at a distance and even posing a threat as their reckless driving frequently causes road accidents. Despite their act of presence, they resembles the figure of Georg Simmel's 'stranger': 'the fundamentally mobile person comes into contact, at one time or another, with every individual, but is not organically connected, through established ties of kinship, locality, and occupation, with any single one' .(Simmel 1950: 404).

Troops in Bosnia-Herzegovina constructed a parallel layer of geography in the space they shared with locals. Troops at the Cherbourg docks constructed a parallel layer of time. Even when a deployment is not constructed as an occupation in legal and political terms, troops remain occupiers in a spatial sense. As occupiers, they are not 'at home' but in a place where they possess certain measures of power and authority and which they can leave at will (though normatively at the will of the organization rather than the individual). Therefore, they appropriate the place linguistically, stamping names from their own language and culture on the foreign space, as a means of re-establishing a usable conceptual home. It is rare that these names outlive the occupation, though there are notable exceptions, such as Omaha Beach in France in

1944 and Arizona Market in Bosnia-Herzegovina in 1996. In renaming places, the occupier increases the distance between military and civilian zones of action and reinforces the dichotomy between inside and outside. This phenomenon appears to be a constant throughout the two case studies and is likely to hold true for other military deployments.

The language of fraternization and its overwhelmingly sexual connotations were established in the occupations of 1945 but have continued to feature in military operations since then. A significant difference in 1995 is the extent to which this has been removed from frontstage to backstage. Where Allied soldiers were supplied with the phrases of sexual encounter as they entered France, NATO soldiers in Bosnia-Herzegovina were enjoined to restraint, even at times threatened with being sent home to explain any inappropriate liaison to their wives. The militaries of 1990s western democracies recognized that they were working within a limited war rather than total war. As a result, they were more aware that the direct gaze of domestic public opinion was upon them, and they were conscious that the limited operations in which they engaged overseas should not alter or threaten social relations at home. Cynthia Enloe astutely points out that relations between governments can be contingent on the integrity of marriages up and down the international pyramid .(Enloe 2000: 11). The sexual dimension of fraternization has therefore become even more informal.

If a sexual encounter is to be construed as legitimate rather than forcible, it must be based on consent, conceived as a negotiation between two individuals of equal status. However, relations are frequently constructed from unequal power positions (Pateman 1980). Language inequality may be a significant element in this, since both parties to a relationship must share a language if they are to produce and understand an agreement to consent. It is noticeable that language for obtaining female sexual consent was absent from Second World War military vocabulary instruction. By contrast, it was prolific in language for initiating an encounter, for example through complimenting the female body or enquiring into a woman's availability. When the foreigner does not speak the language of the other, as is frequently the case in sexual fraternization, it is unclear whether the encounter can result in meaningful consent.

In military operations other than a hostile invasion, if the off-duty sexual activities of troops are expected to be consensual, so is the operation itself. The principle of peacekeeping requires that the foreign military force is present with the belligerents' consent, although it is understood that consent may be given grudgingly, contested or denied

(Ratner 1995). Even in peace enforcement settings such as IFOR, which do not legally require the consent of the belligerents, military forces recognize the need to work with the consent of local populations where possible, for the sake of security and to facilitate reconstruction and civil affairs work. The privilege and asymmetric power of military forces raise the same problems of language and consent. It is not entirely clear that consent is possible without language, and consent is likely to be more meaningful if it is based on a *mutual exchange* of language where both partners are willing to cross the language barriers.

Communicating through intermediaries

Military planners are often taken by surprise at the scale of their language needs. The same surprise seems present in both our case studies, 50 years apart: military occupation in Europe in the 1940s and peace operations in Bosnia-Herzegovina in the 1990s. Undoubtedly, the major issue for the military is what in modern terms is conceived as the problem of capacity. Planners suddenly realize that they need large numbers of people to meet the pressing needs of the conflict. How will they identify and assemble enough people with a suitable range of skills?

An initial response is to look for linguists who are 'ready to go', already equipped by family background, education, training or personal experience to carry out the tasks that require language expertise. The second response is to find ways of training people in the skills required. In the case of languages, the need may be urgent, but the time needed to develop adequate language competence is relatively long. It may be readily achievable to provide personnel with cultural briefing and a sense of the society with which they are expected to engage, but it requires months and even years of intensive training to be able to communicate at a high level in a foreign language. Moreover, language competence is only one part of what a linguist requires to function in a conflict situation. Apart from personal qualities such as courage, ingenuity and an ability to build relationships, linguists may be required to deploy a wide range of professional expertise, to translate, interpret, investigate, interrogate, liaise or resolve problems.

A first issue, then, is to adopt strategies to address the problems of capacity. Perhaps strategies may be too ambitious a term for the responses developed under acute pressure of time. In both our case studies, there was an overriding need to 'get on with the job' even if the means at hand were less than ideal. The inevitable result was a good deal of 'ad hoc-ery' and 'bricolage', cobbling together approximate solutions from available resources and frequently riding roughshod over policies and procedures designed for more settled circumstances. Makeshift arrangements frequently highlight the tensions and conflicts that may be less perceptible in stable systems. Underlying social issues of identity and power may be expressed in a culture, often in indirect forms that can prove a linguistic minefield for the unwary. Ad hoc solutions may have long-term consequences, particularly for individuals. For example, some interpreters hired under the pressure of need may turn the opportunity into a longer-term career, perhaps as a professional translator or interpreter. At a later stage of the operation, more robust procedures are likely to be developed, which approach the status of capacity-building strategies, for example, for recruitment and staff development.

A second issue in meeting language needs is that the procurement of skills is constrained by the availability of personnel. Languages are embodied in people, and unlike materiel people are multipurpose assets. They come with a baggage of family relationships, networks of friends and a personal history. They can carry out a very wide range of tasks. In both contexts examined here, military commanders were required to weigh their operational language needs against the different national, social and professional profiles of the language intermediaries who could meet them.

The language intermediaries themselves often experienced their allocated roles as conflicted and chaotic. They struggled to make sense of their role and relate it to their other identities. For military personnel, the role of interpreter might offer opportunities for self-development, but it might also limit their career prospects. Language skills are an asset in specific tasks, and may provide the entry to more senior responsibilities, but they may equally trigger a round of repetition without career progression. The specific language skills may cease to be an asset when the conflict subsides and military priorities move to a different part of the world. Military linguists must therefore balance their military duties with delivering professional language work. Usually they are clear that they are a soldier first and a linguist second. Their next deployment may easily be one without any language responsibilities. But their language loyalties may also have deeper roots. And the boundary between soldiering and 'languaging' may not be so clear-cut.

For civilian interpreters, the role of interpreter might be a professional one, learned and practised in other institutions such as public administration, the courts or educational establishments. The issues they face relate to how far they should adapt their professional norms and practices to match the military requirements. For other interpreters, their role might be economically attractive, as it was for many locally-employed staff in occupied European countries or in Bosnia-Herzegovina. But they also need to balance the carrying-out of effective language duties for the foreign forces with their place in their own society, with their networks of family, friends and obligations. These tensions bear directly on the nature of the language intermediary and where her or his loyalties lie.

In addition to their respective allegiances with their own community and with their employer, interpreters for the military face a professional issue of allegiance. They have a loyalty to the text, which requires them to strive not only for linguistic accuracy but also for a position of neutrality without regard to the impact of their words on the context. They have a loyalty to the employer for whom they are acting as an intermediary, which requires them to produce work that helps to achieve the aims of the employer. In the case of a military employer, the aims will often be performative, where a text is intended to produce a particular effect on intended readers, or where the choice of language may be a matter of life or death. And thirdly, intermediaries may have a loyalty to the professional role to which they are assigned by an institutional process, such as a trial in court. The way these questions of loyalty are negotiated continues to pose challenges for the profession of interpreter.

The conference interpreting paradigm was not available in 1945, and the Nuremberg trials were an influential catalyst in developing this paradigm. It was of evident value in this highly structured institutional context, but was in many ways exceptional at this time. Conference interpreting does not provide an appropriate framework for all situations. Certainly, it played little part in most day-to-day language work in 1945, even if the emerging paradigm began to take shape at Nuremberg. And it was conspicuously absent from the hasty bricolage of Bosnia-Herzegovina in the early 1990s. The paradigm seems inappropriate for a military interpreter, whose first duty is to serve her or his country, but it may offer an aspiration for civilian interpreters, who are employed for their specific expertise. To some extent the aspiration became a more realistic one in the later stages of the Bosnian intervention, as the tides of conflict ebbed, though perhaps only for a minority of the interpreters.

An alternative paradigm now available is public service interpreter, which seeks to bring together interpreting for the courts, the police, the health services and others. The experience of establishing an Interpreters' Pool to service war crimes cases across the British occupied sector provides a good example of how systems were put in place incrementally to support court interpreting. A Master Interpreter was appointed to ensure quality and standards. He gradually developed a workable system, which included a cadre of tried and trusted interpreters to supervise the work of less experienced staff. A structured procedure was introduced to provide training and mentoring on the job, so as to make best use of the limited and uneven resources available. This experience laid the basis of professional criteria for court interpreters, who were enjoined to translate faithfully, maintain confidentiality and behave impartially. It is at the origin of the ethical standards set out by the UK National Register of Public Service Interpreters, which requires that 'practitioners shall interpret truly and faithfully what is uttered, without adding, omitting or changing anything' (National Register of Public Service Interpreters 2011).

In addition to purely professional criteria, interpreters are also subject to a range of other requirements. In British-occupied Germany in 1945, interpreters had to be security-cleared, socially acceptable and multi-tasking, to adapt to very different tasks in the same day. Concerns for security are highly situational. Whereas German nationals could not be used as court interpreters in the early stages, as the occupation developed, the restriction was relaxed. For the most part, linguistic accuracy and neutrality were only perceived to be in conflict when local German civilians were employed. In Bosnia-Herzegovina in the 1990s, on the other hand, largely untrained interpreters were initially recruited, with relatively little attention paid to their ethnic background. Their English-language competence stood as a proxy for neutrality. As with German Jewish refugees in 1945, speaking English well was often felt by the military to connote a degree of sympathy with British culture and values, which indicated a desirable neutrality, if not assimilation. Of course, there were tasks that initially could not be assigned to locally employed staff, but later the same tasks were often entrusted to them as the security situation eased.

A strict professionalism is made more complex by the frequent combination of other kinds of mediation that interpreters are required to carry out for the military, whether as liaison officers, investigators or 'fixers'. Whereas liaison, interrogation and investigation duties would normally be carried out by military interpreters, there was a degree of overlap with the tasks allocated to civilian interpreters working in the field, who were often asked to provide specialist knowledge or suggest solutions to problems arising.

There are major differences in the demography of civilian interpreters. The interpreters in 1945 were predominantly male, and many of them were of German Jewish origin. In Bosnia-Herzegovina, on the other hand, some two-thirds of them were female and most were of local origin. It is noticeable that in both cases many interpreters were drawn from subordinate groups and that their lack of status was regarded as wholly consonant with the low level of importance commonly attached to interpreting. This may well have been compounded by the lower status of the spoken word, an ephemeral presence that is transmitted by 'lips', as US military slang would call interpreters.

Looking at the two cases together, the problematic identity of the interpreter emerges as a key feature. In 1945, with military interpreters, the identity issues seem related to the uncertainty about their role within the military and within the mission and whether language competence gave them power in the military hierarchy. In the case of Jewish refugees, their role may have enabled them to 'belong', paradoxically helping them to belong to a country by virtue of speaking the language of its enemy. In Bosnia-Herzegovina, with locally-recruited interpreters, the identity issue centres on their relationships with both the military and their local communities and the status which was accorded to them by both. Whether this uncertainty is experienced as a threat or an opportunity depends on very specific conditions and varies greatly between individuals. Perhaps the interpreters should be seen as early exemplars of the hybridity which has more recently been identified as a key feature of the post-colonial condition and lived out alternatively as a curse or a blessing. They may be problematic because of their intermediary status, but they also symbolize the specific circumstances of the conflict. Without the particular intervention, there would be little need for German speakers in the 1940s or Serbo-Croat speakers in the 1990s. And, when the operation ceases, so does their role. They are in that sense the spirit of the conflict, embodying the disruptions which war has brought to their societies.

Lessons learned

What our case studies have revealed for future conflicts and armed interventions is the pervasive nature of language issues in war and occupation. This should not be surprising since language is the very stuff from which human communication is made, and the post-Babel condition of communication is that it is carried through many different languages. The contact between different languages is an almost universal characteristic of making war and building peace, with the exception of some civil wars which are conducted between opponents who share the same language. Language issues are much more extensive than could easily be regulated by explicit policy, but in examining the complex practical situations in which languages play a tangible part it is clear that there are lessons still to be learned.

In seeking to identify lessons arising from the two conflicts, it has become clear that the ability to learn lessons is itself a pivotal issue. As each conflict has progressed, the organization of language preparation and support has markedly improved in the light of experience. The early attempts to cope, often in an ad hoc way, were succeeded by better organized and stable systems. This was not a linear process, and at different stages some lessons were not learned or not passed on. More significant, perhaps, is the limited ability to draw lessons from one conflict and apply them to another. This may not be surprising in the light of historical changes which make each conflict different from previous ones. However, this study has compared two very different operations: mass armies occupying defeated belligerents in a world war and professional armies building peace in a small regional conflict. The lessons which are common to both conflicts demonstrate that issues of languages and cultures are pervasive and fundamental. They have rarely been given a level of priority and investment that matches their importance.

In grouping the findings, it is apparent that languages have a particularly crucial role to play in four major areas of conflict: the gathering and interpretation of intelligence; preparation and support for forces operating in conflict zones; engagement of military forces with civilian populations; and the use of intermediaries to enable effective communication. Each of these areas presents particular issues, and the way they were addressed in each case has been shown to provide both positive and negative lessons, with successful innovations as well as significant shortcomings. From the perspective of military planners, the key lessons derived can be summarized in a few points:

1. In intelligence, translation is not transparent. It involves the knowledge and judgement of several people who have been involved in gathering, transcribing and interpreting a text. These contributions should be managed and documented so that the process is visible to the end user.
2. Expertise in languages and cultures cannot be acquired at short notice. Military planners depend on expertise that has been built up over a long period, much of it developed outside the armed forces in secondary and higher education. They need to support the maintenance in their country of a minimum of expertise related to

any part of the world, which can then provide expertise to future deployments.

3. The armed forces need to be more conscious of how their understanding of the hostile 'other' has actually been constructed and therefore of the limitations that it might well have. They need to be particularly aware of the risks of reducing the 'foreign' to a familiar pattern, which can be easily understood but may not grasp key differences in thought or behaviour.

4. For the majority of troops, language preparation before deployment should focus on meta-language, aiming to give them an awareness of how to use the language resources at their disposal and develop linguistic good manners, including in English, as well as learning some elements of the particular language they are likely to encounter. Training in general language awareness could be included in basic training, since many personnel will deploy at some time in their careers to a foreign country.

5. Armed forces need to become aware of the linguistic effects of their presence in another country. The way in which they occupy and name the spaces they hold has an impact on the local population, as does their attitude to local languages and their use of particular materials in those languages.

6. Cultural training makes a valuable contribution to establishing good relations with the civilian population, especially important where hearts and minds are at stake. It is central to developing personal and professional relationships based on mutual consent.

7. The professional status of translators and interpreters in conflict situations is complex and does not easily fit into the established paradigms. Further work is needed to develop an appropriate model for civilian interpreters working for the military.

8. Most foreign deployments are likely to mean in practice the recruitment of locally-based interpreters. It would be useful to prepare a toolkit which involves:

   • training provided to military personnel on how to work effectively with interpreters, what to expect from language-mediated encounters and how to treat interpreters outside these encounters;
   • recognition of the duty of care and protection that the employer should exercise, including health and safety;
   • awareness of the kinds of personal and social problems the interpreter is likely to face and the issues of trust and security that need to be managed as a result;

- testing of locally-recruited civilians to ensure they have requisite competence for the tasks;
- providing training in professional practice and language proficiency, including work with speakers who have diverse accents and language backgrounds;
- embedding these requirements in third-party contracts for agencies recruiting interpreters for military use;
- employing a 'language management' officer, who does not necessarily need to speak the language, but who is clear about how language resources on the ground should be managed and is able to develop a 'language management plan'.
- instituting a 'language debriefing' mechanism which will feed into the corporate memory.

Underlying these findings is an awareness of the challenging and often unexpected nature of conflict. Plans and policies often prove inadequate or even mistaken in the light of practical experience of conflict, and it is difficult to see how military forces can prepare adequately for what they do not expect. Conversely, an improved capacity in languages and cultures can go a long way towards attenuating the uncertainties.

Recent work within NATO forces suggests that these 'soft' issues may be receiving more attention. Within NATO, a Joint Doctrine Note has been produced on the significance of culture to the military (Ministry of Defence, Development Concepts and Doctrine Centre 2009), and work is currently under way to develop a Doctrine Note on language support. Within the British armed forces, a significant innovation has been undertaken with the establishment in 2007 of the Defence Operational Languages Support Unit, designed to generate, sustain and manage operational language capability. The British Ministry of Defence has introduced financial rewards for personnel who learn languages of particular current importance. The impetus for these changes has largely stemmed from the pressures of military involvement in Iraq and Afghanistan, rather than from lessons learned in 1995, or even 1945.

Within civilian organizations, the issues of languages in conflict are receiving wider attention, mainly as a result of activities by professional organizations and groups. The Association internationale des interprètes de conférence (AIIC) has undertaken research and advocacy in support of interpreters in war zones (Moser-Mercer and Bali 2008; Kahane 2009), recognizing an ethical responsibility towards locally recruited interpreters. In a more campaigning mode, the *Red T* group has launched an initiative for the protection of translators and interpreters (http://www. red-t.org). It brings together advocates and volunteers to raise awareness, defend basic human rights and promote the safety of translators and interpreters at risk. Several newspapers have highlighted the risks to interpreters in Afghanistan (Butt 2011; Haynes, Deborah 2011; Savage 2011), and their concerns have been echoed on military blogs (UK Forces Afghanistan 2011) and elsewhere.

However, the lessons to be learned from the studies presented here are not confined to military planners. The armed forces are deeply embedded in wider society, and in each conflict it has emerged clearly how far the capabilities of the military are dependent on the education and cultural expertise of the society from which they are drawn. At one end of the spectrum, British officers in 1945 benefited from the knowledge of French and France they had acquired at school and in their personal life. At the other end, the military in 1995 was hampered by the dearth of people in Britain with any knowledge of Serbo-Croat. The battle for hearts and minds is becoming an increasingly important dimension of war and peace support operations, rendering expertise in languages and cultures all the more crucial. This suggests that policy makers in government, especially in the area of education, need to take a clearer view of the strategic value of linguistic and cultural diversity within civil society. Recent initiatives in Britain to support languages and area studies at university level outside the mainstream European cultures have contributed to alleviating this lack of expertise. However, the quantity and diversity of potential conflict zones around the world means that any emerging conflict risks provoking a new crisis of understanding. To reduce this risk will require very substantial public investment in education and research, and may well need to be undertaken on an international scale. In view of the increasingly international nature of conflicts and of the language issues they raise, countries may now need to seek international solutions. Increased cooperation in developing expertise in language education and research is certainly a productive route for improved language capability in war and conflict. It also seems likely to be the best route by which wider and deeper knowledge of languages and cultures can contribute to successful post-conflict operations, and to peace-building.

References

Ackerman, Spencer. 2010. 'Petraeus: I'll Change Afghanistan's Rules of War'. *Wired: Danger Room*, 29 June. http://www.wired.com/petraeus-ill-change-the-rules-of-war-in-afghanistan/ (accessed 28 February 2011).

Ad Hoc Group on Cooperation in Peacekeeping. 1997. 'Lessons Learned in Peacekeeping Operations'. http://152.152.94.201/docu/peacekeeping_lessons/peacekeeping-lessons-eng.pdf (accessed 14 July 2009).

Alderson, J. Charles (ed.) 2009. *The Politics of Language Education: Individuals and Institutions*. Clevedon: Multilingual Matters.

Althusser, Louis. 1984. *Essays on Ideology*. London: Verso.

Anderson, Benedict. 1991. *Imagined Communities*. London and New York: Verso.

Andreas, Peter. 2007. *Blue Helmets and Black Markets: the Business of Survival in the Siege of Sarajevo*. Ithaca, NY: Cornell University Press.

———. 2009. 'Symbiosis Between Peace Operations and Illicit Business in Bosnia'. *International Peacekeeping* 16 (1): 33–46.

Andrew, Christopher. 2002. 'Bletchley Park in Pre-War Perspective'. In *Action This Day*, edited by Michael Smith and Ralph Erskine: 1–14. London: Bantam.

———. 2010. *The Defence of the Realm: the Authorised History of MI5*. London: Penguin.

Apter, Emily. 2006. *The Translation Zone*. Princeton: Princeton University Press.

Askew, Louise. 2012. 'Clinging to a Barbed Wire Fence: the Language Policy of the International Community in Bosnia-Herzegovina since 1995.' PhD thesis, University of Nottingham.

Baker, Catherine. 2010. ' "It's Not Their Job to Soldier": Distinguishing Civilian and Military in Soldiers' and Interpreters' Accounts of Peacekeeping in 1990s Bosnia-Herzegovina'. *Journal of War and Culture Studies* 3 (1): 137–50.

Baker, Mona. 2006. *Translation and Conflict: A Narrative Account*. London and New York: Routledge.

———. 2010a. 'Interpreters and Translators in the War Zone: Narrated and Narrators'. *The Translator* 16 (2): 197–222.

———. 2010b. 'Narratives of Terrorism and Security: "Accurate" Translations, Suspicious Frames'. *Critical Studies on Terrorism* 3 (3): 347–64.

Barkawi, Tarak. 2006. *Globalization and War*. Lanham: Rowman and Littlefield.

Barry, Ben. 2008. *A Cold War: Front Line Operations in Bosnia 1995–1996*. Stroud: Spellmount.

Barry, Robert L. 1999. 'Lessons Learned from Bosnia'. *Helsinki Monitor* 3: 100–2.

Bazdulj, Muharem. 2007. 'Bosanski, hrvatski i srpski jezik se razlikuju u tri posto'. *BH Dani*, 31 August. http://www.bhdani.com/default.asp?kat=txt&broj_id=533&tekst_rb=4 (accessed 11 September 2007).

Bermann, Sandra, and Michael Wood. 2005. *Nation, Language and the Ethics of Translation*. Princeton: Princeton University Press.

Biddiscombe, Perry. 2007. *The Denazification of Germany: a History 1945–50*. Stroud: Tempus.

Bieber, Florian. 1999. 'Consociationalism: Prerequisite or Hurdle for Democratisation in Bosnia? The Case of Belgium as a Possible Example'. *South-East Europe Review* 2: 79–94.

BILC. 2004. 'Minutes of Steering Committee Meetings.' Bureau for International Language Co-Ordination, 7–10 June. http://www.bilc.forces.gc.ca/conf/2004/strcomm/SC_2004.pdf (accessed 13 October 2011).

Bloxham, Donald. 2001. *Genocide on Trial: War Crimes Trials and the Formation of Holocaust History and Memory*. Oxford and New York: Oxford University Press.

——. 2003. 'British War Crimes Trial Policy in Germany, 1945–1957: Implementation and Collapse'. *Journal of British Studies* 42 (1): 91–118.

Bodleian Library. 2007. *Instructions for British Servicemen in Germany*. 2007. Oxford: Bodleian Library.

Bonsall, Arthur. 2008. 'Bletchley Park and the RAF Y Service: Some Recollections'. *Intelligence and National Security* 23 (6): 827–41.

Bosch, Dick. 2009. 'A Cross-Cultural Training Model for the Dutch Military: a Possible Framework'. Paper presented at Culture in Conflict Symposium, UK Defence Academy, 17 June.

Bose, Sumantra. 2002. *Bosnia after Dayton: Nationalist Partition and International Intervention*. London: Hurst.

Bougarel, Xavier. 2007. 'Death and the Nationalist: Martyrdom, War Memory and Veteran Identity among Bosnian Muslims'. In *The New Bosnian Mosaic: Identities, Memories and Moral Claims in a Post-War Society*, edited by Xavier Bougarel, Ger Duijzings and Elissa Helms: 167–92. Aldershot: Ashgate.

Bourke, Joanna. 1999. *An Intimate History of Killing: Face-to-Face Killing in Twentieth Century Warfare*. London: Granta.

Bower, Tom. 1995. *Blind Eye to Murder: Britain, America and the Purging of Nazi Germany – A Pledge Betrayed*. London: Little, Brown.

Bracewell, Wendy. 2009. 'Balkan Travel Writing: Points of Departure'. In *Balkan Departures: Travel Writing from Southeastern Europe*, edited by Wendy Bracewell and Alex Drace-Francis: 1–24. New York and Oxford: Berghahn.

Bratt Paulston, Christina. 1997. 'Epilogue: Some Concluding Thoughts on Linguistic Human Rights'. *International Journal of the Sociology of Language* 127: 187–95.

Brossat, Alain. 1994. *Libération, fête folle, 6 juin 1944–mai 1945: mythes et rites, ou le grand théâtre des passions populaires*. Série Mémoires 30. Paris: Editions Autrement.

Browder, Dewey A. 1998. *Americans in Post-World War II Germany*. Lampeter: Edwin Mellen Press.

Brown Mason, John. 1950. 'Lessons of Wartime Military Government Trainers'. *Annals of the American Academy of Political and Social Science* 267: 183–92.

Brumfit, Christopher, and Keith Johnson. 1979. *The Communicative Approach to Language Teaching*. Oxford: Oxford University Press.

Brunt, Rodney. 2006. 'Special Documentation Systems at the Government Code and Cypher School, Bletchley Park, during the Second World War'. *Intelligence and National Security* 21 (1): 129–48.

Bureau, Olivier. 1999. 'Social Patrol'. *SFOR Informer*, 3 March.

Butt, Riazat. 2011. 'Khan's Kitchen: the Difficult Life of an Afghan Interpreter for the British Military'. *The Guardian*, 30 August. http://www.guardian.

co.uk/news/blog/2011/aug/30/khan-kitchen-difficult-life-afghan-interpreter-british-military (accessed 16 September 2011).

Butterfield, Ardis. 2009. *The Familiar Enemy: Chaucer, Language and Nation in the Hundred Years War*. Oxford: Oxford University Press.

Calvocoressi, Peter. 1980. *Top Secret Ultra*. London: Cassell.

CILT. 1982. *Serbo-Croat*. Language and Culture Guide 23. London: Centre for Information on Language Teaching and Research.

Clayton, Aileen. 1980. *The Enemy is Listening*. London: Hutchinson.

Coles, Kimberley. 2007. *Democratic Designs: International Intervention and Electoral Practices in Postwar Bosnia-Herzegovina*. Ann Arbor: University of Michigan Press.

Cooper, Kanty. 1979. *The Uprooted*. London: Quartet Books.

Cooper, Robert Leon. 1989. *Language Planning and Social Change*. Cambridge: Cambridge University Press.

Coulmas, Florian (ed.) 1991. *A Language Policy for the European Community: Prospects and Quandaries*. Berlin: Mouton de Gruyter.

Council for Cultural Cooperation. 2001. *Common European Framework of Reference for Languages: Learning, Teaching, Assessment*. Cambridge: Cambridge University Press.

Craig, James. 2006. 'Introduction'. In *The Arabists of Shemlan: MECAS Memoirs 1944–78*, edited by Paul Tempest. Vol. 1: 1–11. London: Stacey International.

Crossey, Mark. 2005. 'Improving Linguistic Interoperability'. *NATO Review* (Summer), http://www.nato.int/docu/review/2005/issue2/english/art4.html (accessed 26 August 2011)

Dandeker, Christopher, and James Gow. 1997. 'The Future of Peace Support Operations: Strategic Peacekeeping and Success'. *Armed Forces and Society* 23 (3): 327–47.

Defrance, Corinne. 1994. *La politique culturelle de la France sur la rive gauche du Rhin, 1945–55*. Strasbourg: Presses universitaires de Strasbourg.

DeGroot, Gerard. 2001. 'A Few Good Women: Gender Stereotypes, the Military and Peacekeeping'. *International Peacekeeping* 8 (2): 23–38.

De Jong, Erika. 1992. *An Introduction to Court Interpreting: Theory and Practice*. Lanham: University Press of America.

Department of Defense. 1995. *Bosnia Country Handbook*. [Washington DC]: US Department of Defense for Peace Implementation Force (IFOR).

Donnison, F. S. V. 1961. *Civil Affairs and Military Government, NW Europe 1944–45*. London: HMSO.

———. 1966. *Civil Affairs and Military Government: Central Organization and Planning*. London: HMSO.

Dragovic-Drouet, Mila. 2007. 'The Practice of Translation and Interpreting during the Conflicts in the Former Yugoslavia (1991–1999)'. In *Translating and Interpreting Conflict*, edited by Myriam Salama-Carr, 29–40. Amsterdam: Rodopi.

Duffey, Tamara. 2000. 'Cultural Issues in Contemporary Peacekeeping'. *International Peacekeeping* 7 (1): 142–68.

Duncanson, Claire. 2009. 'Forces for Good? Narratives of Military Masculinity in Peacekeeping Operations'. *International Feminist Journal of Politics* 11 (1): 63–80.

Elliott, Geoffrey, and Harold Shukman. 2003. *Secret Classrooms: a Memoir of the Cold War*. London: St Ermin's.

Enloe, Cynthia. 1990. *Bananas, Beaches and Bases: Making Feminist Sense of International Politics*. Berkeley: University of California Press.

——. 2000. *Maneuvers: the International Politics of Militarizing Women's Lives*. Berkeley: University of California Press.

Eytan, Walter. 1994. 'The Z Watch in Hut 4, Part II'. In *Code Breakers: the Inside Story of Bletchley Park*, edited by Harry Hinsley and Alan Stripp: 57–60. Oxford: Oxford University Press.

Finocchiaro, Mary, and Christopher Brumfit. 1983. *The Functional–Notional Approach: From Theory to Practice*. Oxford: Oxford University Press.

Fishman, Joshua A. 1972. *Language and Nationalism: Two Integrative Essays*. Rowley: Newbury House.

——. 1974. *Advances in Language Planning*. The Hague: Mouton.

Flanders, Dalma. 2004. 'Intelligence WAAFs in Y Service'. *WW2 People's War*. http://www.bbc.co.uk/ww2peopleswar/stories/43/a2423143.shtml (accessed 20 June 2008).

Footitt, Hilary. 2011. ' "Russia of the Mind": Learning Languages in the Cold War'. In *The Lost Decade: the 1950s in European History, Politics, Society and Culture*, edited by Heiko Feldner, Claire Gorrara and Kevin Passmore: 101–17. Cambridge: Cambridge Scholars Publishing.

Fortna, Virginia Page, and Lise Morjé Howard. 2008. 'Pitfalls and Prospects in the Peacekeeping Future'. *Annual Review of Political Science* 11: 283–301.

Foster, Benjamin. 2006. 'The NUPOSA Programme for US Undergraduates 1965–66'. In *The Arabists of Shemlan: MECAS Memoirs 1944–78*, edited by Paul Tempest. Vol. 1: 185–90. London: Stacey International.

Frankfort, T. 2002. 'Peacekeeping and Humanitarian Action'. In *Srebrenica: Reconstruction, Background, Consequences and Analyses of the Fall of a Safe Area*. Amsterdam: Netherlands Institute for War Documentation. http://srebrenica.brightside.nl/srebrenica/toc_frame.html (accessed 14 July 2009).

Frantzen, Henning A. 2005. *NATO and Peace Support Operations, 1991–1999: Policies and Doctrines*. Abingdon: Frank Cass.

Freedman, Maurice. 2000. *Unravelling Enigma: Winning the Code War at Station X*. Barnsley: Leo Cooper.

Fry, Helen. 2007. *The King's Most Loyal Enemy Aliens*. Stroud: Sutton Publishing.

——. 2009. *Churchill's German Army*. Stroud: The History Press.

——. 2010. *Denazification: Britain's Enemy Aliens, Nazi War Criminals and the Reconstruction of Post-War Europe*. Stroud: The History Press.

Funtowicz, Silvio O., and Jerome R. Ravetz. 1993. 'Science for the Post-Normal Age'. *Futures* 25 (7): 739–55.

Gaiba, Francesca. 1998. *The Origins of Simultaneous Interpretation: the Nuremberg Trial*. Ottawa: University of Ottawa Press.

Gatalo, Veselin. 2004. *SFOR: siesta, fiesta, orgasmo, riposo*. Sarajevo and Zagreb: Zoro.

Gemie, Sharif, and Luare Humbert. 2009. 'Writing History in the Aftermath of "Relief" '. *Journal of Contemporary History* 44 (2): 309–18.

Goedde, Petra. 1999. 'From Villains to Victims: Fraternization and the Feminization of Germany, 1945–47'. *Diplomatic History* 23 (1): 1–20.

——. 2003. *GIs and Germans: Culture, Gender and Foreign Relations, 1945–1949*. New Haven and London: Yale University Press.

Gollancz, Victor. 1947. *In Darkest Germany*. London: Gollancz.

Gollin, Sandra M., and David Hall. 2011. *Language for Specific Purposes.* Basingstoke: Palgrave Macmillan.

Gonzáles, Roseann Dueñas, Victoria F. Vásquez, and Holly Mikkelson. 1991. *Fundamentals of Court Interpretation: Theory, Policy and Practice.* Durham, NC: Carolina Academic Press.

Goodman, S. M. 1947. *Curriculum Implications of Armed Services Education Programs.* Washington DC: American Council on Education.

Greenberg, Robert. 2004. *Language and Identity in the Balkans: Serbo-Croatian and its Disintegration.* Oxford: Oxford University Press.

Gröschel, Bernhard. 2009. *Das Serbokroatische zwischen Linguistik und Politik.* Munich: Lincom Europea.

Hammond, Andrew. 2007. *The Debated Lands: British and American Representations of the Balkans.* Cardiff: University of Wales Press.

Hansen, Annika S. 1997. 'Political Legitimacy, Confidence-Building and the Dayton Peace Agreement'. *International Peacekeeping* 4 (2): 74–90.

Hawkesworth, Celia. 1986. *Colloquial Serbo-Croat.* London and New York: Routledge and Kegan Paul.

Haynes, Deborah. 2011. 'Taleban Target Britain's Army of Interpreters'. *The Times,* 1 August.

Haynes, Dina Francesca. 2010. 'Lessons from Bosnia's Arizona Market: Harm to Women in a Neoliberalized Postconflict Reconstruction Process'. *University of Pennsylvania Law Review* (158) 6: 1780–829.

Headrick, Daniel. 1991. *The Invisible Weapon: Telecommunications and International Politics, 1851–1945.* New York and Oxford: Oxford University Press.

Heazle, Michael. 2010. 'Policy Lessons from Iraq on Managing Uncertainty in Intelligence Assessment: Why the Strategic/Tactical Distinction Matters'. *Intelligence and National Security* 25 (3): 290–308.

HEFCE. 1995. *Review of Former Soviet and East European Studies.* London: HEFCE.

Heiser, Sandrine, and Hans-Gerg Merz. 2009. 'Un an d'occupation française en Allemagne. Vue d'ensemble sur l'exposition présentée au palais Berlitz du 15 juin au 5 juillet 1946'. *Revue historique des armées* 256: 88–93.

Helm, Sarah. 2005. *A Life in Secrets: the Story of Vera Atkins and the Lost Agents of SOE.* London: Little, Brown.

Herval, René. 1947. *Bataille de Normandie: récits de témoins.* Paris: Editions de Notre Temps.

Hill, Marion. 2004. *Bletchley Park People: Churchill's Geese that Never Cackled.* Stroud: Sutton Publishing.

Hill, Michael. 2009. *The Public Policy Process.* 5th edn. London: Longman.

Hillel, Marc. 1983. *L'occupation française en Allemagne, 1945–9.* Paris: Balland.

Hinsley, Harry, C. A. G. Simkins, and Michael Howard. 1979–90. *British Intelligence in the Second World War.* London: HMSO.

——, and Alan Stripp. 1994. *Code Breakers: the Inside Story of Bletchley Park.* Oxford: Oxford University Press.

Hoare, Oliver. 2000. *Camp 020: MI5 and the Nazi Spies.* Richmond: Public Records Office.

Howard, Les. 2006. *Winter Warriors: Across Bosnia with the PBI.* Brighton: Book Guild.

Hudemann, Rainer. 1997. 'L'Occupation française après 1945 et les relations franco-allemandes'. *Vingtième Siècle. Revue d'Histoire* 55: 58–68.

Human Rights Watch. 2002. *Hopes Betrayed: Trafficking of Women and Girls to Bosnia and Herzegovina for Forced Prostitution*. Washington DC: Human Rights Watch.

Inghilleri, Moira. 2005. 'The Sociology of Bourdieu and the Construction of the "Object" in Translation and Interpreting Studies'. *The Translator* 11 (2): 125–45.

——. 2007. 'National Sovereignty Versus Universal Rights: Interpreting Justice in a Global Context'. *Social Semiotics* 17 (2): 195–212.

——. 2008. 'The Ethical Task of the Translator in the Geo-Political Arena: from Iraq to Guantánamo Bay'. *Translation Studies* 1 (2): 212–23.

——. 2009. 'Translators in War Zones: Ethics under Fire in Iraq'. In *Globalization, Political Violence and Translation*, edited by Esperanza Bielsa and Christopher Hughes: 207–21. Basingstoke: Palgrave Macmillan.

——. 2010. ' "You Don't Make War without Knowing Why": the Decision to Interpret in Iraq'. *The Translator* 16 (2): 175–96.

Jackson, John. 2002. *The Secret War of Hut 3*. Milton Keynes: Military Press.

Jašarević, Larissa. 2007. 'Everyday Work: Subsistence Economy, Social Belonging and Moralities of Exchange at a Bosnian (Black) Market'. In *The New Bosnian Mosaic: Identities, Memories and Moral Claims in a Post-war Society*, edited by Xavier Bougarel, Ger Duijzings and Elissa Helms: 273–93. Aldershot: Ashgate.

Johnston, Nicola. 2007. 'Peace Support Operations'. In *Inclusive Security, Sustainable Peace: A Toolkit for Advocacy and Action*. London: International Alert and Washington DC: Women Waging Peace.

Jones, Francis. 2004. 'Ethics, Aesthetics and *Décision*: Literary Translating in the Wars of the Yugoslav Succession'. *Meta: journal des traducteurs/Meta: Translators' Journal* 49 (4): 711–28.

Kahane, Eduardo. 2007. 'Interpreters in Conflict Zones: the Limits of Neutrality'. *Communicate!* (Summer). http://www.aiic.net/ViewPage.cfm/page2691.htm (accessed 2 September 2011).

——. 2009. 'The AIIC Resolution on Interpreters in War and Conflict Zones: Thoughts Towards a New Ethical, Contractual and Political Understanding with Society'. *Communicate!* (Spring). http://www.aiic.net/ViewPage.cfm/page3196.htm (accessed 28 October 2011).

Kaplan, Robert B., and Richard B. Baldauf. 1997. *Language Planning from Practice to Theory*. Clevedon: Multilingual Matters.

——, Richard B. Baldauf, Anthony J. Liddicoat, Pauline Bryant, Marie-Thérèse Barbaux and Martin Pütz. 2000. 'Current Issues in Language Planning'. *Current Issues in Language Planning* 1 (1): 1–10.

Karton, Joshua. 2008. 'Lost in Translation: International Criminal Tribunals and the Legal Implications of Interpreted Testimony'. *Vanderbilt Journal of Transnational Law* 41 (1): 1–54.

Kent, Vanessa. 2007. 'Protecting Civilians from UN Peacekeepers and Humanitarian Workers: Sexual Exploitation and Abuse'. In *Unintended Consequences of Peacekeeping Operations*, edited by Chiyuki Aoi, Cedric de Coning and Ramesh Thakur: 44–66. Tokyo: United Nations University Press.

Kilcullen, David. 2007. 'Religion and Insurgency'. *Small Wars Journal Blog*, 12 May. http://smallwarsjournal.com/blog/religion-and-insurgency (accessed 16 September 2011).

Kleinman, Sylvie. 2009. 'Un brave de plus: Theobald Wolfe Tone, Alias Adjutant-General James Smith, French Officer and Irish Patriot Adventurer, 1796–8'.

In *Franco-Irish Military Connections, 1550–1945: Proceedings of the Vincennes Conference, September 2007*, edited by Nathalie Genêt-Rouffiac and David Murphy: 163–88. Dublin: Four Courts Press.

Kordić, Snježana. 2010. *Jezik i nacionalizam*. Zagreb: Durieux.

Kostić, Roland. 2007. 'Ambivalent Peace: External Peacebuilding, Threatened Identity and Reconciliation in Bosnia and Herzegovina'. PhD thesis, Uppsala University.

Krulak, Charles C. 1999. 'The Strategic Corporal: Leadership in the Three Block War'. *Marines Magazine* (January). http://www.au.af.mil/au/awc/awcgate/usmc/strategic_corporal.htm (accessed 12 October 2011).

Lévi-Strauss, Claude. 1966. *The Savage Mind [La pensée sauvage]*. Trans. John Weightman and Doreen Weightman. London: Weidenfeld and Nicolson.

Lewin, Ronald. 1978. *Ultra Goes to War: the Secret Story*. London: Hutchinson.

Liddicoat, Anthony J., and Richard B. Baldauf (eds) 2008. *Language Planning and Policy: Language Planning in Local Contexts*. Clevedon: Multilingual Matters.

Liddy, Lynda. 2005. 'The Strategic Corporal: Some Requirements in Training and Education'. *Australian Army Journal* 2 (2): 139–48.

Lipsky, Michael. 1983. *Street Level Bureaucracy*. New York: Russell Sage Foundation.

Loewe, Michael. 1994. 'Japanese Naval Codes'. In *Code Breakers: the Inside Story of Bletchley Park*, edited by Harry Hinsley and Alan Stripp: 257–63. Oxford: Oxford University Press.

Lovrenović, Ivan. 2002. 'Moj jezik bosanski'. *BH Dani*, 19 April. http://www.bhdani.com/arhiva/253/kraj.shtml (accessed 18 September 2007).

Lüdi, Georges, Lukas A. Barth, Katharina Höchle and Patchareerat Yanaprasart. 2009. 'La gestion du plurilinguisme au travail entre la "philosophie" de l'entreprise et les pratiques spontanées'. *Sociolinguistica Jahrbuch* 23: 32–52.

Lüdi, Georges, and Monika Heiniger. 2007. 'Sprachpolitik und Sprachverhalten in einer zweisprachigen Regionalbank in der Schweiz'. In *Mehrsprachigkeit am Arbeitsplatz*, edited by Shinichi Kamryama and Bernd Meyer. Frankfurt am Main: Peter Lang.

Maček, Ivana. 2009. *Sarajevo under Siege: Anthropology in Wartime*. Philadelphia, PA: University of Pennsylvania Press.

Macintyre, Ben. 2006. 'The Truth That Tin Eye Saw'. *The Times*, 10 February.

Malcolm, Noel. 2002. *Bosnia: a Short History*. 3rd edn. London: Pan.

Mayer, Felix. 2001. *Language for Special Purposes: Perspectives for the New Millennium*. Vol. 1. Tübingen: Gunter Narr Verlag.

McFate, Montgomery. 2004. 'The Military Utility of Understanding Adversary Culture'. *Joint Force Quarterly* 38: 42–8.

———. 2005. 'Anthropology and Counterinsurgency: the Strange Story of their Curious Relationship'. *Military Review* (March–April): 24–38.

McGregor, Joan. 1996. 'Why When She Says No She Doesn't Mean Maybe and Doesn't Mean Yes: a Critical Reconstruction of Consent, Sex, and the Law'. *Legal Theory* 2: 175–208.

Mikkelson, Holly. 2000. *Introduction to Court Interpreting*. Manchester: St Jerome.

Millar, Sharon, and Astrid Jensen. 2009. 'Language Choice and Management in Danish Multinational Companies: The Role of Common Sense'. *Sociolinguistica Jahrbuch* 23: 86–103.

Millward, William. 1994. 'Life In and Out of Hut 3'. In *Code Breakers: the Inside Story of Bletchley Park*, edited by Harry Hinsley and Alan Stripp: 17–29. Oxford: Oxford University Press.

Ministry of Defence, Development Concepts and Doctrine Centre (2009). *The Significance of Culture to the Military: Joint Doctrine Note/1/09*. Bicester: DSDA Operations Centre.

Mombert, Monique. 1995. *Jeunesse et livre en zone française d'occupation, 1945–9*. Strasbourg: Presses universitaires de Strasbourg.

Morrison, Leigh. 2009. 'Talking the Talk at the Defence School of Languages'. *Royal Navy History*. http://www.royal-navy.org/lib/index.php?title=Talking_the_talk_at_the_Defence_School_of_Languages (accessed 13 October 2011).

Moser-Mercer, Barbara, and Grégoire Bali. 2008. 'Interpreting in Zones of Crisis and War: New Technologies and Online Learning Can Be Tailored to the Urgent Needs of People About to Begin Work in These Difficult Situations'. *Communicate!* (Summer). http://www.aiic.net/ViewPage.cfm/page2979.htm (accessed 16 September 2011).

Muckle, J. Y. 1992. *Schools, Polytechnics and Universities Where Russian is Taught: a United Kingdom List*. Nottingham: Bramcote Press.

Muckle, James. 2008. *The Russian Language in Britain: a Historical Study of Learners and Teachers*. Ilkeston: Bramcote Press.

Mujkić, Asim. 2007. 'We, the Citizens of Ethnopolis'. *Constellations* 14 (1): 112–28.

Murray, G. 1978. 'The British Contribution'. In *The British in Germany: Educational Reconstruction after 1945*, edited by Arthur Hearnden: 64–94. London: Hamish Hamilton.

Murray, J. H. 1997. 'Operation Resolute: Some Observations'. *Australian Defence Force Journal* 126: 29–33.

National Archives. 2010. 'Subseries Within WO 208: Prisoners of War Section'. http://www.nationalarchives.gov.uk/catalogue/DisplayCatalogueDetails.asp?CATID=73078&CATLN=4&FullDetails=True&j=1 (accessed 4 May 2010).

National Register of Public Service Interpreters. 2011. 'Code of Professional Conduct 2011'. http://www.nrpsi.co.uk/pdf/CodeofConduct07.pdf (accessed 25 May 2011).

NATO. 1949. 'Final Communiqué of the First Session of the North Atlantic Council (Terms of Reference and Organisation)'. http://www.nato.int/cps/en/natolive/official_texts_17117.htm (accessed 13 October 2011).

——. 2010. *Glossary of Terms and Definitions*. http://www.nato.int/docu/stanag/aap006/aap-6-2010.pdf (accessed 4 June 2011).

NIOD. 2002. *Srebrenica: Reconstruction, Background, Consequences and Analysis of the Fall of a Safe Area*. Amsterdam: Netherlands Institute for War Documentation. http://srebrenica.brightside.nl (accessed 5 February 2009).

Norris, David A. 1993. *Teach Yourself Serbo-Croat*. London: Hodder and Stoughton.

Oswald, John. 2004. 'Wartime Memories'. *BBC: WW2 People's War*. http://www.bbc.co.uk/ww2peopleswar/stories/34/a3189134.shtml (accessed 4 May 2010).

Palmer, Jerry. 2007. 'Interpreting and Translation for Western Media in Iraq'. In *Translating and Interpreting Conflict*, edited by Myriam Salama-Carr: 13–28. Amsterdam: Rodopi.

Parry, Albert. 1967. *America Learns Russian*. Syracuse: Syracuse University Press.

Pateman, Carole. 1980. 'Women and Consent'. *Political Theory* 8 (2): 149–68.

Patterson, Michael. 2008. *Voices of the Code Breakers*. Cincinnati: David and Charles.

Pattinson, Juliette. 2011 [2007]. *Behind Enemy Lines: Gender, Passing and the Special Operations Executive*. Manchester: Manchester University Press.

Pelican, Fred. 1993. *From Dachau to Dunkirk*. London: Vallentine Mitchell.

Pisac, Andrea. 2011. 'Trusted Tales: Authority and Authenticity in Literary Representations from Ex-Yugoslavia.' PhD thesis, Goldsmiths College, London.

Pouligny, Béatrice. 2006. *Peace Operations Seen from Below: UN Missions and Local People*. London: Hurst.

Pratt, Mary Louise. 1992. *Imperial Eyes: Travel Writing and Transculturation*. London and New York: Routledge.

Pupavac, Vanessa. 2006. 'Discriminating Language Rights and Politics in the Post-Yugoslav States'. *Patterns of Prejudice* 40: 112–28.

Quinn-Judge, Paul. 1995. 'US Military Steps up Deployment Effort'. *Boston Globe*, 5 December.

Rafael, Vicente. 2007. 'Translation in Wartime'. *Public Culture* 19 (2): 239–46.

——. 2009. 'Translation, American English, and the National Insecurities of Empire'. *Social Text 101* 27 (4): 1–23.

Ramsbotham, Oliver, Tom Woodhouse, and Hugh Miall. 2005. *Contemporary Conflict Resolution*. 2nd edn. Cambridge: Polity.

Ratner, Steven. 1995. *The New UN Peacekeeping: Building Peace in Lands of Conflict after the Cold War*. London: Macmillan.

Reckitt, Basil. 1989. *Diary of Military Government in Germany, 1945*. Ilfracombe: Arthur H. Stockwell.

Reinisch, Jessica. (ed.) 2008. 'Relief in the Aftermath of War'. Special Issue of *Journal of Contemporary History* 43 (3).

Ricento, Thomas (ed.) 2006. *An Introduction to Language Policy: Theory and Method*. Malden, MA: Blackwell.

Roland, Ruth. 1999. *Interpreters as Diplomats*. Ottawa: Ottawa University Press.

Rubin, Joan, Björn H. Jernudd, Jyotirindra Das Gupta, Joshua A. Fishman and Charles A. Ferguson (eds) 1977. *Language Planning Processes*. The Hague: Mouton.

Rubinstein, Robert A. 2008. *Peacekeeping under Fire: Culture and Intervention*. Boulder: Paradigm Press.

Said, Edward. 1985. *Orientalism*. Harmondsworth: Penguin.

Salama-Carr, Myriam. 2007. 'Introduction'. In *Translating and Interpreting Conflict*, edited by Myriam Salama-Carr: 1–9. Amsterdam: Rodopi.

——. (ed.) 2007. *Translating and Interpreting Conflict*. Amsterdam and New York: Rodopi.

Sampson, Steven. 2002. 'Weak States, Uncivil Societies and Thousands of NGOs: Western Democracy Export as Benevolent Colonialism in the Balkans.' In *The Balkans in Focus: Cultural Boundaries in Europe*, edited by Barbara Törnquist-Plewa and Sanimir Resic. Lund: Nordic Academic Press. http://www.anthrobase.com/Txt/S/Sampson_S_01.htm (accessed 29 November 2010).

Sands, Robert. 2009. 'The Importance of Culture General in Promoting Cross-Cultural Competence'. Paper presented at Culture in Conflict Symposium, UK Defence Academy, 17 June.

Savage, Michael. 2011. 'MoD Discloses that 21 Interpreters Have Been Killed in Afghanistan'. *The Times*.

Schechner, Richard. 2002. *Performance Studies: an Introduction*. London and New York: Routledge.

Schiffman, Harold F. 1996. *Linguistic Culture and Language Policy*. London: Routledge.

Sharman, Claire Louise. 2007. 'War Crimes Trials between Occupation and Integration: the Prosecution of Nazi War Criminals in the British Zone of Germany.' PhD thesis, University of Southampton.

Simmel, Georg. 1950. *The Sociology of Georg Simmel*. Trans. Kurt Wolff. New York: Free Press.

Simms, Brendan. 2002. *Unfinest Hour: Britain and the Destruction of Bosnia*. Harmondsworth: Penguin.

Simon, Sherry (ed.) 2005. *Translation and Social Activism*. Special Issue of *TTR: Traduction, Terminologie, Rédaction* 18 (2).

Skillen, Hugh. 1990. *The Y Compendium*. Ipswich: Ipswich Book Company.

Skinner, William, and Thomas F. Carson. 1990. 'Working Conditions at the Nuremberg Trials'. In *Interpreting: Yesterday, Today and Tomorrow*, edited by David Bowen and Margareta Bowen: 14–23. Binghamton: State University of New York.

Skutnabb-Kangas, Tove, and Robert Phillipson (eds) 1994. *Linguistic Human Rights: Overcoming Linguistic Discrimination*. The Hague: Mouton.

Spender, Stephen. 1946. *European Witness*. London: Hamish Hamilton.

Spolsky, Bernard. 2004. *Language Policy*. Cambridge: Cambridge University Press.

——. 2005. 'Language Policy'. In *ISB4: Proceedings of the 4th International Symposium on Bilingualism*, edited by James Cohen, Kara T. McAlister, Kellie Rolstad, and Jeff MacSwan: 2152–64. Somerville, MA: Cascadilla Press.

——. 2009. *Language Management*. Cambridge: Cambridge University Press.

Stahuljak, Zrinka. 2000. 'Violent Distortions: Bearing Witness to the Task of the Wartime Translators', *TTR: Traduction, Terminologie, Rédaction* 13 (1): 137–51.

——. 2010. 'War, Translation, Transnationalism: Interpreters In and Out of the War (Croatia, 1991–1992)'. In *Critical Readings in Translation Studies*, edited by Mona Baker: 391–414. London and New York: Routledge.

Stankovic, Milos. 2000. *Trusted Mole: a Soldier's Journey into Bosnia's Heart of Darkness*. London: HarperCollins.

Stech, Frank J. 1995. 'Sociopolitical Stresses and the RMA'. *Parameters* (Summer): 47–54.

Stewart, Bob. 1993. *Broken Lives: a Personal View of the Bosnian Conflict*. London: HarperCollins.

Stofft, William A, and Gary L. Guertner. 1995. 'Ethnic Conflict: The Perils of Military Intervention'. *Parameters* (Spring): 30–42.

Szepesy, James E. 2005. 'The Strategic Corporal and the Emerging Battlefield'. Master's thesis, The Fletcher School, Tufts University.

The Times. 1948a. 'Alleged Cruelty to Germans: British Officer Charged'. 3 March.

The Times. 1948b. 'Lieut. R. O. Langham Acquitted Not Guilty of Cruelty to S.S. Men'. 1 April.

Thomas, Edward. 1994. 'A Naval Officer in Hut 3'. In *Code Breakers: the Inside Story of Bletchley Park*, edited by Harry Hinsley and Alan Stripp: 41–9. Oxford: Oxford University Press.

Thomson, Andrew. 1996. 'Over There 1944–45: Americans and the Liberation of France: Their Perceptions of and Relationships with France and the French.' PhD thesis, University of Kent.

Tipton, Rebecca. 2011. 'Relationships of Learning between Military Personnel and Interpreters in Situations of Violent Conflict'. *The Interpreter and Translator Trainer* 5 (1): 15–40.

Tomlinson, Kathryn. 2009. 'How Societies Operate'. Paper presented at Culture in Conflict Symposium, UK Defence Academy, 17 June.

Torriani, Riccarda. 2005. 'Nazis into Germans: Re-Education and Democratisation in the British and French Occupation Zones, 1945–9'. PhD thesis, University of Cambridge.

Truchot, Claude, and Dominique Huck. 2009. 'Le traitement des langues dans les entreprises'. *Sociolinguistica Jahrbuch* 23: 1–31.

Tymoczko, Maria. 2000. 'Translation and Political Engagement: Activism, Social Change and the Role of Translation in Geopolitical Shifts'. *The Translator* 6 (1): 23–47.

——. 2007. *Enlarging Translation, Empowering Translators*. Manchester: St Jerome.

——. 2009. 'Translation, Ethics and Ideology in a Violent Globalizing World'. In *Globalization, Political Violence and Translation*, edited by Esperanza Bielsa and Christopher Hughes: 171–94. Basingstoke: Palgrave Macmillan.

UK Forces Afghanistan. 2011. 'Afghan Interpreters, the Forgotten Heroes'. *The Official Blog of UK Forces in Afghanistan*, 1 June. http://ukforcesafghanistan.word press.com/2011/06/01/afghan-interpreters-the-forgotten-heroes/ (accessed 16 September 2011).

Venuti, Lawrence. 2008. *The Translator's Invisibility: a History of Translation*. London and New York: Routledge.

Watt, Donald Cameron. 1989. 'An Intelligence Surprise: the Failure of the Foreign Office to Anticipate the Nazi-Soviet Pact'. *Intelligence and National Security* 4 (3): 512–34.

Weinberger, Sharon. 2008. 'Military Research: the Pentagon's Culture Wars'. *Nature* (455): 583–5.

Welchman, Gordon. 1982. *The Hut Six Story: Breaking the Enigma Codes*. London: Allen Lane.

Wendt, Alexander. 1992. 'Anarchy is What States Make of It: the Social Construction of Power Politics'. *International Organization* 46 (2): 391–425.

Whitteaker, Kelly. 2002. 'Romanian Engineers De-Launch Perie Bridge'. *SFOR Informer*, 29 August. http://www.nato.int/sfor/indexinf/146/p04a/t02p04a.htm (accessed 29 November 2010).

Whitworth, Sandra. 2004. *Men, Militarism, and UN Peacekeeping: a Gendered Analysis*. Boulder: Lynne Rienner.

Willis, F. Roy. 1968. *France, Germany and the New Europe, 1945–67*. Stanford: Stanford University Press.

Woodward, Rachel, and Trish Winter. 2007. *Sexing the Soldier: the Politics of Gender and the Contemporary British Army.* London and New York: Routledge.

Wright, Sue. 2004. *Language Policy and Language Planning.* London: Palgrave Macmillan.

Ziemke, Earl F. 1975. *The US Army in the Occupation of Germany, 1944–6.* Washington DC: Center of Military History.

Zink, Harold. 1957. *The United States in Germany 1944–55.* New York: Van Nostrand.

Index